Panchayati Raj Institutions and Rural Development

Panchayati Raj Institutions and Rural Development

Narratives on Inclusion of Excluded

Edited by
Bishnu C. Barik
Umesh C. Sahoo

RAWAT PUBLICATIONS
Jaipur • New Delhi • Bangalore • Mumbai • Hyderabad • Guwahati

ISBN 81-316-0107-2

Published by
Prem Rawat for **Rawat Publications**
Satyam Apts, Sector 3, Jawahar Nagar, Jaipur 302 004 (India)
Phone: 0141 265 1748 / 7006 Fax: 0141 265 1748
E-mail: info@rawatbooks.com
Website: www.rawatbooks.com

New Delhi Office
4858/24, Ansari Road, Daryaganj, New Delhi 110 002
Phone: 011 2326 3290

Also at Bangalore, Mumbai, Hyderabad and Guwahati

Typeset by Rawat Computers, Jaipur
Printed at Chaman Enterprises, New Delhi

To

Prof. S.P. Punalekar
Former Director, Centre for Social Studies, Surat

commemorating his contributions to the growth of
School of Social Sciences,
Swami Ramanand Teerth Marathwada University,
Nanded

Contents

Acknowledgements

This volume grew out of a National Seminar on "Panchayati Raj Institutions and Rural Development in Western India" organised by the School of Social Sciences, Swami Ramanand Teerth Marathwada University, Nanded (Maharashtra) during February 24-25, 2006 with financial support from the Indian Council of Social Science Research, New Delhi and Swami Ramanand Teerth Marathwada University, Nanded. We express our sincere gratitude to both the institutions for this gesture.

We owe a lot to Prof. Partha Nath Mukherji, former Director, Tata Institute of Social Sciences, Mumbai and former President of Indian Sociological Society, New Delhi for agreeing to our request to be the chief guest at the inaugural function and delivering the keynote address at the seminar; Prof. B.S. Baviskar, former President of Indian Sociological Society to be the guest of honour at the valedictory function and delivering his concluding remarks; and Prof. S.A. Suryavanshi, Vice-Chancellor, Swami Ramanand Teerth Marathwada University for presiding over the inaugural function of the seminar. We express our sincere thanks and gratitude to all three dignitaries for their kind presence and thought-provoking addresses.

Over 25 participants representing various professional and academic groups from six states (Himachal Pradesh, Gujarat, Andhra Pradesh, Orissa, Maharashtra and Goa) deliberated on the various sub-themes of the seminar. We express our sincere thanks to all delegate friends and more particularly Dr. (Mrs.) Gopelwar Banmala, Prof. P.N. Gautam and Dr. R. Siva Prasad for acting as chairpersons in the technical sessions. Dr. Santosh Kumar deserves our special thanks for taking down emerging points in all the technical sessions and writing the first draft on the perspective of the seminar.

It is a fact but not exaggeration to mention that the seminar could not have been decently organised without the enthusiasm shown in and hard work put in by the colleagues in the School: Dr. P.M. Katare, Dr. E.N. Ashok Kumar, Dr. A.I. Shaikh, Ms. U.S. Sarode and Dr. G.S. Yelne and of course our students. We express our sincere thanks to all of them.

We owe a special debt to Dr. J.M. Waghmare, the Founder Vice-Chancellor for his constant support for conducting academic activities at the School; and to our teacher Prof. Jagannath Pathy for his continued encouragement and deep interest in our academic pursuits.

In this era of e-communication, we cannot ignore the help in e-mailing and downloading the files from Internet by Mr. Ranjeet G. Dharmapurikar, Information Scientist in our university library and Mr. Ramesh D. Gandle, typist in our School, in helping us in editing the manuscripts on computer. No doubt, both the above tasks by nature were arduous and time-consuming but both Mr. Dharmapurikar and Mr. Gandle handled it with patience and care. Both of them deserve our thanks.

Finally, we express our sincere thanks to Mr. Pranit Rawat, Rawat Publications, Jaipur for arranging publication of the volume in record time with commitment.

Editors

Contributors

B.S. Baviskar, Senior Fellow, Institute of Social Sciences, New Delhi.

Partha N. Mukherji, Professor, S.K. Dey Chair, Institute of Social Sciences, New Delhi.

Bishnu C. Barik, Director, School of Social Sciences, S.R.T.M. University, Nanded.

Rajendra B. Patil, Professor, Department of Sociology, Shivaji University, Kolhapur.

Sarjerao A. Salunkhe, Professor, Department of Sociology, Shivaji University, Kolhapur.

Siva Prasad R., Reader, Department of Anthropology, University of Hyderabad, Hyderabad.

Gaurang R. Sahay, Reader, Department of Rural Studies, Tata Institute of Social Sciences, Mumbai.

Bibhuti B. Mohanty, Professor, Department of Sociology, Pondichery University, Puducherry.

Aureliano F. Fernades, Reader, Department of Politics, Goa University, Goa.

Satyakam Joshi, Associate Professor, Centre for Social Studies, University Campus, Surat.

Umesh C. Sahoo, Reader, School of Social Sciences, S.R.T.M. University, Nanded.

Santosh Kumar, Professor and Head, Research Division, Mahatma Gandhi Labour Insitute, Thaltej Road, Ahmedabad.

Kunj Behari Nayak, Lecturer, Department of Sociology, Amaravati University, Amaravati.

Archana Kamble (Jagatkar), Lecturer, Department of Sociology, The New College, Kolhapur.

Manish K. Thakur, Senior. Lecturer, Department of Sociology, Goa University, Goa.

Ozmond R. D'Souza, Research Scholar, Department of Political Science, University of Hyderabad, Hyderabad.

1

Introduction: Panchayati Raj Institutions and Rural Development

Contextualising the Discourse

B.C. Barik, Santosh Kumar and U.C. Sahoo

School of Social Sciences, Swami Ramanand Teerth Marathwada University, Nanded organised a national seminar on "Panchayati Raj Institutions and the Rural Development in Western India" on the 24th and 25th January 2005 at the campus of the University. Five technical sessions were held, in addition to inaugural and valedictory, during the two-day seminar. This report is being presented in the form of an essay to encapsulate the essence of the papers and the discourse permeated in seminar. The authors, nevertheless, would agree that the essence of the seminar is present in the essay.

Democracy and decentralisation are often presented as the *sine qua non* of the rural development and the poverty reduction programmes. Democratic decentralisation, it is argued, results in a state apparatus more responsive to local needs and aspirations. This in turn produces systems of governance that are more effective. Panchayati Raj Institutions (PRIs), in the context of rural India, are these systems of governance, which respond to the needs of the democratic decentralisation.

Democratic decentralisation can be defined as a meaningful authority devolved to local units of governance that are accessible and accountable to the local citizenry, who enjoy political rights and liberty. It thus differs from the vast majority of earlier efforts at decentralisation in developing areas (which go back to the 1950s in India), which were largely initiatives in public administration without any serious democratic component (Blair, 2000: 23). If one must locate PRIs in the given definitional format, the periodic elections provide an important means of ensuring government responsiveness and accountability on broad social issues. "At the same time", as Blair argues, "elections are crude instruments of popular control, since they occur at widely spaced intervals... and address only the broadest issues" (ibid.: 27).

In the rural context, arguments encouraging democratic decentralisation are often associated with improvements in public accountability, environmental sustainability and the empowerment of poor and vulnerable groups. Central to this is the notion that large and centrally administered bureaucracies represent an inefficient and potentially destructive means of allocating resources and generating wealth within the society. The solution, it is argued, is to make governments more accountable and more responsive to local people.

Studies on decentralisation show that the devolution can enhance rural livelihoods in a variety of ways. First, the establishment and empowerment of local resources user groups can improve the ways in which poor people are often disproportionately dependent (IFAD, 2001). Second, and related, collaboration between public agencies and local resources users can produce 'synergistic' outcomes, in which citizens and civil servants co-operate to provide goods that would be unobtainable were they acting alone. Third, the democratisation and empowerment of local administration bodies can enhance representation and participation in decision-making fora, particularly among groups that have been traditionally marginalised by local political processes (Blair, 2000).

This increased participation offers significant benefits in itself. One, participation in local, democratically elected bodies can lead to improvements in self-identity and worth, which can help to break down customs of inequality and discrimination. Second, membership in local administrative bodies can provide important skills that can be transferred to other walks of life. Regulations stipulating the inclusion of such groups (reservation policy) can help to ensure that poor and marginalised group have a voice in local bodies. Among some of the successful cases of democratic decentralisation, the systems of local democratic governance have also been shown to improve the efficiency and responsiveness of public officials (Blair, 2000; Crook and Manor, 1998; Manor, 1999).

Stating the Indian context, during the 1950s, there was a need felt by the Government of India to formally decentralise governance and devolve power by introducing the Panchayati Raj Institutions (PRIs) as institutions of local self-governance, following the Balwantrai Mehta Committee's recommendations after reviewing the Community Development Programme, to enable the rural masses to participate in the micro-planning and implementation of the various development schemes. By the early 1960s, many states had taken the necessary legislative measures to establish PRIs, but there was scarcely any representation of the women in the elected panchayats.

In order to make PRIs more responsive and productive in its socio-economic responsibilities, the varied committees and the recent 73rd Constitutional Amendment hailed important landmarks its democratic decentralisation, devolution of power, financial autonomy and provided space for participation of the women and the marginalised sections in the decision-making process at the grassroots level. Over the years, despite the constitutional provisions and several other recommendations, the ground reality shows the inadequacy of the PRIs to become pro-people, people-centred and innovative in approach because of the age-old inequality, domination, subjugation and subordinated relations in terms of gender, caste, class and power in rural landscape. Besides, politicisation of the democratic institutions, frequent interference by the bureaucrats, irregularity in holding elections, etc., have posed a major threat for sustaining the democratic local self-governance system, which called for a review and introspection.

The studies conducted over several states across the country project different tinges, scenarios and with varied concentrations. Some states have exhibited wonderful results, while in some others it appeared marred due to the politicisation, which made these bodies dysfunctional. The one-third representation to the women and the proportional representation to the marginalised castes and sections remained more quantitative and its qualitative aspects remained to be appreciated.

It is against this background of the macro-theoretical framework and actuality at the ground level that the seminar found itself located in. The seminar intended to address the questions highlighted in the foregoing passages in the limited context of the western India, however, the proceedings were generalised at the broad-based and national level. The present volume contains the papers which tried to cover the range of topics such as (i) conceptual issues of the PRIs, (ii) empowerment of the members and the development, (iii) PRIs and the issues of human rights, (iv) impact of the PRIs on rural governance, (v) PRIs and the governance in the tribal societies, to list a few. With this backdrop, the seminar proposed to address the following major areas:

1. *PRIs and the Civil Society: Issues, Strategies and Ways:* This theme focused upon the civil society's role in capacity building of elected representatives and their participation in planning, implementation and management of government-sponsored rural development programmes. The theme also covered the interface between the government and the civil society.
2. *PRIs and Empowerment of the Members:* The topic sought to critically examine the provisions made in the 73rd Constitutional Amendment and reservation of women and marginalised sections, and the extent of their participation and bottlenecks, if any, faced by them in decision-making processes, implementation of developmental programmes, and bringing socio-economic transformation of rural India.
3. *Finances and PRIs: Strategies, Policies and Self-Reliance:* This theme discussed the devolution of financial powers by the state and the strategies on PRIs own self-finance schemes in

the development of rural society. The subject also covered areas of mobilisation of resources.

4. *Rural Development Programmes and the PRIs: Allocation of Schemes and Utilisation Pattern:* The focus was on deliberation on allotment of various rural development programmes by the central and the state governments and other agencies to the PRIs. It also focused upon the various stakeholders, specially panchayat members, in implementing the schemes for alleviation of rural poverty.
5. *Panchayati Raj and Human Rights:* The area under focused attention was effectiveness of rights of people to participate in decentralised governance systems such as Gram Sabha, Gram Panchayat and other tiers. It also deliberated upon the PRIs' role to ensure people's basic rights in education, health service, food, housing and employment, etc., in governance processes.

The keynote address delivered by Prof. P.N. Mukherjee set the agenda for the two-day reflective session. The address essentially scanned the emergence of the modern-day institutions of the local self-governance from the historical, nationalist, political sociology and political economy perspectives and in a dialectical framework. It deliberated on a range of issues, and initiated the discussion with the mentioning of the debate on the parliamentary democracy versus participatory democracy. He focused his attention on the debate from the standpoint of the nationalist leaders, thinkers and the policy framers of the pre-independent India and the debate that was ensuing regarding the issue of the model of democracy India in the post-colonial era would or should adopt. In the post-independent period the compulsions of the political economy and the other considerations led India to adopt the parliamentary democracy, but was this model really conducive to Indian political system, questioned Prof. Mukherjee, given the history where the processes of the local governance rather than the institutions of local governance from the participatory stance were always held high.

The development scenario in independent India, when the first two Five-Year Plans were mainly focused on the nation and infrastructure building, did not venture much on the institutional aspects of the institutions of the local self-governance, until the launching of the Community Development Programme and its subsequent review by Balwantrai Mehta Committee. The recommendations of the Committee formed the basis for the institutionalisation of the local self-governance through the Panchayati Raj Institutions (PRIs) in India with a much concerted and articulated approach. It determined the functional necessity of the management of the rural development. There was also a functional need of PRIs for the administration of the rural development programmes. Hence, the panchayat was seen as an end as well as means in itself. As an end, it was an inevitable extension of the democracy, and as a means, it would continue to discharge obligations entrusted to it by the national and the state governments. Its sphere was not yet transferred to its exclusive jurisdiction, however, as both as an end as well as means, Panchayati Raj was expected to contribute to the philosophy as well as the practice, rewarding to the rural development. And, hence, once again, the development imperative, for which the panchayats should become an instrument, took higher note rather than of democratic governance in itself.

Critiquing the post-Balwantrai Mehta Committee panchayat system, a noted Gandhian, Siddharaj Dhaddha, observed that the vary foundation of the structure of the Panchayati Raj was missing. The purpose of the decentralisation was not merely to help development but also to define and create an integrated structure of self-governing institutions from the villages and small towns to upward national levels to enable these people manage their own affairs. The Panchayati Raj should be foundation of the *swaraj* and that is how the Balwantrai Mehta Committee had missed an opportunity in putting the democracy in sound footing.

After several committees that tried to understand and recommend for the enhancing the functional and structural aspects of the Panchayati Raj, the efforts of Rajiv Gandhi in understanding the leakages and the shortfalls led to the 73rd Amendment to the Constitution of India. Rajiv Gandhi understood how the power brokers had been contracted out the tasks of rural development and the several other vices that had gripped the PRIs. Hence, with the Constitutional Amendment, two essential aspects were taken care of: first was that the preparation of the plan for the economic development was done through the social justice and human rights perspectives and second, it delegated powers and functions related to the implementation of the schemes for the economic development.

The most important consequence of the Constitutional Amendment was that will it enhance the will power to the people and provide structural framework for all the future developments. At least the people could demand an audience with the government, if it was not paying any heed to the people's demands. Hence, the studies, the observations and the understanding should locate Panchayati Raj as a process, as a contention, and a dialectic. The role of the civil society must also be scrutinised in the context of the PRIs. The concluding part of the keynote address was on setting the research agenda with regard to the PRIs in the various academic institutions.

The four sessions of the seminar deliberated on the various themes, as outlined in the foregoing paragraphs. The common string that bound the various presentations was the understanding of the decentralisation process in its several manifestations. The Constitutional Amendment was celebrated as a step towards democratic decentralisation, as it made provisions for:

(a) the establishment of the Gram Sabha as the lowest decision-making unit within the three-tier administrative system, at the village, administrative block and the district;
(b) regular elections every five years; and
(c) reservation for not less than one-third seats for the women as members and as chairpersons at the three levels and also for the SCs, the STs and other backward castes.

Villagers, as members of the constitutionally recognised Gram Sabha, could now formally, by a call of votes, accept or veto development programmes and projects. By making the provisions for women's reservation and also for other marginalised groups, the legislation on PRIs also made way for many women and people from the SCs/STs to represent the Gram Sabha as sarpanch or head of the Gram Panchayat. As per the Maharashtra Human Development Report, 2002, women constitute over 40 per cent of the chairpersons of Panchayat Samitis and 29 per cent of the sarpanchas of the Gram Panchayats. Similarly, representation of the SCs/STs has increased by 14 per cent and many of them have also been elected from the unreserved posts. The common voice that however emerged from various presentations from all over the country, was that such representations have not necessarily translated into the empowerment of women, SCs and STs. The Gram Sabhas have often reflected and reproduced the caste and class dynamics of the villages.

The academics brought the points to the fore that there have been instances when an SC or a backward caste sarpanch also happened to be 'front' for the persons belonging to the dominant castes, making it difficult for the incumbent to discharge his/her duties as sarpanch effectively. Similarly, even though women sarpanchas are no longer unheard of, this had not necessarily led to the a consequent rise in the women's effective participation in meetings and activities of the Gram Sabha/Gram Panchayat – at times their husbands attend the meetings. From human rights perspective, the panchayats have not proved fully competent as far as the protection of human rights was concerned. In most of cases the elections for the reserved seats led to violence and there were instances when a dalit woman or man found to contesting the election was paraded naked.

The participants argued that the framework provided through the Constitutional Amendment was on the whole good, however not good enough for the empowerment of the women and marginalised sections. This abysmal performance in participants in the institutions of local self-governance had its causality in the amendments itself, and the state governments' legislations defined the level of participation of citizens and limiting it to a merely consultative role rather than assigning them decision-making powers in village governance. It appears that enskilling representatives and people in participatory methods, citizens' education and awareness, training and sensitising local officials, interlinkages with universities, participatory budgeting and most importantly accountability of elected officials to the Gram Sabha could bring to fruition the process triggered by the Constitutional Amendment Act. The participants debated that to make it possible, it was time that the Constitutional

Amendment itself underwent a radical revision. Decentralisation needed to be unmasked of the pretensions. One could not afford a proliferation of new, formal institutions, which would only aggravate an already iniquitous situation. Silverlining in such scenario would appear only when all the facts are laid threadbare, and then policies were made in a transparent manner on a realistic premise.

Serious discussion also took place on the papers on the PRIs in the tribal societies from the viewpoint of PESA (Act No. 40 of 1996) and the question raised whether the modern and the traditional panchayats could co-exist in the Scheduled Areas. Traditionally, the tribal communities had their own systems of governance, justice and customary practices governing their own lives, resources and economies. Since the British rule, different policies adopted by the governments had only deprived them of rights to their livelihood and access to the resources. The introduction of statutory panchayats had further contested/weakened the tribal institutions and unity. The PESA Act envisaged that the state's legislations should be in consonance with the customary laws, social and religious practices and traditional management practices of community resources. The tenor of the Act 40 of 1996 did not anywhere match with the ground-level realities. In fact, these were contrary to what was stated. When the states did not fulfil their obligatory functions to whom else could the tribals look for? This also brought to the fore the question of compatibility of the traditional tribal system of governance, political and judicial institutions with the structures introduced by the government. The participants agreed that, in spite of these pressing issues, the PESA has opened up the possibilities of self-rule in tribal villages. Tribal population is slowly understanding the importance of PESA and becoming conscious about their rights and responsibilities. They are trying to exercise their rights and compelling government officials to solve their problems. One the other hand, it is also true, as has been stated earlier, that the PESA is not being implemented in its true spirit. Politicians and bureaucrats are apathetic to PESA. Gram Sabhas are not held as per the PESA's provisions and there seems to be a lack of information on the part of the villagers and the elected representatives of the tribal panchayats. Another problem is that the provisions, which have been there in PESA, do not collaborate with the national laws pertaining to the land acquisitions, market regulation and moneylending. There is an anomaly on the part of the legislation, which has hampered the implementation of PESA. It was noted that due to external forces such as outsider invasion, market penetration and differentiation of tribal communities on socio-economic lines, there has been some bottlenecks in the implementation of the PESA, which required political will and people's participation.

The seminar was concluded on the agenda for the academic institutions for taking the process of decentralisation ahead through the meaningful research. After the Gulbenkian Committee Report that declared the blurring of the boundaries of the various disciplines of the social sciences, it was of critical significance that a multidisciplinary approach emerged in understanding the decentralisation process and its true implementation.

References

Blair, Harry (2000), "Participation and Accountability at the Periphery: Democratic Local Governance in Six Countries", *World Development*, 28 (1): 21-28.

Crook, Richard C. and Manor, James (1998), *Democracy and Decentralisation in South Asia and West Africa*, Cambridge: Cambridge University Press.

IFAD (2001), *Rural Poverty Report 2001: The Challenges of Ending Rural Poverty*, Oxford: Oxford University Press for IFAD.

Manor, James (1999), *The Political Economy of Democratic Decentralisation*, The Directions in Development Series, Washington D. C.: World Bank.

2

Including the Excluded, Empowering the Powerless

Case Studies of Panchayati Raj in Maharashtra

B.S. Baviskar

For a long time social scientists have been interested in understanding the distribution of power in society. It is agreed that in no society power is equally distributed. While some people enjoy or exercise greater power, many others have hardly any power. How to explain this inequality in the distribution of power in a given society? Of course, the distribution of power in a society may change over a period of time. The question is how to explain such changes? What are the forces and processes underlying such changes?

In the literature one finds two major schools of thought debating this issue in the 1950s and 1960s. They could be identified as elite theorists and pluralists. The elite theorists such as C. Wright Mills (1956) and others argued that political power always went to those who enjoyed high status and wealth. In other words, the upper classes always rule. As against this view, the pluralists, represented by Robert A. Dahl (1961) and Nelson W. Polsby (1962) and others, argued that it was too simplistic a view to assume that the upper classes always enjoyed grater power. According to them, the distribution of power in a society was generally determined by the combination of resources and skills enjoyed by people. There are many resources other than status and wealth, which enabled people to acquire power. Besides, the skills for using one's resources are not evenly distributed nor are they necessarily acquired by one's status and wealth. Thus, not just status and wealth but a plurality of factors enabled people to acquire power. This was the pluralist view.

The Indian Constitution introduced in 1950 adopted adult franchise, thus creating a political resource for all citizens.

When the Indian parliament passed the 73rd Constitutional Amendment Act in 1992 reserving seats for women, Scheduled Castes (SCs) and Scheduled Tribes (STs) in Panchayati Raj Institutions (PRIs), it was in a sense following the pluralist line. It was creating another resource through reservation in the hands of these deprived sections to enable them to acquire some power even if they did not enjoy high status and wealth.

Of course, occupying formal positions of power is not enough. That does not make one necessarily powerful. The real test of power, as Max Weber told categorily, is one's ability to influence decision-making in a public action affecting the community. The formal position only gave an occupant a better opportunity to participate in the decision-making process. The pluralists always emphasised the importance of studying the process of decision-making for this purpose. It follows that if we want to find out whether the women, SCs and STs have been empowered or not, we must study the process of decision-making at the various levels of PRIs. If we find these sections influencing the decisions in panchayats, that will be the proof of their empowerment and a sign of their being included overcoming their earlier state of exclusion.

Thus, the main objective of our research was to find out the degree of inclusion of the hitherto excluded groups and categories such as SCs, STs and women in the rural power structure. What was the extent of their empowerment?

We thought that this could be found out only by going to the field. That is why, in our preparatory meetings, we decided to undertake case studies in particular districts and follow the method of intensive fieldwork or participant observation. In view of this objective, I decided to study three Gram Panchayats (village councils) in Chalisgaon taluka of Jalgaon district in Maharashtra.

The Background

Maharashtra is known to be a progressive state in the field of Panchayati Raj. It had introduced the three-tier Panchayati Raj system in 1962 with great deal of enthusiasm. The state authorities did not hesitate in delegating requisite powers to the newly created Gram Panchayats (GP), Taluka Panchayat Samitis (TPS) and Zilla Parishads (ZP). Excepting on one occasion (1979-92) they also held elections to these bodies on time. In fact, the state decided to reserve 30 per cent seats for women in PRIs on its own initiative in 1991, a year before the passage of the 73rd Constitutional Amendment.[1]

After the creation of the unilingual state of Maharashtra with Bombay as the capital on 1 May 1960, the Congress which had suffered serious setback in the general elections of 1957, again emerged as the dominant party and the Chief Minister Yeswanth Rao Chavan as the acknowledged leader of the party and the government in the state. In line with the Nehruvian vision of that time, Chavan advocated creation of a democratic socialist Maharashtra with the help of newly emerging PRIs and rural co-operatives. While PRIs were looked upon as the instruments to extend democracy to the masses in the rural areas, co-operatives such as the network of co-operative sugar factories and district central co-operative banks were expected to usher in the area of economic prosperity and egalitarian society. The Congress Party controlled not only the state government but also the PRIs and the co-operatives. The dominance of the Congress Party coincided with dominance of the Maratha caste which enjoyed a decisive dominance in the state as a whole, largely due to its numerical strength, economic and political clout, and relatively high ritual status. Both the PRIs and the co-operatives were looked upon as the entry points and training grounds for the younger political leadership emerging in the rural areas. Thus, the Congress Party and its predominantly Maratha leadership continued to control PRIs, co-operatives and the state government until the early 1990s. However, the Shiv Sena and Bharatiya Janata Party (BJP) soon started challenging its position. They finally succeeded in ousting the Congress from power in the state in 1995 and claimed share in controlling PRIs and co-operatives in some districts. This significantly changed the political scene in the state.

When the elections to PRIs were held in 1995 (soon after the passing of 73rd amendment), a fragmented picture emerged with control over PRIs being shared by the Congress, BJP and Shiv Sena. The split in the Congress Party in 1999 and emergence of the Nationalist Congress Party (NCP) under the leadership of Sharad Pawar have further fragmented the local political scene. In the elections to 27 ZPs held in February 2002, only in five any single party had a majority on its own. Besides, in four more ZPs, the Shiv Sena-BJP alliance had clear majority. In the 18 ZPs the verdict was fractured (for details see Palshikar, 2002: 1278).

In the elections to the Jalgaon ZP held in February 2002 Shiv Sena-BJP combine won a clear majority with 11 and 27 seats respectively out of the total of 68 seats. In the Chalisgaon TPS the total of 14 seats were shared as follows: NCP 6, BJP 4, Shiv Sena 2, Congress 1, and Independent 1. Any ideologically rational combination proved to be impossible. So, the leaders of NCP and BJP set aside their ideological baggage and decided to come together. The Sabhapathi's post was reserved for an ST candidate. There was only one ST candidate (Hiraman Govinda Sonavane, a Bhil) among the 14. He was elected on the NCP ticket. Being the only eligible candidate his getting elected as the Sabhapati was a forgone conclusion. The NCP struck a deal with the BJP for a stable majority by offering them the post of Upa-Sabhapati. Thus, Ananda Fakira Patil, a BJP Maratha candidate from Pilkhod, was elected as Upa-Sabhapati unopposed. Both parties, which had fought a bitter election campaign against each other, now come together claiming that they did so in the interests of the development of Chalisgaon taluka. Such are the compulsions of pragmatic politics at the local level in Maharashtra.

Soon after his election as Sabhapati, Sonavane was taken in a procession in the town and felicitated with garlands and words. At the party leader Shubash Chavan's house, in the presence of a large crowd of party followers, Sonavane was welcomed by the party leader's wife in the traditional Maharashtrian style by performing 'arti'. Sonavane, a poor Bhil from Londhe village, could hardly control tears in his eyes. Sonavane is 29 who studied upto 12th class. He was a gram panchayat member for two years. Otherwise, he is a novice in the taluka level politics. He will therefore be guided by the senior leaders of the party. He seems to be quite happy in the symbolic trappings of office. The honour of holding public office and the respectful attention bestowed upon him, the official vehicle, the honorarium and allowances will all mark a big change in his lifestyle. In the process he will also learn rules of the political game and may acquire certain political skills. At the moment the symbolic aspects of power appear to be more important to him. Of course, it is not a small gain for a tribal from a poor family.

According to the project design, I selected the following three Gram Panchayats in Chalisgaon taluka for intensive study: (1) Mandurne where an OBC woman is the sarpanch, (2) Alwadi where an SC woman is the sarpanch, and (3) Pilkhod where a dominant caste man (Maratha, OBC) is the sarpanch. The detailed analysis follows.

Mandurne: The Village

Mandurne is situated on the left bank of the Girna river on the border between Jalgaon and Nashik districts. It is a medium size village with 1,547 voters. The caste-wise distribution of voters is shown in Table 1.

Mandurne is a clear case of decisive dominance of the Malis. They are overwhelming in numbers, and own most of the land. On the other hand, although the Bhils and Muslims have some numerical strength, they are poor, do not own any land, and are economically dependent on the Malis. Unlike most of the villages in Maharashtra, where the Marathas enjoyed Patilki vatan (village headmanship), in Mandurne the Malis have traditionally enjoyed both the positions of Police Patil and Mulki or Revenue Patil. In order to proclaim their special status, the Malis use Patil as their surname, which is common among the Marathas all over Maharashtra.

Table 1
Caste Distribution of Voters in Mandurne

Caste	*Traditional occupation*	*Reservation category*	*No. of voters*
Mali (gardeners)	Agricultural cultivation	OBC	713
Bhil	Agricultural labour	ST	230
Muslims*	Crafts and agricultural work	—	205
Maratha	Agricultural cultivation	—	196
Mahar (neo-Buddhists)	Agricultural labour	SC	65
Bhavsar	Crafts and agri labour	OBC	30
Kumbhar	Potter	OBC	26
Beldar	Earth work	OBC	25
Bhoi	Grain parcher	OBC	19
Koli	Water carrier, agricultural labour, fishing	ST	09
Nhavi	Barber	OBC	07
Bhikshu	Monk	—	06
Sutar	Carpentry	OBC	05
Shimpi	Tailoring	OBC	03
Mang	Rope-making, playing music	SC	03
Chambhar	Leather worker	SC	03
Bhangi	Scavenger	SC	02
Total			1,547

* A cluster of three castes.

Until the early 1950s Mandurne was like any other dry village, neither poor nor prosperous. But, in the fifties, a few enterprising Mali farmers obtained permits to lift water from the Girna river, laid long pipelines to irrigate their fields, and started cultivating sugarcane. Soon it became a prosperous village. They set up a school, which was gradually upgraded up to 10th standard. Recently, farmers in Mandurne are sliding into gradual economic decline for two reasons. With inadequate and scanty rains in recent years the government has imposed severe restrictions on lifting water from the Girna river bed. This has curtailed the acreage under sugarcane and other irrigated crops, resulting in an economic loss to the farmers. The second reason for the economic ruin of some families was addiction to alcoholism. Recently, there has been an attempt to create awareness about this problem through religious preaching and thus wean away people from drinking. Some families have joined the Vaishnavite Warkari sect, which advocates vegetarianism and teetotalism. How strong is the impact of the movement, is yet to be seen.

Mandurne Panchayat

Following the example of the neighbouring villages, viz., Pilkhod, Saygaon and Tamaswadi, people in Mandurne also decided to reach a consensus in the panchayat elections held in April 2000. Accordingly, a general meeting of all the villagers was held and it was agreed to allot six seats to Malis and one each to Marathas, Muslims and Bhils & (ST). Since the post of sarpanch was reserved for a woman OBC candidate, it was given to Devakabai Chhagan Patil belonging to the Mali caste. The composition of the Gram Panchayat is shown in Table 2.

Although elected on the basis of village-wide consensus, the GP is now divided into two factions. Five members support the sarpanch. The remaining three are in the opposition, though they appear to be rather mild opponents.

The sarpanch Deavakabai is educated up to 4th standard. She narrated the background of her unopposed election. There was a general agreement in the village for sometime to elect her husband (Chhagan Narayan Patil) as the sarpanch. They thought it was his turn this time. But, the sarpanch's post was reserved for an OBC woman. Then, the choice fell on her. If not the man, let his wife be elected, the villagers said. At first, she was reluctant. But, she was persuaded to accept. She accepted only because her election was unopposed. She was not interested in fighting the election. Their's is a leading family in the village and has supported sarpanch candidates a number of times in the past. This was another reason for accepting the offer. She wanted to maintain the family tradition. However, the main reason was her husband's support. He agreed to help in her work, particularly in dealing with the outside world – school teachers, contractors, government officials and others.

Table 2
Composition of Mandurne Gram Panchayat

Name	*Designation*	*Age*	*Caste*	*Reservation category*	*Education*	*Occupation*
Devakabai Chhagan Patil	Sarpanch	35	Mali	OBC (W)	Std IV	Agriculture
Suresh Raja Ram Patil	Upa-Sarpanch	40	Mali	OBC	Std X	Agriculture
Vikram Sukhdev Patil	Member	50	Maratha	General	Std IV	Agriculture
Danged Atmaram Patil	Member	30	Mali	OBC	Std X	Agriculture
Pratap Vikram Patil	Member	32	Mali	OBC	Std XII	Agriculture
Jamid Nathu Mansuri	Member	35	Muslim	General	Std VII	Mattress maker
Nimba Thanha Bhil	Member	40	Bhil	ST	Std IV	Agricultural labour
Vatsalabai Laxman Mahajan (w)	Member	40	Mali	OBC	Std IV	Agriculture
Dagubai Bahurao Mahajan (w)	Member	50	Mali	OBC (W)	Illiterate	Agriculture

Devakabai is literate and well informed on panchayat matters. She chairs the meetings – her husband never attends meetings since he is not a panchayat member and she signs all papers. He deals with people, particularly men. This overcomes her limitations as daughter-in-law of the village.

The arrangement seems to have worked smoothly. Chhagan Patil is educated upto 10th standard. He is a well-to-do farmer with irrigated land and large poultry in partnership with an affinal relative. Devakabai donates all her honorarium to the panchayat. With that money they have purchased a public address system for the panchayat. Two other members have donated ceiling fans for the office. The panchayat participated in the state level village cleanliness campaign and competition with great enthusiasm. The leaders offered their own tractors and bullock carts free of charge to level the village lanes and remove the garbage. They were disappointed when they did not get the prize.

When there was shortage of drinking water in Mandurne and the surrounding villages, and their own panchayat well dried up, they promptly solved the problem by paying a farmer in the neighbouring village to buy water from his well for the session, with the result that Mandurne people were getting daily supply of water while several neighbouring villages had to go without it for several days. On the whole, there is overall approval among the villagers of the arrangement worked out by the sarpanch and her husband. The panchayat is functioning smoothly, although one of the opposition members in the panchayat was murmuring to me about the absurdity of the arrangement. Why should there be a reservation for women if they cannot do the work, he asked.

According to some villagers, there is nothing wrong in this arrangement. This is bound to happen in the transition period. Earlier young women never entered the public sphere. Now, they have come out and attend public meetings. That itself is a big change for the village like Mandurne. The next woman sarpanch will perhaps do all the work herself without depending too much on the man in the family. Devakabai's is really a case of proxy sarpanch but luckily for her and the village the panchayat work has not suffered. Of course, the objective of empowering women is far from fulfilled. Devakabai is sarpanch for name's sake. The other two woman members of the panchayat are not very different. They attend the panchayat meetings but rarely open their mouth. They do not air their views even on matters affecting women such as low attendance of girls in school and lack of proper toilet facilities for women.

There is one ST member belonging to the Bhil tribe. He has not been empowered at all. Although studied upto 4th class, he is a poor agricultural labourer. There is not enough work in the village. So, he migrates to Gujarat for sugarcane harvesting for six months in a year. That income helps him to support his family. Being away for six months, he is not active in the panchayat work. Besides he has no ideas, energy and initiative to do anything for his community. Inspite of reservation and government's tribal welfare programmes, Bhils have remained uneducated, backward and poor unlike the Mahars (SC) who are far more advanced.

Mandurne Gram Panchayat is functioning smoothly, thanks to the effective leadership of Chhagan Patil and the efficient Gram Sevak. Of course, the objective of including the excluded and empowering the women and STs is far from achieved. The dominant caste and patriarchy continue to rule in the village. The women and STs have willingly submitted to their rule accepting continuation of their traditional subordination.

Alwadi: The Village

Alwadi is a relatively small village with a population of 1,088 according to the 1991 census. Its location has advantages as well as disadvantages. It is situated close to the reservoir of the dam on the Manyad river. Its wells are always full due to percolation of water from the reservoir. This has enabled the farmers to cultivate irrigated cash crops such as sugarcane, which has led to marked prosperity of the village and particularly of its farmers. Throughout the summer of 2002, when many neighbouring villages where faced with acute shortage of drinking water, Alwadi never faced any scarcity. On the other hand, being at least 6 kms away from the main road, Alwadi suffers physical inconvenience due to difficulties of communication and a sense of isolation. Being small in size means having smaller number of voters (only 800), which does not give Alwadi people any political clout to bargain for political positions. In every election, they complained, the political parties including BJP, Congress and Shiv Sena do not take their claims for party tickets seriously.

In Alwadi, the Marathas enjoy a decisive dominance due to their overwhelming numerical strength, economic power arising out of near monopoly of landownership, and high social status as Marathas. Bhils and Mahars are in good numbers but smaller than the Marathas. They are economically poor and dependent for employment on the Marathas.

Most of the 640 hectares of its cultivated land is irrigated and used for sugarcane cultivation which has contributed largely to the prosperity of the Marathas and others. There are 106 wells, with equal number of electric motor pumps to lift water. Twenty-one TV sets, 18 telephones, 21 motorcycles and 7 tractors and some other signs for material prosperity. As against this, the primary school is only upto 4th standard. There are not enough children to enable the school to open higher classes, with the result that boys and girls have to commute to neighbouring Saygaon village to study in higher classes. The caste distribution of voters in Alwadi is shown in Table 3.

Table 3
Caste Distribution of Voters in Alwadi

Caste	*Traditional occupation*	*Reservation category*	*No. of voters*
Maratha	Agricultural cultivation	–	354
Bhil	Labour	ST	210
Mahar (neo-Buddhists)	Agricultural labour	SC	117
Nandiwale	Worship of Nandi, agricultural labour	OBC	50
Koli	Water carrier, fishing, agricultural labour	ST	39
Sutar	Carpentry	OBC	10
Muslim	Agricultural labour	–	06
Mali	Agricultural cultivation	OBC	05
Dhangar	Shepherds	OBC	05
Mang	Rope making, playing music	SC	02
Gosavi	Mendicant	OBC	02
Total			800

Alwadi Panchayat

Being a small village Alwadi was for many years part of a joint panchayat with another small village (Deshmukhwadi) in the neighbourhood. The joint panchayat was divided into two separate panchayats in 1993. The second election to the separate panchayat was held in June 2000 and the sarpanch and upa-sarpanch were elected in September 2000 for period of five years. The composition of the Gram Panchayat is shown in Table 4.

In the June 2000 elections to the panchayat two panels of candidates were in the fray, one led by a BJP worker and the other put up by an NCP sympathiser. Elections are usually not fought on party lines. But, the two rival factions were known for their different political affiliations. The BJP leader's panel won five seats while the NCP worker's could win only two seats – both Marathas but one man and one woman. In the meetings, the man is mildly critical of the ruling group. The woman does not utter a word.

Madhukar Uttamrao Shinde is the leader of the ruling faction. He is a rich farmer educated upto 11th standard and active in BJP politics. He tried for a TPS ticket but the party favoured a candidate from Philkod. He was complaining that the claims of workers in small villages were always ignored. Since it was known that the sarpanch's post was reserved for an SC woman, Shinde and his group encouraged and supported Satabai Dhanraj Ahire – a Mahar woman. She is illiterate and poor, depending mainly on working as agricultural labourer with her husband. They are often helped by the Shinde family in times of need. With Satabai in the sarpanch's chair, Shinde and his supporters thought that they could steer the panchayat work smoothly according to their plans.

In return, for playing the game according to the group's design, Satabai has earned several benefits. These benefits are both social and economic. She sits in the main chair while presiding over the panchayat meeting. She does not talk much, but seems to understand the issues involved. Everybody addresses her with respect due to the chair. Being a former, untouchable who was not even allowed to enter higher caste houses, this must be a very satisfying experience for Satabai. When the meetings are in session, her husband Dhanraj Ahire takes around and watches the proceedings

Table 4

Name	*Designation*	*Age*	*Caste*	*Reservation category*	*Education*	*Occupation*
Satabai Dhanraj Ahire	Sarpanch	55	Mahar	SC (W)	Illiterate	Agriculture
Gorakh Malji Patil	Upasarpanch	36	maratha	OBC	Std VII	Agriculture + Contractor
Madhukar Uttamrao Shinde	Member	42	Maratha	OBC	Std XI	Agriculture
Valmik Dala Patil	Member	41	Maratha	General	Std IV	Agriculture
Karbhari Irbhan Pawar	Member	27	Bhil	ST	Std X	Agriculture
Popat Ganpat Patil	Member	45	Maratha	OBC	Std XI	Agriculture
Chitrakalabai Pralhad Patil (w)	Member	47	Maratha	General (w)	Illiterate	Agriculture

from a distance with a certain degree of pride. Going to the TPS office at Chalisgaon to attend meetings and to meet senior officials must also be a satisfying experience for a woman of Satabai's background. Of course, she is always escorted by someone, either the Gram Sevak or the panchayat's peon, who is also a Mahar.

Satabai has also received some material benefits. She gets a modest amount as honorarium for being a sarpanch, which is important for a poor family. She has also obtained a bicycle for her daughter who commutes to the neighbouring village for attending school since Alwadi school has no provision for higher classes. This is under a government scheme to enable girls from poor families to continue their education by using the facilities in the neighbouring villages.

Satabai has also succeeded in persuading the panchayat to construct a cement concrete platform to arrange social functions for her Mahar community. She is now trying to get a community hall constructed. A drain has already been constructed in the Dalit locality by the panchayat for removal of dirty water.

The panchayat has also accomplished other works for the village as a whole such as adding a class room to the school building and constructing dwellings for the poor under the Indira Awas Yojana. In all these achievements of the panchayat the Gram Sevak, Pandurang Mahadu Ahire's role has been crucial. He is hardworking and dedicated to panchayat work. Last year, he won the award for a model Gram Sevak in the taluka. He was judged the best among 80 Gram Sevaks.

The Bagul episode provides evidence of empowerment of Dalits at the village level, thanks to Panchayat Raj. Ashok Bagul is a peon in the panchayat office. He is a Mahar (SC) like Satabai. They may even be related to each other. One issue about his duties has been discussed in panchayat meetings several times. In the case of village drains the panchayat policy is that each household should clean that portion of the drain in front of their own house. This leaves the question of cleaning that portion of the drain which is not near anybody's house. Who should clean that portion? The panchayat cannot afford to employ somebody to do that work. It has no funds.

The panchayat members suggested that this work should be entrusted to Bagul since he does not have much work as a peon in the panchayat office. Besides, the cleaning of a certain portion of the village drain, that too on certain days in a week, will not be too much of a burden on him. Bagul argued that cleaning village drains was not part of a peon's duty, and that the panchayat should find some other solution. The issue was discussed in several monthly meetings of the panchayat. The same arguments were repeated every time by both the parties. The members used all means of persuasion, appeal for larger interests of the village, and subtle threats of harassment. Under constant pressure, Bagul would agree to do the work, but did not do it in practice. He even approached the panchayat employees' union at the taluka level. The union leaders felt that Bagul was defying the panchayat's orders because of silent support from the sarpanch. Sarpanch Satabai denied such a blame. They asked her to openly order him in the presence of all. Her reply was, since she did not order anyone, why should she order Bagul? "Let the panchayat pass a resolution and follow it with an office order." They cannot pass such a resolution. They know that cleaning drains is not peon's duty.

The Bagul episode illustrates an example of Dalit empowerment. Despite tremendous pressure by the panchayat leaders, Bagul tried to defend himself against what he considered to be injustice and dared to report the matter to the union leaders at the taluka level. What gives him so much courage? First, he is a Mahar inspired by Ambedkar's teachings to fight against injustice. Second, he feels confident because the sarpanch is a fellow Dalit. Perhaps, he expects her to stand by him if the matter reaches a critical point.

In the actions of Satabai and Bagul one sees the beginning of Dalit empowerment, thanks to the 73rd Amendment.

As against this, see the record of Kabhari Pawar, the Bhil (ST) member of the panchayat. He is very passive and hardly takes any interest in panchayat work. He does not seek panchayat benefits either for himself or for his community. Such is the contrast between Mahars and Bhils. When I asked Pawar why he was not active in panchayat work, and why he did not try to obtain benefits for his community – the Bhils, he just shrugged his shoulders saying he was not interested. "Besides", he said, "the Bhils won't appreciate if I tried to do anything for them. Then, why bother?" A Mahar member would not have reacted like this.

Pilkhod: The Village

Pilkhod is located on the right bank of the Girna river, 22 kms from Chalisgaon, the taluka town. The road from Chalisgaon to Pilkhod is connected to the national highway (Mumbai-Agra Road) at a distance of 30 kms near Malegaon town in Nashik district.

In 1991, the village had a population of 3,736. Currently, it is estimated to be around 5,500. The caste distribution of voters in Pilkhod is shown in Table 5.

Most of the land in the village is owned and cultivated by the Marathas and Malis. Landownership among other caste groups is marginal. They depend for their livelihood on crafts and services in addition to agricultural labour.

Pilkhod, as a whole, has proposed since 1968 with the introduction of electricity in the village which enabled many farmers to instal, electric pumps on their wells to cultivate irrigated cash crops such as sugarcane, bananas and vegetables. With economic prosperity, there have also come about other changes in the village. The village school has been upgraded upto XII standard. The water supply scheme was set up in 1982. There are branches of two banks. More than 200 households have TV sets and over 50 have telephones. Frequent buses are available to travel in the direction of both Chalisgaon and Malegaon. Everyday, more than 450 copies of local newspapers are sold in Pilkhod and its neighbourhood. There is also an agricultural school and an Industrial Training Institute (ITI) providing specialised vocational training to boys and girls from Pilkhod and surrounding villages.

The relationship between the Marathas and Malis in Pilkhod is marked by a subtle distrust and rivalry, if not open hostility. Both the major groups are more or less balanced in terms of numerical strength, landownership and social status. However, they differ in two respects. Traditionally, the Marathas occupied positions of

Table 5
Caste Distribution of Voters in Pilkhod

Caste	*Traditional occupation*	*Reservation category*	*No. of voters*
Maratha (Kunabi Patil)	Agricultural cultivation	OBC	669
Mali (gardners)	Agricultural cultivation	OBC	512
Koli	Water carrier, fishing, agricultural labour	ST	382
Muslim	Agri work, crafts and petty trading	-	259
Bhil	Labourer	ST	257
Mahar (neo-Buddhists)	Agricultural labour	SC	167
Teli	Oil pressing	OBC	63
Wani	Trading	—	42
Sonar	Goldsmith	OBC	40
Nhavi	Barber	OBC	38
Gosavi	Mendicant	OBC	30
Chambhar	Leather work	SC	26
Jain	Business	—	21
Shimpi	Tailoring	OBC	20
Sutar	Carpentry	OBC	20
Mang	Rope making, plying music	SC	13
Brahman	Priest	—	12
Gond	Agricultural labour	ST	10
Dhivar	Fishing	OBC	09
Mahanubhav	Monk	—	08
Marwari	Business	—	07
Bhoi	Grain parcher	OBC	07
Rajput	Agricultural cultivation	OBC	07
Panchal	Iron craftsman	OBC	06
Dhobi	Washerman	OBC	05
Leva Patil	Agricultural cultivation	—	03
Garudi	Snake charmer/ magician	OBC	02
Total			2,635

power in the village. They had the hereditary claim to the offices of Police Patil and Revenue Patil. This gave them access to and contacts with government administration at the taluka and district levels. This also gave them the confidence of being superior to others as they were the rulers, so to say. The other difference was that all Malis belonged to the Mahanubhav (Vaishnavite) sect preaching and practising strict vegetarianism and teetotalism. This religious cult enabled them to be industrious and parsimonious which improved their economic condition. Some Maratha families lost their fortunes due to addiction to alcohol. When the democratic politics emerged and hereditary claims to power (including the officers of Police Patil and Revenue Patil) were abolished, with their improved economic condition, the Malis started asserting claims to a legitimate share in the village power structure.

The Gram Panchayat elections in 1995 gave indication of intense rivalry between Marathas and Malis. Two panels of candidates were put up, one led by a Maratha and the other by a Mali candidate with representatives of some other castes. The elections created tremendous bitterness between the two groups. The results were mixed, with Malis having an edge over the Marathas who felt outmanoeuvred.

Unfortunately, for both the dominant rival groups, the post of sarpanch was reserved for a woman of ST category. A Koli woman (the only ST female in the panchayat) was elected sarpanch. The Malis tried to control panchayat affairs through manipulation and backseat driving. The sarpanch was poor and illiterate. Her husband was also illiterate. The Marathas also tried to take advantage of the situation. In the process the rivalry between Marathas and Malis intensified to such an extent that for the first time in living memory there was a complete breakdown of social intercourse between the two. They stopped attending social events such as marriage and funeral in the homes of the rival caste members. This had never happened in the past. The Malis were very unhappy when the Marathas stopped all social interactions with them. They decided to retaliate by boycotting the elections to the village co-operative credit society. When non-cooperation between the two caste groups reached extreme limits in created unpleasantness all over which led to some rethinking in both the camps.

The hostility between the two groups further intensified during the TPS elections in 1997. Prakash Ramchandra Baviskar of the Mali caste was the Congress candidate. The BJP put up a Maratha, Ananda Fakira Patil. Both belonged to Pilkhod. In the bitterly fought contest the Mali candidate won defeating his Maratha rival.

The atmosphere of hostility and distrust had an adverse impact on the functioning of the panchayat. The Gram Sevak took advantage of the situation and misappropriated a sum of a few lakhs of rupees (estimated to be over Rs. 7 lakhs) from funds received under the Indira Avas Yojana and similar other development projects. The Gram Sevak could do this due to two reasons. The sarpanch was an illiterate poor woman belonging to Koli caste legally recognised as ST. Her husband was also illiterate. The Gram Sevak could pressurise her in giving her thumb impression on cheques and other documents, saying that it was government order which she could not refuse. He also gave her some money from time to time to overcome her reluctance to cooperate. Perhaps, one or two panchayat members were also involved. The Gram Sevak could indulge in such a big fraud because of lack of vigilance on the part of most members as they were engaged in fighting among themselves.

When the fraud come out it opened the eyes of the panchayat members and other village leaders. Some of them took initiative in bringing the two rival caste groups together in the wider interests of the village community. It was acknowledged that the village as a whole suffered because of their enmity, and unity among them was imperative to save the village from further ruining. Thus, the leaders of the two dominant groups – Marathas and Malis – came together and complained to the higher authorities about the fraud. The government sent a special audit team which established the fraud and the Gram Sevak was suspended from service. Appropriate legal action against the Gram Sevak is in progress at the usual slow pace.

The panchayat members passed a no-confidence motion against the ST woman sarpanch for being a party to the fraud. But she could not be removed from the post of sarpanch, as there was no other female panchayat member belonging to a Scheduled Tribe. So the Koli woman continued to function as sarpanch till the end of the term although no-confidence motion was passed against her. The big fraud and the events surrounding it vitiated the atmosphere in the village and brought all development of the panchayat to a standstill.

The events relating to Pilkhod Gram Panchayat during 1995-2000 had far reaching consequences for the village as a whole during the next election. When the election to the panchayat approached in April 2000, the entire village community had a meeting to decide on a strategy. There was an overwhelming demand to have uncontested or unopposed election. But, how to reach a consensus among nearly 2,600 voters belonging to two religious communities (Hindu and Muslim) and more than 20 caste group? And, how to bring together two equally strong main contenders – Marathas and Malis?

One thing was clear. The events of the previous five years had taught them a lesson. The fight between the two rival dominant groups, Marathas and Malis, not only deprived them of any share in power, but the development work of the whole village also suffered and the unscrupulous petty bureaucrat cheated them by misappropriating huge funds. They did not want this to be repeated. A compromise had to be reached on the posts of sarpanch and ten other panchayat members.

After a great deal of debate, it was agreed that the major caste group in the village will nominate one member each irrespective of their individual numerical strength among the voters. Thus the top ten caste groups (in the terms of their members) were to contribute one member each (see Table 5). The Muslims, irrespective of difference among them, were treated as one caste group. The Bhils and Kolis, the only two ST groups, had three reserved seats. The Kolis were allotted two seats and Bhils one, partly because Kolis were slightly larger in number than the Bhils. Thus, except the Kolis, all other caste groups, including the Muslims, got one seat each. Although the members were relevant in selecting the top ten groups, they were ignored in allotting the seats. Each caste group was given one seat, irrespective of its numerical strength. Thus, Marathas and Malis got only one seat each even though they had over 500 voters each. Similarly, Sonars (Goldsmith) and Nhavis (Barber) also got one seat each even though they had less than 50 voters each. Mahars (neo-Buddhists), Muslims, Telis and Wanis were also allotted one seat each. It means all castes were considered equal in the distribution of power above a certain threshold. Only Kolis got two seats because of reservation.

The question of selecting a candidate from each caste was left to individual castes. For this purpose, each caste group held discussions in its own ranks in general meeting in small groups and agreed upon one candidate to be nominated on its behalf. Thus, when all castes gave the names of their agreed candidates, they were asked to file their nomination papers. No one else filed any nomination. Since there were no other nominations, there was no contest and all the candidates were declared elected unopposed.

The choice of sarpanch was also decided by arriving at a consensus. Since the post was reserved for an OBC this time, the choice was mainly confined the two dominant caste groups, viz., Malis and Kunabi Patils (i.e., Marathas). It was agreed to share the office equally between the two groups for half the period each. Accordingly, Raosaheb Dharma Patil, a Kunabi Patil (OBC), was elected sarpanch unopposed in September 2000. The understanding is that he will resign after two-and-a-half years, and will be replaced by Kknath Jamrao Patil (OBC) by electing him unopposed for the remaining term of two-and-a-half years.

When the neighbouring villages of Mandurne, Tamawadi and Saygaon came to know about the way the people of Pilkhod had handled their panchayat elections, they also decided to follow the path of consensus in place of contest though with one difference. instead of asking individual caste groups to nominate a chosen candidate after holding its own internal discussions, the names of candidates representing different caste groups were decided in the general body meeting of the village community as a whole.

Pilkhod Panchayat

Pilkhod being a larger village and having a larger panchayat provides a different kind of example for study. Composition of Pilkhod Gram Panchayat is shown in Table 6. Not only that it has a larger budget, larger staff, and larger number of clients and complaints to handle, there is also a far greater complexity in each of its functions.

Just supplying water on a daily basis to such a large population during the time of scarcity can be a tension-ridden task. There are complaints galore every day. Even seeing that all the streetlights work can be difficult at times. Keeping such a populous place clean is often difficult.

During the summer of 2002 water supply was the most critical issue. The sarpanch and panchayat members often met on daily basis and discussed the strategy to be adapted to keep the population satisfied. It was not easy.

On the inclusion/exclusion or empowerment issue there is a mixed picture. Let us bring with the negative example. There are four women among 11 members in the panchayat. One woman is Koli (ST), doubly deprived or excluded being a woman and a tribal. She is educated and intelligent and understands what is going on in the panchayat. But she keeps herself aloof and avoids getting involved. She attends meetings, but avoids expressing her views. She is scared of getting involved in village politics. Among the three other women, who are all OBC, two are illiterate and rarely speak. The third woman is educated but very shy to speak in a meeting. For all these women coming to the panchayat office, sitting with seven men from different castes and age groups and taking tea with them is itself a new experience. No village woman ever comes to the panchayat office on her own. She will send a male member if she had any work. Given the tradition, active participation by these women is difficult. Another reason for their passivity could be their nomination instead of election. In the election based on compromise they did not willingly come forward to contest the election. They were persuaded to file nomination and were elected without doing anything. They all belong to small and marginal artisan castes who have very little stake in the village problems. They all expressed anguish over difficulties faced by women in toilet matters. This is a problem common to most villages. Women have no convenient places to ease themselves. Again, they say this quietly, but do not raise their voice with determination to compel the panchayat leaders to take some action.

Table 6
Composition of Pilkhod Gram Panchayat

Name	*Designation*	*Age*	*Caste*	*Reservation category*	*Education*	*Occupation*
Raosaheb Dharma Patil	Sarpanch	51	Maratha	OBC	Std XI	Agriculture
Mango Punju Yashod	Upa- Sarpanch	62	Mahar	SC	Std VII + teacher training	Retd Teacher
Purushottam Randas Deo	Member	40	Wani	General	Std X	Contractor
Eknath Jamrao Mali	Member	47	Mali	OBC	Std XI	Agriculture
Dagadu Kashinath More	Member	35	Koli	ST	Std X	Bus driver
Shaikh Iqbal Shaikh Sandu	Member	58	Muslim (Manyar)	General	Std IV	Dari weaver
Rajdhar Rajaram Bhil	Member	60	Bhil	ST	Std V	Agricultural labour
Meenabai Nimba Sonar	Member	42	Sonar	OBC (W)	Std XI	Housewife
Sarubai Baburao Chaudhari	Member	55	Teli	OBC (W)	Illiterate	Agriculture
Rukhmabai Dagadu Chitte	Member	57	Nhavi	OBC (W)	Illiterate	Agriculture
Indubai Babulal More	Member	45	Koli	ST (W)	Std VIII	Agriculture

There are two ST men, one a Bhil and the other a Koli. Both are educated and articulate. They often participate in discussions. But they are not taken seriously. They have no following even in their own community. In other words, they do not have even a nuisance value. They too do not seem to have been empowered. They might have acquired some status by their membership of the panchayat where prominent people sit. But, the sarpanch and others do not attach much weight to their views.

The only positive example of inclusion and empowerment is the Upa-sarpanch, Mango Punju Yashod, a Mahar (SC) member. He is 62. Has retired after 38 years of a teaching career in different primary schools. In addition to being a good teacher and organiser he is also a social worker. After retirement in 1999 he is devoting all his time and energy to social work, mostly for his own Mahar community. He has set up a credit society for poor Mahars and collected a capital of Rs. 4 lakhs. He is also working for the construction of a community hall in the Mahar colony. He has been a vocal and active member of the panchayat after his election in 2000. As a panchayat member he has used his position to get a protective wall constructed in the area where Mahar women go for their toilet needs. According to the government directive, 22 per cent of all grants received under Jawahar Rojgar Yojana have to be used for the welfare of SC/ST population in the village. Most panchayats do not implement this directive. He constantly reminds the Pilkhod panchayat about this.

Yashod is vocal and articulate and expresses his views in meetings constructively with clarity. He often questions the sarpanch and the Gram Sevak about some of their decisions whereas most others keep quiet. Naturally, the sarpanch does not like him.

As a panchayat member, Yashod (popularly addressed as Guruji in the village) does not seek any personal benefit for himself. He does seek benefits for his Mahar community. But he is also willing to work for the village community as a whole. Whenever there is a crisis, he is willing to join the team to tackle it. Whether it is a new water supply scheme, or getting a health centre for the village, or persuading people to pay their house tax and water supply bills, he is ready to contribute his bit in whatever way possible.

Among all the three panchayats, Yashod Guruji emerges as the best example of empowerment under Panchayati Raj. Why is so? Again, one has to go back to his being a Mahar and the influence of Ambedkar's teachings. Being educated and respected as a teacher, he does not suffer from any inferiority complex and speaks and acts confidently in any situation. Education and a certain degree of awareness about social issues seem to make a difference in the case of Yashod Guruji.

Conclusion

We have seen a variety of responses to the process of inclusion or empowerment. The provisions of 73rd Constitution Amendment Act are common to all the three panchayats. Then, how to explain the differential responses?

First, let us understand that the process of empowerment is not one quantum jump. You do not jump from a zero power situation to an all-power situation. Empowerment is a long journey and there are several stages in its path. Let us try to identify these stages. In my view, there are at least five stages in this process:

1. *Opening up or coming out:* When women who never came out of their homes acquire enough courage to come out and sit in a public office along with strangers belonging to different castes and age groups, it is a first step in empowerment. This applies also to ex-untouchable men and women who come out and occupy seats as equals in a panchayat at meeting.
2. *Acquiring symbolic features of power*: A woman or a Dalit man may not take decisions and may accept decisions taken by others. However, presiding over a meeting and signing the papers as an office bearer is also a sign of empowerment, however limited it might be. Satabai may be putting her thumb impression on papers recording decisions taken by village notables. But for a former untouchable it is a stage in empowerment.
3. *Using power for one's self or one's family*: When Satabai obtained a bicycle for her daughter under the girl's education scheme, it was an important stage in her empowerment. It

made her learn the process of acquiring tangible benefits by using her position of power.

4. The next stage is *to use power for the benefit of one's own community*, i.e., using power for higher purpose. Satabai got platform constructed for the Mahar community. Yashod Guruji succeeded in getting a protective wall constructed for the Mahar women's toilet needs. He was pressurising the panchayat to spend 22 per cent of the Jawahar Rojgar Yojana grant for the welfare of SCs and STs.
5. Finally, when the women and Dalit members are able *to work for the village community as a whole*. That is the ultimate test of empowerment, i.e., when they transcend the boundaries of their limited constituencies and work for the community as a whole. It also implies acceptance by the community of their larger role. Yashod Guruji is gradually moving in that direction.

These stages need not occur discretely or sequentially. They are presented here mainly for analytical or heuristic purposes. They may also overlap in real life.

How to explain the differential responses of panchayat members to the process of empowerment? It really depends on the nature of obstacles one has to overcome and the degree of favourable conditions available to the panchayat members.

Gender disabilities are a major obstacle to overcome. Same is the case with ex-untouchables or Dalits. The obstacles they face in being accepted, as community leaders are equally formidable. Given the long history of oppression of women and Dalits in our society it will take quite sometime for these sections to acquire and exercise power given by the constitutional amendment.

Poverty is another obstacle. A panchayat member gets only Rs. 10 as 'sitting fee' for attending a meeting. If he is an agricultural labourer he will lose Rs. 50 as his daily wage. How will he feed his family with 10 rupees? No wonder, he decides not attend the meeting. Both the Bhil members of Mandurne and Alwadi gave this reason for their absence from meetings. On the other hand, Yashod Guruji gets a modest pension. He does not go out for work. He has all this time for social work.

Education makes a lot of difference. Greater the education, greater will be the possibility of empowerment. Throughout the fieldwork and interviews with all sections of society education was emphasised. No one opposed reservation for women or SCs and STs. But putting minimum as an eligibility condition was a universal demand. Again, Yashod Guruji is effective as a panchayat member largely because of his educational background.

Social background of a member also counts a lot. Among the SCs and the STs of Maharashtra the Mahars are far ahead of others in education, social reform, employment, cultural achievements and political organisation, thanks to Ambedkar's legacy. When they sit in panchayat meetings, all this background enables them to perform their role confidently and effectively as compared to, say, the Bhils. Satabai may be illiterate, but she is doing better than the Bhil men and OBC women.

All the factors listed above taken together boil down to acquiring resources and skills. If women and Dalits succeed in acquiring some of these resources and skills, they will be successful in their march on the path of inclusion and empowerment.[2]

Notes

1. The positions of panchayat members are reserved for different categories of population such as Other Backward Classes (OBCs), Scheduled Castes (SCs) and Scheduled Tribes (STs), according to their proportion in the village population. In the case of women it is 33 per cent throughout.

   For the offices of sarpanch and Upasarpanch there is a system of rotation among eight categories such as (1) OBC, (2) OBC -Women, (3) SC, (4) SC-women, (5) ST, (6) ST- women, (7) Open/General-women.

   Women are eligible to contest for positions reserved for them and also for those which are unreserved provided they belong to that category.

   For example, an ST woman can contest for a post reserved for ST- women as well as for a post reserved for ST where both men and women would be eligible. She can also contest under Open/ General, and Open/General-women.

But she is not eligible to contest under the remaining four categories, viz., OBC, OBC-women, SC, SC-women.

This paper is a part of the larger research project on 'Inclusion of Excluded Communities through Panchayati Raj' undertaken by the Institute of Social Sciences, New Delhi.

2. I am grateful to Professor A.M. Shah for his valuable comments and suggestions on the earlier draft.

References

Dahl, Robert A. 1961. *Who Governs? Democracy and Power in an American City*. New Haven: Yale University Press.

Mills, C. Wright. 1956. *The Power Elite*. New York: Oxford University Press.

Palshikar, Suhas. 2002, "Triangular Competition and Bipolar Politics: Elections to Local Bodies in Maharashtra", *Economic and Political Weekly*. 37: 1273-80.

Polsby, Nelson W. 1962. *Community Power and Political Theory*. New Haven: Yale University Press.

3

Representative and Participatory Democracy

Indigenisation of Indian Democracy*

Partha Nath Mukherji

Let me begin by saying that the theme of the seminar is indeed a very vital one because it relates to the future of India. What kind of democracy and development are we going to have in future in the context of the rapid transformation that is taking place all over the world and in our country? Today, we figure in the international discourse as a country that is destined to be a superpower in a decade or two. There is an all-round confidence and a spirit of optimism amongst us today that we shall face the challenges ahead to become one of the foremost nations in the coming years. It is in this context that the theme acquires signal importance, for it is not easy to anticipate the manner in which the forces of development will sweep the country affecting the vast masses of our people. We pride ourselves to be the most complex and unique democracy in the world, an enigma for the western democratic world. We have not ceased recreating and evolving our democracy.

---

* Slightly modified version of the keynote address delivered at the National Seminar on *Panchayati Raj Institutions and Rural Development in Western India* (January 24-25, 2005), organised by the School of Social Sciences, Swami Ramanand Teerth Marathwada University, Nanded.

The theme of Panchayati Raj is part of that story. Are we going to make ourselves a unique democracy? Although many of us may be familiar with the evolutionary tract of our political institutions, my intention here is to provide a framework within which we ought to look at the evolution of Panchayati Raj and how this institution will grow and develop. Thousands of years of history have seen our panchayats functioning at the grassroots level. True, there are scholars who have doubted its democratic character. The fact remains, however, that no matter what was the nature of panchayats, elected or not, this was the institution in place for millennia. It did exist as a durable institution and survived through the ravages of time. It witnessed invasions, and went on adapting itself to the changing circumstances. It was British colonialism that made it an instrument of revenue collection in a manner that was not done before. The British used it in the manner they deemed fit consistent with their colonial objectives. This was reason enough for the Indian nationalist movement to 'restore' the institution as the primary democratic unit for the future polity. Gandhi, as we all know, was vociferous about its potential for true democracy.

The Early Phase of Alternative Discourses

What I wish to present here is the evolution of this institution, not as chronological history, but as a process that is encountering the contradiction between participatory and representative forms of democracy. The democratic institutions that we adopted at the turn of 1947 were the legacy of a distorted representative democracy of the Westminster variety adapted to colonial rule. Through the Government of India Act of 1935 the British introduced limited franchise, inducting us into a structure of political power that ultimately became the basis of our political system. In effect, on the one hand, this entrenched political system, which evolved out of the colonial dispensation, was in place until 1947 and had to be handed over into independent India. Whilst at the same time, a live alternative discourse on Panchayati Raj as India's indigenous grassroots local level participatory democracy, remained strong, resilient and vibrant. It argued for the village panchayat as a primary unit of self-government over which the superstructure of a self-governing political system could be erected.

The indigenous political system in the imagination of our nationalist leadership, particularly following Mahatma Gandhi, was that of an inversion of the pyramidal representative form of democracy as practised in Britain. This is a very important point to keep in mind. I am suggesting that from day one of our independence till we passed the path breaking 73rd and 74th amendments to our Constitution, there has been a constant dialectic spanning over four decades between the colonially inherited representative form of democracy and the indigenous participatory democracy. It is to be expected – now that this contradiction has acquired a structural basis for playing itself out – that a balance will be achieved between the inherited, adapted parliamentary institutions and the indigenous evolving Panchayati Raj Institutions (PRIs) over a period of time.

Why is it that in spite of the strong nationalist discourse in favour of a more participatory indigenous panchayati form of democracy, we opted for the western type parliamentary form? The reasons are not difficult to appreciate. First, to design an altogether new structure of democracy in the indigenous format for the new nation was a stupendously complex job, particularly since our's is a country with immense diversity with millennia old accretions of inequities. Second, historically, the evolution of the parliamentary form of democracy in Britain was associated with the industrial revolution. As such, it was perceived as the engine of industrial revolution and western modernity. India was in a hurry to make up for the lost time under colonialism that had aborted its march towards modernity. The country had myriad problems of poverty, food shortages, industrial growth, health, education, etc. to attend to. I recall Prime Minister Nehru remarking once, that India needed to catch up in ten years what Britain had achieved in 100 years! Could the sea of villages be garnered through panchayats to address the tall tasks of modern nation-state building? Quite understandably, the nationalist elite under Nehru's leadership did not have the confidence that a polity based on scattered decentralised panchayats would be capable of delivering the required growth momentum to the urgent tasks of the nation.

The strategy of rapid rural and industrial development appeared consistent with centralised planning through Five-Year Plans crafted in the Planning Commission. In the First Five-Year Plan agriculture and rural development found priority. The Community Development Programme was introduced to bring about rural development. Nehru conceived rural infrastructures in terms of large dams for irrigation and hydel power, romantically, as the temples of modern India.

In the Second Five-Year Plan the emphasis shifted to industrial development. It was realised that imports of manufactured goods was costing heavy to the exchequer and was keeping India dependent on advanced western countries. Imported technology and science were proving very expensive; hence, India had to develop import substitution industrialisation (ISI) to become a self-reliant economy and nation. We could not wait and lag behind others. We had to develop to produce the much-needed wealth to combat poverty and inequalities. So, there was an element of extreme urgency to increase the pace of development.

The alternative discourse took off from Gandhi. M.N. Roy, Tagore, Chittaranjan Das, Rajagopalachari, Vinoba Bhave, Jayaprakash Narayan were either a part of this discourse or came close to it. Gandhi, as one who piloted the Indian national movement, was very clear about the Westminster model in its colonial incarnation – it was a highly centralised system of power. His was a fundamentally different position. He looked "upon an increase of power of the state with the greatest fear because, although while apparently doing good by minimising exploitation, it does the greatest harm to mankind by destroying individuality which lies at the root of all progress". He further argued, since "centralisation cannot be sustained and defended without adequate force", it was inconsistent with a non-violent society (cited in Ghosh, 2000: 1-2).

Gandhi believed that the real development of India could be possible through its indigenous political system in which the centralised state would wield only such power as was not possible to be handled by lower tiers of participatory governance. The state was not the architect of development. It was the people who had to work out their own development. More positively, Gandhi was for a multi-layered autonomous vertical integration of political institutions constituting the political system, with its base as India's villages and its superstructure at the Centre – manifesting a descending level of power over the people as we move from the base to the superstructure. He believed, "if the village perishes, India also will perish". Gandhi, like many others, drew inspiration from the long tradition of panchayats in the Indian civilisation, aborted at times by invasions and distorted by British imperial interests.[1] He clearly envisaged the village panchayat as an elected body enjoying its legislative, administrative and judicial autonomy, as the best guarantee of "perfect democracy based upon individual freedom" (Gandhi, 1942: 12).

Tagore expressed strong views very similar to Gandhi. He was critical of the way the British were trying to manipulate the panchayats to serve their political ends. In no uncertain terms he observed:

> "At one time, panchayat was our own institution. Now, it is going to be a product manufactured in the office of the government. The two cannot be the same thing. The power of the panchayat that does not flow from the will of the people, but originates from the delegation of authority by the government will be nothing but a curse on the people", because, he argued, "the people exercising power of such panchayats would act as the agents of government" (cited in Ghosh, 2000: 5).

Ghosh points out that for the great poet "small rural communities did not depend upon the central power for their social, economic, religious or cultural pursuits. Basic public functions like providing facilities for education and health or supply of drinking water, or settlement of local disputes, the community did not depend upon the state...In such a society the individual was conscious of his *duties* to the community and the role he should play for the sustenance of communal life" (Ghosh, 2000: 5; italics mine). The poet argued that authority delegated to village panchayats by an imperial power would amount to making them act as the agents of the colonial government.

M.N. Roy, one of the tallest Marxists India has produced, who served as a member of the Comintern, but later gave up Marxism to establish the philosophy of radical humanism, echoed identical concerns about the Westminster form of democracy. He argued while power had a legitimate place in history, it was how power was distributed, shared, and exercised that really mattered. Commenting on Roy's political thinking, Ghosh points out that he was against the concentration of power in the hands of the privileged few, which the representative form of democracy fosters. By a system of delegation of authority the parliamentary system atomises the citizen and robs him of any kind of control over the state. This leads to a disjuncture between the state and society (Ghosh, 2000: 8). Roy observes:

> So long as the state is not coterminous with society, it remains an instrument of power in the hands of some section of society...To be real democracy must be direct...In so far as democracy is not government of the people and by the people, it is not democracy (cited in Ghosh, 2000; Roy, 1960: 67).

Roy went to the extent of preparing a draft constitution for of what he called 'organised democracy'. He believed that a truly democratic state might emerge only if it was based on the foundation of the 'local republic', which could "combine all functions of the state as they affect the local life" (ibid.: 72).

While Tagore's critique was specific to the way the British dispensation was fiddling around with our traditional panchayat institution, Gandhi and M.N. Roy were theorising at a more abstract universalistic level of participatory democracy. Both Tagore and Gandhi were carrying on serious rural experimentation – the poet in Sriniketan and the Mahatma in Sevagram. Had Tagore survived longer the influence of the duo in the shaping of the future polity might have made a qualitative difference in our Constitution-making process.

The burden of this short discussion on the three Indian stalwarts is to substantiate the fact that there was a strong discourse on installing participatory democracy, bottom-up, during the nationalist movement, which the dominant political elite, already saddled with power in the extant colonial institutional transplants, were unable to pursue for reasons I have mentioned above. Almost by default, the entrenched, colonially constructed, highly elitist model of representative democracy became the obvious choice of the political elite socialised in this system.

Quite apart from the fact that the nationalist political elite had dilemmas that restrained them from creating a new political system, there was a stream of thinking, very vibrant and not least, irrelevant, that must be taken into account. There was strong rejection of the Panchayat Raj formulations by Gandhi from Babasaheb Ambedkar, who was convinced that in such a decentralised polity, the fate of the socially discriminated Scheduled Caste untouchables would be sealed in the hands of the upper castes. His strident opposition to this idea was made in no uncertain terms, when he stated:

> I hold that these village republics have been the ruination of India. I am therefore surprised that those who condemn provincialism and communalism should come forward as champions of the village. What is the village but a sink of localism, a den of ignorance, narrow mindedness and communalism? I am glad that the Draft Constitution has discarded the village and adopted the individual as unit (cited in Jain, 1967: 128).

When it was brought to the notice of Gandhi that the framers of the Constitution of free India had no place for the panchayats, he was very upset. The debate sparked off by the position taken up by Baba Saheb was a source of grave anxiety and could not be dismissed, but it was not reason enough to reject the whole paradigm of participatory democracy. This resulted in the insertion of a face saving Article 40 in the Constitution to appease the Mahatma. This Article 40 would have far-reaching consequences for the evolution of democracy in India. It read:

> The State shall take steps to organise Village Panchayats and endow them with such powers and authority as may be necessary to enable them to function as *units of self-government* (quoted in ibid.: 59; emphasis added).

It was this single insertion in the Constitution that provided the necessary scope for the process of progressive democratic decentralisation to operate continuously over time, allowing the space for the alternative discourse of participatory democracy to evolve in a dialectical relationship with the entrenched forces of the centralised representative democracy.

After Gandhi, Gandhians like Vinoba, Jayaprakash Narayan, Siddharaj Dhaddha and a host of others continued in their attempts to chart out an alternate agrarian communitarian system through a non-political organisation the Sarva Seva Sangh (approximating the Lok Sevak Dal) of Gandhi's conception. The *sarvodaya bhoodan gramdan* movement, after a spirited beginning, lost out to the dominant forces entrenched in the Westminster legacy and to the violent Maoist inspiration for revolutionary transformation.

The Praxis of Nation-State Building and the Compulsions of Revisiting the Panchayati Raj

Caught up in the glare of the western liberal democratic paradigm of modernity India's nationalist elite leadership was naturally impatient to catch up with the more advanced countries using science and technology to improve production in industry and agriculture. It introduced anti-feudal land reforms by abolishing landlordism and introducing ceiling in landholdings, so that surplus lands thus obtained would be redistributed amongst the landless and the poor peasants. On the one hand, agriculture had to be given a boost in view of its pathetic performance under conditions of colonial exploitation. Massive irrigation projects with hydroelectricity generation, introduction of modern inputs of chemical fertiliser, hybrid seeds, pesticides, use of tractors etc. figured as priorities to be pursued. For this, factories for chemical fertilizers, pesticides, major and minor irrigation schemes had to be established. On the other hand, import substitution industrialisation (ISI) policy was vigorously undertaken to reduce the massive expenses involved in purchasing technology, also symbolising the country's endeavour to reduce its dependence on Western countries. It is in this context that one has to visualise, and perhaps appreciate, how panchayat and people's participation got relegated to the background.

It is under such compulsive circumstances that a veteran American extension expert Albert Mayers, in the district of Etawah in Uttar Pradesh, initiated India's rural development programme in 1952 under the inspiration of the nationalist leader and Chief Minister of Uttar Pradesh Gobind Ballabh Pant. The concept of the multipurpose Village Level Worker (VLW) was tried and conceptualised. Through extension methods various activities like agricultural demonstrations, soil conservation, improvement in animal husbandry, and village sanitation were initiated. Social education was developed for preparing the people's participation in development. While he appreciated the Gandhian focus on small communities, his values relating to containment of spiralling needs did not find favour with Mayers as he felt "that would mean imposing a very low ceiling on material adequacy and welfare" (quoted in Jain, 67: 57).

Around the same time, by mid-1951, Paul Hoffman, President of the Ford Foundation provided the support for fifteen pilot projects, in the pattern of Etawah in different states. Concurrently, a pioneering experiment had evolved out of a rehabilitation programme for displaced persons from Pakistan in Nilokheri near Karnal under the dynamic and inspired leadership of S.K. Dey. Imbued with Gandhian values Nilokheri developed on a more indigenous pattern. The newly appointed friendly U.S. ambassador to India pledged fifty million dollars, which led to the launching of fifty-five blocks of the Community Development Programme on October 2, 1952, Gandhi's birth anniversary (Dey, 1961: 67-71). Inaugurating the programme Nehru spoke:

> The work we are about to start today is in the service of the Motherland, in the service of the land of which we are all part. We should serve her with hard work, with the sweat of our brow. If necessary, we shall shed our blood, so that millions of our countrymen may go forward and that there may be an end to their trials and tribulations (quoted in Jain, 1967: 62).

The nationalist elite was caught between two equally major imperatives of rural India: (a) to unleash rapid rural development in order to pick up the sagging rural economy, and (b) to create conditions for the proper operation of self-governing local communities. Obviously, initially, they lacked confidence in the local communities to steer rapid development, which involved the introduction of modern agricultural science and technology. This also becomes clear from the objectives of the First Five-Year Plan relating to the programmes, which make the following points: (1) "Within the broad framework of national priorities, the actual programmes in localities should be determined by local needs." (2) "Unless people feel that a programme is theirs and value it as a practical contribution to their own welfare no substantial results will be gained." (3) "People's participation must be not only in project execution but project planning." (4) "If the people are to be trained to be builders of the future, the works have to be entrusted, even at a certain risk, to the people themselves through their representative agencies, the Government organisation furnishing them technical assistance and essential finance" (quoted in Taylor, 1965: 3).

Some of the extremely perceptive observations of the Ford Foundation Consultant Sociologist Carl C. Taylor are illuminating. The Community Development Programme in India was "the most gigantically planned and governmentally administered programme of its kind in the history of the world" (ibid.: 4). It sought revolutionary changes to be brought about by evolutionary methods in a society that was highly stratified (ibid.: 50). In order to achieve these ends, two principles and methods were involved: that of community development and of extension. While extension work related to the introduction of specific practices relating to agriculture, health, animal husbandry, sanitation, education and so on, it logically implied the existence of local groups functionally relevant and specific to these interests. In such a context the concept of leadership was functional to the tasks of carrying forward extension services. These groups were the agents of change from within the community that identified with the benefits of extension method associated with bringing about change in new practices (in agriculture, animal husbandry etc.). In contrast, community development involved the mobilisation of the whole community for the general benefit of the community. Community development methods correspondingly would mean discovering leadership that was functional to the role of community organisation. Clearly, an extension worker in community development was different from the 'specific purpose' extension worker. The VLW was an extension consultant of sorts whose job was to tie up with specific purpose extension workers by identifying rural leadership functional to specific extension works, not so much to identify community leaders.

Taylor found the roles of the VLW and extension workers getting more and more unsatisfactory with the expansion of the programme. He also viewed the mobilisation of community development as a movement, counterproductive, as this often ran counter to the role of the extension programmes. What came out as his most important conclusion found place in his epilogue and, surprisingly, not in the body of his report. He was clear that unless reforms in the institution of landownership took place at a meaningful level the efforts at Community Development Programme were unlikely to yield expected results.

It is generally commented that the extension approach in the Community Development Programme targeted the asseted and excluded the assetless families, creating problems of widening disparities, already compounded by a caste hierarchy. The local communities and groups, in course of time, began to be used as unpaid instruments of development programmes and projects not of their own choice.

First Evolutionary Landmark Towards Panchayati Raj

The Community Development Programme phase, more or less, covered the period of the First Five-Year Plan. This model ran out of steam preparing the ground for the setting up of the Balwant Rai Mehta (a respected Gandhian) Committee (1957) (BRMC). It was realised that in the rural development efforts put in so far, public involvement was not representative enough and as such was not effective. The BRMC evaluated the Community Development

Programme and the National Extension Service (NES) and concluded that "development cannot progress without responsibility and power. Community development can be real only when the community understands its problems, realises its responsibilities, exercises necessary powers through its chosen representatives and maintains a constant and intelligent vigilance on local administration." Given this objective, "an early establishment of statutory elective local bodies and *devolution* to them of the necessary resources, and power and authority", was recommended (in Mehta, 1978: 2-3; emphasis added). It is significant that the term 'devolution' had already figured. This is how the three-tier system of PRIs came to be established – the Village Panchayat (at the village level), Panchayat/Block Samiti (at intermediate level) and the Zilla Parishad (at district level). The Committee further proposed the disaggregation of the State Plan into District Plans. The Panchayat Samiti at the block level was the strategic level for formulating village level planning in preparation for the District Plan. Comprehensive village planning would take into account "the needs of the entire community, weaker sections like tenant-cultivators, landless workers and artisans" (ibid.: 2). The decentralised administrative system of the state was to be under the elected bodies. It is important to recall that Rajasthan was the first state to adopt the new scheme of Panchayati Raj (October 2, 1959, Gandhi's birth anniversary) following the formulation by the BRMC. Andhra Pradesh followed soon.

The experience from this restructuring of democratic and administrative institutions was significant. The development model consisted of an intensive phase of rural community development with a higher level of resources provided by the state, to be followed up by a second phase of development with a much reduced level of state contribution, with the expectation that by that time people's initiative would foster further growth through spontaneous internal mobilisation of resources. Reality proved otherwise. The post-intensive phase of the development blocks was characterised by inexplicably low levels of activity in terms of people's participation and motivation. Balwant Rai Mehta observed that a change had to take place from a government programme with people's participation to a people's programme with government participation. While the Community Development Programme was to continue, it was now to be canalised through newly created rural institutions of Panchayati Raj.

As a follow-up of the experiences of the Panchayati Raj during the Second Five-Year Plan period, the President of the All India Panchayat Parishad, Jayaprakash Narayan, organised an important seminar at Udaipur in January 1964. Balwant Rai Mehta, then Chief Minister of Gujarat, attended. The Ministry of Community Development, Panchayati Raj and Cooperation also participated. Besides these, there were 11 representatives from different states. The broad consensus reached was a strong echo of Article 40 of the Constitution that "Panchayati Raj institutions should act as units of self-government at the village, block and district levels" (Narayan et al 1970: 8). Within six months of the seminar, the Consultative Council on Panchayati Raj, a non-official advisory body of the Union Ministry of Community Development, Panchayati Raj and Cooperation, formed a committee consisting of 11 members with Balwant Rai Mehta as chairman. The committee endorsed the general principles formulated by the Udaipur seminar and drew five lists detailing the powers and functions of each of the three tiers on the basis that "each tier of the Panchayati Raj should be entrusted with those functions which it can discharge efficiently on its own" (ibid.: 8). Two successive conferences of State Ministers of Community Development and Panchayati Raj (1965 & 1966) "put a finish to it by noting that, as per advice of Union Law Ministry, there was no need to amend the Constitution to give effect to the 'concept' of Panchayati Raj as enunciated by the Udaipur seminar" (bid: 8, 9). This was the period of political confusion just after Nehru's death with Lal Bahadur Shastri having to face the first Indo-Pakistan war.

Second Landmark

It is not surprising that during the Indira Gandhi's regime, spanning January 1966 till March 1977, the discourse on democratic decentralisation got numbed. She followed a path of deliberate centralisation of power culminating in the National Emergency (1975). It was only when the electorally triumphant newly formed

Janata Party assumed power that we find the Asoka Mehta Committee (December 1977) once again given the responsibility of reopening the issue of Panchayati Raj. By this time, the Panchayati Raj Institutions (PRIs) were almost in shambles in several states, with a weak resource base, with elections indefinitely postponed by some state governments, and supercession of some of the important tiers of Panchayati Raj. Asoka Mehta very perceptively drew attention to the contradiction between representative and participatory democracy when he observed:

> The lukewarm attitude of the political elite at higher levels towards strengthening of the democratic process at the grassroots was generally the crux of the matter. Of particular significance in this connection is the relative cooling of enthusiasm of the MPs and MLAs in some states towards Panchayati Raj, because they would perceive a threat in emerging Panchayat Raj leadership to their position in their respective constituencies (Mehta, 1978: 6).

The most significant feature of the Asoka Mehta Committee report was the linking of "institutions of democratic decentralisation with socially motivated economic development" (ibid.: 175). It held that "Panchayat Raj, like democracy at the national and state levels, is both an end and a means. As an end, it is an inevitable extension of democracy; as a means, it would continue to be responsible for discharging obligations *entrusted to it by the national and State Governments* in spheres not yet transferred to its exclusive jurisdiction. Altogether, both as an end and a means Panchayat Raj should contribute to the philosophy as well as practice of a rich rewarding life in rural India" (ibid.: 176; emphasis added).

In contrast to the key importance given to the block-level Panchayat Samiti by Balwant Rai Mehta in the formulation of district plans, it was suggested that "the district should be the first point of decentralisation, under popular supervision, below the State level" (ibid.: 178).

Paradoxically, the Asoka Mehta Committee's report represented a reverse trend in the democratisation process, when compared to the Balwant Rai Mehta Committee's report, which envisaged district plans coming from the involvement of the intermediate level of the Panchayat Samiti. It viewed the importance of panchayats in the somewhat myopic perspective of their role in rural development. The Committee's recommendations invoked a strong dissenting note from its veteran Gandhian member Siddharaj Dhadda. He pointed out that the "very foundation of the structure of Panchayati Raj was missing". He argued that the "purpose of decentralisation was not merely to help development, however it is defined, but the creation of an integrated structure of self-governing institutions from the village and small town onwards to the national level in order to enable the people to manage their own affairs". He had used all his persuasive powers to impress upon the Committee for the "recognition of the village, functioning through the Gram Sabha, i.e., the village assembly consisting of all voters in the village, as the primary unit of Panchayati Raj and as the foundation on which the upper tiers should rest and from which they would derive strength and vitality". He regretted that "apart from a casual and patronising reference to the Gram Sabha as 'deserving genuine encouragement', its place as an organic and vital part of Panchayati Raj does not find place in the recommendations". He bemoaned the fact that "the Committee has missed a great opportunity of putting democracy on a sure footing" (ibid.: 174). Little did Dhadda know that his observations would find a votary in a future prime minister.

The Historic Moment

The Gandhian position was consistent with the Udaipur seminar and the spirit of Article 40 of the Constitution. It was left to Rajiv Gandhi to unambiguously define the context that compelled him to invoke the spirit of Article 40. His question was simple and to the point: how is it that so much money is provided by the government for the uplift of the rural poor, but at the end of the day only 10 percent of this finds its way to the target group (10 paises in a rupee)? It is symbolically significant that he traced his steps to the All India Panchayat Parishad – where Jayaprakash Narayan, S.K. Dey, Balwant Rai Mehta, Siddharaj Dhadda, and host of others had persistently pursued the spirit of Article 40 – to pave the way for the establishment of Panchayati Raj. What he uttered in its 13th meeting (September 1986) will go down in the history of democratisation in India. He said:

> If we continue to devise schemes from above large sections of the population will be left high and dry, and flow of benefits from development will pass over their heads like water on a duck's back, for it is not possible for the government agencies to reach each and every individual and to guide him and tell him to do this or that (cited in Bandopadhyay, 2004: 148).

Rajiv Gandhi further pointed out that it was quite "apparent that if our district administration is not sufficiently responsive, the basic reason is that *it is not sufficiently representative*" (ibid.: 150; emphasis added). He did not stop at this. He went on to describe the entrenched structure that had come about thwarting both development and democracy. His oft quoted words is a testimony of his sincerity and resolve to set things right and is worth quoting at length:

> The present chasm between a few elected representatives like MPs and MLAs and the bureaucratic administration; and the vast masses was conveniently filled up by power brokers, the middlemen, the vested interests. The power brokers have established their vice-like grip only because democracy has not functioned at the grassroots. Once the people have their own elected representatives from electorates as small as a hundred to five hundred persons, the source of power will be only as far away as the Panchayat Ghar, not some distant State capital or even more distant capital of the country (cited in ibid.: 154).

What might well have happened during his regime, due to force of circumstances, had to wait till Narasimha Rao assumed office of the Prime Minister heading a coalition, in June 1991. The 73rd and 74th amendments to the Constitution in 1992 were transformatory in nature because for the first time they institutionalised the organs of participatory democracy at a third level of autonomous governance within the state system. I shall confine for the present to the 73rd amendment that relates to Panchayati Raj.

The Constitution mandated that the composition of the membership of the Panchayati Raj Institutions (PRIs) would have

(a) one-third of the seats and one-third of the offices of the PRIs reserved for women; (b) seats reserved for the Scheduled Castes (SCs) and Scheduled Tribes (STs)in proportion to their population in the area; and (c) seats reserved for Other Backward Castes (OBCs) only on the discretion of the states. In this manner the social composition of the PRI bodies has been made consistent with the principles of social justice.

Two important aspects related to the devolution of power at the third level of governance are: (a) the preparation of plans for economic development and social justice; and (b) "the implementation of schemes for the economic development and social justice as may be entrusted to them including those in relation to matters listed in the Eleventh Schedule" (Bandopadhyay, 2004: 155). Two more institutions were created: (a) the State Finance Commission that would provide for a fair share of the state's resources for the PRIs; and (b) the State Election Commission that was entrusted with ensuring regularity and fairness in elections. It was mandated that elections to the PRIs would be direct, underscoring the participatory character of its representativeness.

While it is anybody's guess that the translation of these provisions to operational realities cannot be expected out of a revolutionary sleight-of-hand legislation, the structural changes provide the possibilities and scope for transformations that have already begun taking place, albeit unevenly, in various parts of the country. The interests entrenched in the representative form of parliamentary democracy and the bureaucracy find it hard to devolve power to the PRIs. It is perceived as a zero-sum game. The PRIs, on the other hand, are now becoming conscious that the Constitution has now given the go-ahead to shape their own destinies. It is there to see the slow acquiescence of the entrenched system to the realities of the future. This process of transition into a new accommodation between participatory and representative forms of democracy is a fertile field for urgent research.

One last illustration will make my point clear. There are numerous instances of women *panchas* and *sarpanchas* acting on the dictates of their husbands (*pradhan patis*). These have led to critiques of women's reservation. For sociologists such observations appear transient and superficial. If one visits the process through which the SCs and STs graduated from the phase in which they were being co-opted by upper caste political elites in all the national political parties, to the situation obtaining now when the Bahujan Samaj Party has been recognised as a national party, with a lady Scheduled Caste leader who could become thrice Chief Minister of the biggest state in India, one would understand how unfounded are the critiques of protective discrimination for social justice in defence of women.

Had Babasaheb Ambedkar been alive today, he would have been more than pleased that the PRIs have removed the apprehensions he nurtured when he was framing the country's Constitution. Had Gandhi been alive today, perhaps he would have smiled and said, "I told you. That is why I got you the Article 40. Good you have begun realising. Better late than never".

Note

1. Panchayat has an ancient flavour; it is a good word. It literally means an assembly of five elected by villagers. It represents the system, by which the innumerable village republics of India were governed. But the British Government, by its ruthlessly through method of revenue collection, almost destroyed these ancient republics, which could not stand the shock of this revenue collection (*Panchayat in Pre-Independence Days, Young India,* 28 May 1931: 6-8)

References

Bandopadhyay, D. 2004, 'Panchayat and Democracy' in D. Bandopadhyay and Amitav Mukherjee, *New Issue in Panchayati Raj*, New Delhi, Concept Publication Co.

Bose, N.K. 1957, *Selections from Gandhi*, Ahmedabad, Navjivan Publishing House.

Dey, S.K. 1961, *Panchayati Raj: A Synthesis*, Bombay, Allied Publishers.

Gandhi, M.K. 1942, 'My Idea of Village Swaraj', *Harijan*, 26 July 1942.

— 1931, 'Panchayat in Pre-Independence Days', *Young India*, 28 May 1931.

Ghosh, Budhadeb. 2000, *Panchayati Raj: Evolution of the Concept*, New Delhi, Institute of Social Sciences.

Jain, S.C. 1967, *Community Development and Panchayati Raj in India*, Bombay, Allied Publishers.

Mehta, Asoka, 1978, *Report of the Committee on Panchayati Raj Institutions*, New Delhi, Ministry of Agriculture and Irrigation, Department of Rural Development, Government of India.

Narayan, Iqbal, Sushil Kumar, P.C. Mathur and associates, 1970, *Panchayati Raj Administration: Old Controls and New Challenges*, New Delhi, Indian Institute of Public Administration.

Roy, M.N. 1960, *Politics, Power and Parties*, Renaissance Publishers (cited in Ghosh, 2000).

Tagore, Rabindranath. 1995, (Bengali year 1402), 'Swadeshi Samaj', *Rabindra Rachanabali, Vol. 2*, Shantiniketan, Vishwabharati (cited in Ghosh 2000).

Taylor, Carl C. 1965, *A Critical Analysis of India's Community Development Programme*, New Delhi, The Community Projects Administration, Government of India.

4

Empowerment of Scheduled Castes and Women

A Study of Three Villages in Kolhapur District

R.B. Patil

The 73rd amendment to the Constitution of India in 1992 was a major step towards democratic decentralisation. It has led to greater participation and empowerment of SCs/STs and women in Panchayat Raj Institutions (PRIs) in the country.

The Maharashtra Zilla Parishads and Panchayat Samities Act, 1961 was enacted and accordingly Zilla Parishads and Panchayat Samities were constituted in May 1962. The Maharashtra state adopted three-tier system of Zilla Parishad, Taluka Panchayat and Gram Panchayat. The district was considered as an ideal institution for local development and we notice district oriented approach in Maharashtra (Joshi and Mitragotri, 2000).

Again, the Maharashtra state amended Village Panchayat and Zilla Parishad and Panchayat Samities Act of 1958 and 1961 commensurating with the provisions of 73rd constitutional amendment and this new Act, was enforced in the state from 2nd April 1994.

This paper presents micro-level picture of how sarpanchas in the reserved categories function at the local level and also tries to reflect on the emerging situation and their views. The study is based on the data collected from three villages in Kolhapur district.

Table 1
District-wise Distribution of Sarpanchas in Maharashtra

	District	*Women*		*SCs*		*STs*	
		1992-93	*1999-2000*	*1992-93*	*1999-2000*	*1992-93*	*1999-2000*
1	Thane	1.16	13.73	0.58	2.83	33.18	37.04
2	Raigad	2.94	33.99	1.54	1.36	2.52	8.28
3	Ratnagiri	0.75	26.81	3.77	6.41	0.15	0.59
4	Sidhudurg	0.73	33.02	0.00	5.15	0.00	0.47
5	Nashik	2.08	16.64	1.31	5.15	29.14	28.66
6	Dhule	1.23	26.14	0.62	3.11	37.03	NA
7	Nandurbar	NA	12.45	NA	2.74	NA	66.24
8	Jalgaon	2.08	33.42	0.72	6.37	4.60	9.60
9	Ahmednagar	1.96	30.59	0.89	7.94	6.05	26.96
10	Pune	1.05	27.11	0.53	7.56	4.89	5.11
11	Satara	0.99	20.41	0.76	8.91	0.00	1.36
12	Sangli	0.90	23.83	0.15	9.36	0.45	16.31
13	Solapur	0.78	5.66	0.59	25.82	0.00	11.50
14	Kolhapur	1.69	29.41	1.46	9.41	0.00	9.80
15	Aurangabad	0.00	33.33	2.23	12.03	0.00	4.93
16	Jalna	1.97	37.10	2.62	8.22	1.53	1.16
17	Parbhani	2.27	29.06	4.10	13.53	8.30	4.03
18	Hingoli	NA	28.60	NA	10.48	NA	13.68
19	Beed	2.74	28.47	1.90	14.09	0.00	0.39
20	Nanded	2.16	21.51	2.24	9.20	2.31	13.72
21	Osmanabad	1.86	35.06	0.37	17.69	0.19	1.62
22	Latur	2.55	28.17	1.42	14.08	0.99	1.54
23	Buldhana	1.82	25.81	4.85	7.29	3.52	4.98
24	Akola	2.48	20.60	4.03	6.80	2.28	6.60
25	Washim	NA	30.30	NA	19.13	NA	7.74
26	Amravati	2.88	12.95	5.64	11.51	13.28	9.23
27	Yavatmal	2.35	31.01	1.48	7.81	15.57	18.12
28	Wardha	2.45	27.24	5.93	12.45	9.61	13.04
29	Nagpur	2.56	28.13	6.84	9.64	6.98	11.72
30	Bhandara	1.47	34.95	6.49	12.66	4.08	11.10
31	Chandrapur	0.87	33.54	3.22	14.20	7.93	20.07
32	Gadchiroli	1.29	28.19	4.51	3.52	43.22	46.04
	State	1.74	26.14	2.29	9.59	8.50	12.77

Source: Directorate of Economics and Statistics, Mumbai.

Maharashtra: Women, SC/ST Sarpanchas, 1992-93 & 1999-2000

Table 1 indicates that at the state level there has been an increase in the participation of women, SCs and STs in electoral politics during the period from 1992-93 to 1999-2000. Participation of women is more pronounced than SCs and STs.

The district-wise distribution also reveals the similar trend. The another notable point is that, in some of the districts, there were no sarpanchas from these categories in 1992-93 but this scene has changed in 1999-2000.

Women Sarpanchas in Maharashtra

Aalochana, Centre for Documentation at Pune carried out a study of all women panchayats. In 1993 elections the villages like Salod and Erangaon (Amravati), Vitner and Dudhgaon (Jalgaon), Metikhdea (Yavatmal) and Brahmanagher (Pune) had all women members.

Apart from all-women headed panchayats, there are some examples where women sarpanchas have performed their roles efficiently. These include: Arjunwadao (Dist. Kolhapur) (Karande, 2004), Malwadi (Western Maharashtra) (National Institute of Rural Development, 2004), Paniv (Dist. Solapur) (Patil, 2002). But, at the same time, the outside forces work when women sarpanchas attempt to perform their role which is evident from Tarkarli in Sindhudurg district (Thakkar & Gawankar, 1997), Tirth in Osmanabad district (Mathew, 2001), Abdullat in Kolhapur district, Bhende Khurd in Nagpur district (Thakkar & Gawankar, ibid.), Ghera Purandar in Pune district (Thakkar & Gawankar, ibid.), Erangaon, Belora (Institute of Social Sciences, 2004), Pilkhod in Jalgaon district (Baviskar, 2001), Pethvadaz in Nanded district (Mohanty, 2003) and Panjawadi in Nashik district (Institute of Social Sciences, 2003).

Vasagade Village in Kolhapur District

Population and Social Structure

Vasagade village is situated 15 kms from Kolhapur in the eastern side. It is 1.5 km away from Kolhapur-Hupari road. The population of Vasagade in the last three decades was 5,593 (1981), 6,780 (1991) and 7,517 (2001). There were 1,377 total households in the village (Census 1991) .

The castewise distribution of the voters in Vasagade village clearly reveals that Jains had nearly one-third voters (1540/4775). The other prominent group of voters comes from Mahar caste (1052/4775). The other castes having more number of voters include Maratha (509/4775) and Koli (452/4775).

Political System

The Gram Panchayat in Vasagade was established in 1934. The details regarding sarpanchas, their caste background and tenure are presented in Table 2.

Table 2
Gram Panchayat Vasagade: Sarpanchas

Name	*Caste*	*Period*	*Niyukti*
Dhulagonda Babagonda Patil	(Jain)	1934-38	Sarkarniyukt
Ramagonda Aanna Patil	(Jain)	1938-40	Sarkarniyukt
Ramagonda Aanna Patil	(Maratha)	1940-41	Lokniyukt
Aanna Dhulagonda Patil	(Jain)	1941-45	Lokniyukt
Balagonda Jinagonda Patil	(Jain)	1945-52	Lokniyukt
Aadinath Aappa Khul	(Jain)	1952-56	Lokniyukt
Bapusaheb Sidagonda Patil	(Jain)	1956-65	Lokniyukt
Sidagonda Dada Patil	(Jain)	1966-92	Lokniyukt
Chamundaraya Sidagonda Patil	(Jain)	1992-97	Lokniyukt
Ashok Shamrao Pandharabale	(Mahar SC)	1997-99	Lokniyukt
Prakash alis Popat Siddhu Kamble	(Mahar SC)	1999-2002	Lokniyukt
Sanjay Jnanadev Katakar	(Bhoi, OBC)	Since November 2002	Lokniyukt

The table indicates that with the exception of Maratha sarpanch in 1940-41, SC sarpanchas during 1997-2002 and OBC sarpanch since November 2002, all other sarpanchas were Jains. Thus, the village is dominated by the Jains and it has been reflected in the post of sarpanchas.

Another thing which will have to be noted here is that Bapusaheb Sidagonda Patil was sarpanch for 10 years. His successor Sidagonda Dada Patil was sarpanch for 25 years and then his son Dr. Chamundray became sarpanch for five years. Due to the 73rd constitutional amendment, the village had SC sarpanchas for the first time in the history of Gram Panchayat during 1997-2002 and at present has an OBC sarpanch.

Views on Reservation

There were 15 members (10 men and 5 women) in Gram Panchayat. They were from Jain (4), Mahar (3), Dhanagar (2), and one each from Mang, Chambhar, Lohar, Sonar, Koli and Nhavi caste background.

The members were asked about their opinions on reservation of seats in Gram Panchayats. Majority of them were in favour of reservation. They justified reservation as it gives equal opportunity, chance and right to everyone. As everyone has chance, the backward communities will be able to progress.

Three members have opposed reservation on the ground that untouchability has been removed, and so there should be equality to all castes. As the persons from Scheduled Castes have no capacity, they should not occupy seats in Gram Panchayat body. These people go in the field every day for work. The persons on reservation seats do not attend the meetings and it requires to obtain their signatures after meetings. Whenever the seats are reserved for SCs/OBCs/ women for Panchayat Samiti and Zilla Parishad, the voters do not go for voting. Those who vote for them, in such cases, it is the party which is important and not the person who belongs to SC/ST or is a woman.

The training of Gram Panchayat Administration for the SCs/OBCs/women is required and this viewpoint was expressed by most of the members. But, the trend observed here was that women members have not attended such training programmes. The programme was organised in 1998-99 for three days in eight villages. One of the general caste members expressed that even though training is given to SCs/OBCs/women, they do not have capacity to work in panchayats.

The developmental activities carried out by the present body includes housing scheme for poor, SC colony improvement, employment guarantee scheme, distribution of sewing machines, gutter repairs, drinking water pipeline, community cultural hall, grants to backward classes, and water taps, etc.

The Gram Panchayat members reported that there are no tensions in the relations of SC/OBC with dominant castes. Most of the members have reported that there is improvement in the functioning of Gram Panchayat due to the introduction of the 73rd constitutional amendment. They reported the advantage of all people in the Gram Panchayat administration has been realised. The father-to-son rule in Gram Panchayat as occurred in this village has been discontinued. The new members due to reservation have enthusiasm to do development work.

Two of the members reported that there was no need of reservation for SC sarpanch. The sarpanch from the general caste is able to spend money to get the work done. Due to the constitutional amendment, there is improvement in the standard of living of the individual elected member but there is no progress in the backward community as a whole.

Due to the 73rd constitutional amendment most of the members reported that there is improvement in SC/OBC members. They have got authority, so the attitude of people towards them has changed. At the same time, the SC sarpanch feels, "I am sarpanch. How shall I go to work on the field of others?"

The 73rd constitutional amendment has also improved the status of women. Earlier, the women did not come to panchayat office, but now they have every right to enter the panchayat office and act as members. But, one of the members reported that due to the male-dominated society, the status of women is still restricted to hearth and children.

Sarpanch

The post of Vasagade sarpanch was reserved for SC during 1997-2002. It was decided by the majority party to give chance to two SC members for a period of two-and-a-half years. Accordingly, the post was first held by Ashok Shamrao Pandharbale and then by Prakash alias Popat Siddhu Kamble.

Mr. Pandharbale belongs to Mang community and has studied up to 5th standard. He has a small family. He owns no land. He got elected due to the efforts of the leaders in the village. His co-brother and uncle contested the Gram Panchayat election and were elected as member in 1992. Due to reservation, Pandharbale could get the post of sarpanch.

Pandharbale who was working as farm labourer became sarpanch. After becoming sarpanch, he stopped going to field. The leaders arranged for payment of grocery shop. After the end of his tenure, it became difficult for him to work on the farms of others. He is now staying most of the time at his father-in-law's residence at Kolhapur.

Kamble has studied up to 8th standard. He comes from a joint family. He has 7 gunthas of unirrigated land where the crops of soyabean and wheat are grown. His grandfather got elected during 1945-52 and his father got elected during 1956-60 and 1961-65. Thus, in the earlier generations, SC elected representative used to be members only but now they can become sarpanch. The present sarpanch belongs to Nationalist Congress Party (NCP). He got elected due to the efforts of leaders in the village.

The financial position of the sarpanch is weak. So, in the administration, he cannot take firm stand. He has to get cooperation and guidance of the dominant community members and their leaders. After the tenure of SC sarpanch is over, it became very difficult for the person concerned to work in the fields of others.

One of the villagers commented about SC sarpanch, "the leaders in the village do not appoint a wise SC as sarpanch. On the other hand, SC community does not elect wise man as sarpanch. So, there are problems."

Here, the post of sarpanch is held by an SC. The members technically cooperate with him. But, some members expressed that they spent money for getting elected and 'Sarpanch Chair' has been given to SC. Others expressed that the SC sarpanch is for name's sake only. He has no capacity to get the work done for village. The dominant leaders do this work.

Sangawade Village in Kolhapur District

Population and Social Structure

Sangawade village is situated 15 kms east of Kolhapur. It is 1.5 kms away from Kolhapur-Hupari road. Sangawade is in the south and Vasagade is in the north side of Kolhapur-Hupari road. Sangawade is a famous religious centre of Shri Narsinha temple, so it is also called as 'Narasobache Sangawade'. The population of Sangawade in the last three decades was 3,518 (1981), 3,428 (1991) less due to bifurcation into two villages, viz., Sangawade and Sangawadewadi, and 3,838 (2001).

The village had 2,539 voters. The caste-wise distribution of the voters in Sangawade clearly indicates that Jains (745, i.e., 29.34) had the highest number of voters, which is followed by Maratha (511, i.e., 20.12) and Mahar (498, i.e., 19.61) voters in more or less similar number. This is followed by Mang (141, i.e., 5.55) and then Kumbhar (119, i.e., 4.68) voters. This village has large number of Gurav (113, i.e., 4.45) voters due to its being a religious centre.

Political System

The Gram Panchayat in Sangawade was established in 1927. In the earlier phases the sarpanchas were appointed by the government. The details regarding names of sarpanchas, their caste background and tenure are presented in the Table 3.

The table clearly indicates that Jain, Brahmin, Muslim, OBC, and SC have acted as sarpanch over the years. Two of them have got the post twice. Since 1929, for the first time, a woman became sarpanch. She is an OBC. The tenure of the sarpanch has varied and now it is for five years.

This researcher had an opportunity to meet Mahadeo Gopal Chougule, who acted as sarpanch for two terms from 1967 to 1972 and 1972 to 1976. In this period, the elected representatives were from different caste backgrounds like Maratha, Lingayat, Jain, Mahar, Dhor and Koli. The cluster of houses of different caste groups leads to the fact that the representative of that particular caste group gets elected from their ward. There used to be three representatives from backward castes.

Table 3
Gram Panchayat Sangwade: Sarpanchas

Name	*Caste*	*Period*	*Niyukti*
Vhanagonda Nemagonda Patil	(Jain)	1929-32	Sarkarniyukt
Dattatraya Govind Joshi	(Brahmin)	1932-36	Sarkarniyukt
Bhujagonda Narasgonda Patil	(Jain)	1936-40	Sarkarniyukt
Vhanagonda Nemagonda Patil	(Jain)	1940-45	Sarkarniyukt
Ganapati Balaram Gujar	(OBC)	1945-46	Lokaniyukt
Dhulgonda Babagonda Patil	(Jain)	1946-47	Lokaniyukt
Anna Dada Kusanale	(Jain)	1947-50	Lokaniyukt
Bala Aaba Mulani	(Muslim)	1950-52	Lokaniyukt
Devagonda Balgonda Patil	(Jain)	1952-57	Lokaniyukt
Dada Hari Sawant	(Maratha)	1957-62	Lokaniyukt
Pandit alis Narhar Balaji Kulkarni	(Brahmin)	1962-67	Lokaniyukt
Mahadeo Gopal Chougule, Nhavi	(OBC)	1967 to 7-12-76	Lokaniyukt
Devu Yallappa Mane, Mahar	(SC)	8-12-76 to 31-5-78	Lokaniyukt
Parisa Shantappa Marle,	(Jain)	1-6-78 to 30-11-80	Lokaniyukt
Atmaram Dadu Yadav, Mahar	(SC)	1-12-80 to 27-9-81	Lokaniyukt
Parisa Shantappa Marle	(Jain)	28-9-81 to 26-4-84	Lokaniyukt
Dudhappa Nana Jadhav, Mahar	(SC)	27-4-84 to 24-10-89	Lokaniyukt
Vijay Paygonda Patil	(Jain)	25-10-89 to 24-4-92	Lokaniyukt
Pravin Jinappa Mane, Mahar	(SC)	25-4-92 to 1997	Lokaniyukt
Sanjay Bhupal Biraje, Mang	(SC)	1997 to 2000	Lokaniyukt
Vandana Sonappa Koli, Koli	(OBC)	Since 9-8-2000	Lokaniyukt

Views on Reservation

There were 11 members (7 men and 4 women) in Gram Panchayat. They were from Maratha (4), Mahar (2), and one each from Jain, Mahar, Dhor, Nhavi and Teli caste background.

When question was asked about the opinion of the members regarding reservation of seats in Gram Panchayat, 10 members favoured it. The reasons they put forth were scope for common men and leadership, power to powerless, shifting of power from one class to another class, among the SCs and OBCs we-feeling, prestige to the downtrodden class, social welfare, difficulties of women and SCs/OBCs solved etc.

One member expressed that it is alright reservation for membership but it should not be for the post of sarpanch. The candidates from reserved category have their own limitations; they have no financial strength to work effectively so the highest post of sarpanch should not be reserved at all.

The members expressed that there is need of training for the members who have got elected on the reserved posts as most of them have no experience of the administration of panchayat system. The members of Sangawade Gram Panchayat have participated in the training camp conducted at Uchagaon for three days.

The members felt that the benefits of reservation have not been restricted to the individual family but these have reached to women and SCs/OBC.

The present body of Gram Panchayat has carried out the activities of drinking water supply. Village-well, tar-road construction, bridge on stream, shed for funerals, toilet blocks, pre-primary classes, gutters, bore for drinking water, health clubs, rooms for primary school, community hall for SCs, school compound etc.

To the question, "What type of change has occurred in caste relations due to reservation of seats in Gram Panchayat?", the members responded that there is peaceful co-existence of different castes and no tension in the village.

The members reported that with the introduction of 73rd amendment to the Constitution, there have also been changes in the functioning of Gram Panchayats. There is scope for development. The facility of Gram Sabha gives the people an opportunity to talk.

Woman Sarpanch

Mrs. Vandana Sonappa Koli was the sarpanch of Sangawade. She had studied up to 3rd standard in Kannada. She hardly could read and write in Marathi. She only uses to sign in Marathi. She is a housewife. Her husband used to work in agricultural field as labourer. The family economic condition is not very sound. She used to attend the meetings. But, the main work was being carried out by her husband and the leaders in her party. The role which was expected from the sarpanch was not performed by her as she lacked educational qualification and experience in public life. Here, 'sarpanchpati' having primary level of education acted like a sarpanch in the office. The administration of the village was carried out by other influential members.

The researcher attended the Gram Sabha held on 15th Aug, 2002. It was historic as for earlier Gram Sabha only paper work was done. The corruption charges were alleged on Gram Sevak who was absent in the meeting. The Gram Sabha was held in the presence of acting Gram Sevak. The villagers gave their written complaints and suggestions regarding tax rebate to Amit Spinning Mill. The tax levied was in lakhs. It was alleged that Gram Sevak and some panchayat members gave tax rebate in return of cash payment and it was loss to Gram Panchayat. The other issues raised were pollution of drinking water, road widening, village cleanliness campaign, permission for construction of Maruti temple, grant to backward castes to be used for them only, etc.

The no-confidence motion was passed against the sarpanch by 9 vs. 0 votes in a special meeting held on 13th September, 2002. The sarpanch and one more lady were absent and the meeting was held under the chairmanship of Sanjay Patil, Tahsildar Karveer taluka. After the no-confidence motion, charge was given to deputy sarpanch. In the meantime the complaint regarding corruption charges was enquired by Deputy Chief Officer, Zilla Parishad, Kolhapur. The report was placed before Standing Committee of Zilla Parishad and the charge has been given to deputy sarpanch.

Gadamudashingi Village in Kolhapur District

Population and Social Structure

Gadamudashingi village is situated 7 km from Kolhapur in the eastern side. It is 1 km away from Kolhapur-Hupari road. The population of Gadamudashingi in the last three decades was 7,007 (1981), 9,850 (1991) and 12,716 (2001) respectively. There were total 1231 households in the village.

Political System

The Gram Panchayat in Gadamudashingi was established in 1927. The details regarding names of sarpanchas, their caste background and tenure is presented in Table 4.

Table 4
Gram Panchayat Gadamudashingi: Sarpanchas

Name	*Caste*	*Period*	*Niyukti*
Shivajirao A. Patil	Maratha	1927 to 20-8-1941	Sarkar
Datto Annappa Gurav	Gurav	21-8-41 to 2-10-42	Lok
Yashawant Ramaji Patil	Maratha	3-10-42 to 28-6-52	Lok
Rajaram Janardan Patil	Maratha	29-6-52 to 30-5-61	Lok
Ganapati Pandurang Patil	Maratha	31-5-61 to 24-5-67	Lok
Yashawant Buwaji Patil	Maratha	25-5-67 to 16-1-71	Lok
Shankarrao Maruti Mali	Mali	25-5-71 to 13-8-72	Lok
Krishna Yashawant Patil	Maratha	14-8-72 to 28-5-78	Lok
Ashok Uttamarao Patil	Maratha	29-5-78 to 9-8-83	Lok
Pandit Yashawant Patil	Maratha	10-8-83 to 2-11-89	Lok
Vitthalrao B. Yadav	Maratha	3-11-89 to 5-9-93	Lok
Balaso Ganapati Nagave Ag. Sarpanch	Maratha	6-9-93 to 4-11-93	
Appaso Sambhaji Dhanawade	Maratha	5-11-93 to 6-8-95	Lok
Subhasharao Dagadu Sonule	SC	7-8-95 to 14-7-99	Lok
Bagal Dagadu Kamble	SC	15-7-99 to 6-8-2000	Lok
Shivajirao Krushnat Patil	Maratha	Since 7-8-2000	

The table indicates that most of the sarpanchas at Gadamudashingi were belonging to Maratha caste, which is a dominant caste in the village.

Shivaji Patil is a college educated and young sarpanch coming from Maratha dominant caste background. He has sound financial position with agricultural background. His father Krishnat

Yashawant Patil won the Gram Panchayat election in 1972 and remained sarpanch from 1972 to 1978. His grandfather Yashwant Buwaji Patil was sarpanch during 1967-71. So here, we find a tradition of sarpanch from father to son in three generations. Being educated and knowing the nuances of the Gram Panchayat administration, he controls the meeting effectively.

Gunda Aaba Yayadande, deputy sarpanch hails from Mang community. He works as coal maker in a private factory at Kolhapur. In February 2002, he also contested for Taluka Panchayat (Mudashingi) but lost it. He contested the election as RPI-Athavale group candidate. He could secure only 11.02 per cent votes.

Views on Reservation

There were 17 members (11 men and 6 women) in Gram Panchayat body. Nearly half of them were Maratha (7) and the remaining were from Mang, (3) Lingayat (3), and one each from Gosavi and Chambhar caste background.

Majority of the members favoured the reservation of seats in Gram Panchayat as it gives equal right, an opportunity of development, and expression of opinions. Some members however opposed reservation of seats, as they do not have much knowledge of panchayat administration. Initially, members from reservation category have no interest in social work because they consider "Pota bhal aapan bhal" (satisfaction with own livelihood). They are being considered on the 'use and throw' principle. The members feel that training is necessary for the persons on reserved seats. The participation of women in public sphere was favoured by the members as it gives equal right, women development, and the difficulties of women can only be put forth by them. One member did not favour it on the ground that they do not have knowledge of panchayat administration. The participation of SCs/OBCs in public sphere was favoured by the members as it leads to their development. Some members expressed the view that it does not serve the purpose as they are illiterate, and also lack the knowledge of panchayat administration. Majority of the members reported that the benefits of reservation have reached to SCs/OBCs and women as a class. Some members reported that these have been limited to the individuals who got elected from these categories. All the members reported that harmony has been maintained in the society due to reservation of seats.

The Gram Panchayat members have implemented many government schemes. These include road construction, gutters, drinking water facility, gharkul scheme, Aanganwadi, street-lighting, swachhata abyhiyan, proposal of new Sachiwalaya and Jawahar Rojgar Yojana, etc.

Due to reservation of seats in panchayat the relation between various castes have also improved. The tensions have decreased and it had lead to 'salokha' in castes at village level. One of the members reported that the members from reservation categories look after the interest of their caste only and they have no perspective of development of village as a whole.

Majority of the members reported that there has been improvement in the panchayat administration due to 73rd amendment. They also feel that it has improved the status of SCs/OBCs and women.

The members from SC/OBC category reported that there were no difficulties due to dominant castes in panchayat administration. Similarly, the women members also stated that there were no difficulties due to male-dominated society.

Majority of the members from general castes have favoured SC/OBC/women reservation and their participation. Some members opposed it on the ground that these members do not have capacity and lack knowledge of administration.

An Overview

The percentage of women, SC and ST sarpanchas has increased in all the districts in Maharashtra over the years. There are examples of all women Gram Panchayats, which have done commendable work under their tenure in different aspects. Even, in the case of women sarpanchas, they have performed their role efficiently. At the same time, there are women sarpanchas facing problems. These include their own illiteracy, non-cooperative and corrupt Gram Sevak, male dominance, harassment, pressure of dominant caste leadership on Dalits, and tendency to keep the post of sarpanch in one family etc. In male-dominated Indian society, that too in villages, women sarpanchas are performing their roles and this is an achievement. The situation is changing very fast. Some of the women sarpanchas have done commendable job. They are marching on the challenging road towards empowerment.

The 73rd constitutional amendment opened gates of opportunities in different fronts for women, SCs and STs to enter into Panchayat Raj administration. The study of three villages in Kolhapur district in Maharashtra indicates that because of the amendment women, SCs and OBCs could occupy the position of sarpanchas for the first time in the history of these Gram Panchayats.

The women engaged as housewives under the present study have entered in politics due to enforcement of reservation but their role has remained nominal. This is due to their being less educated and lack of experience in panchayat administration. In most of the cases, they were dependent on their husband or male counterpart for Gram Panchayat activities.

The woman sarpanch at Sangawade played official role in panchayat. Her status moved upward in the village. But, she is unable to take major decisions by herself. At Sangawade the dominant caste men control the Gram Panchayat. The sarpanch is less educated, less experienced in panchayat administration and economically weak, which forces her to take help from outside. She has not become empowered in true sense of term as the real power remained with the dominant caste. The sarpanch is economically dependent on dominant caste for agricultural work. The general trend is that the persons from these categories are from economically poor section. This situation limits their level of performance at the village administration.

The reservation to the post of sarpanch is declared at the time of election. If it is reserved, the dominant caste gives candidature to a financial weak and amenable person with less political skill. The persons elected from reserved categories find difficult in leadership.

Majority of the Gram Panchayat members have favoured reservation of seats while few have opposed it.

Acknowledgements

The data from three village have been collected under the project entitled, "Inclusion of Excluded Communities for Social Cohesion through Panchayat Raj: An All-India Study" by Institute of Social Sciences, New Delhi. The author is thankful to Prof. B.S. Baviskar, Project Coordinator and Dr. George Mathew, Director of the Institute for the financial assistance for carrying out the project in Kolhapur district.

References

Baviskar, B.S., "Pilkhod: From Conflict to Consensus", Institute of Social Sciences, *Panchayati Raj Update*, August 2001.

Institute of Social Sciences, "Sarpanch reinstated after forged resignation letter", *Panchayati Raj Update,* June 2003.

—, "Women Sarpanch Beaten", *Panchayati Raj Update*, June 2004.

Joshi, S.D. and Mitragotri, N.P., "Maharashtra in Status of Panchayat Raj in the States and Union Territories of India". Mathew George. Editor, Institute of Social Sciences & Concept Publishing Company, New Delhi, 2000.

Karande, Prakash, "Sou Sarpanch" , *Lokmat Sakhi* (in Marathi), 2nd September, 2004.

Mathew, George, "Maharashtra's Gram Sevak Raj", *The Hindu*, 13th August, 2001.

Mohanty, B.B.: "Panchayat Raj in Maharashtra and Orrisa", *IASSI*, 2003: 45.

National Institute of Rural Development, "A Dalit Woman Sarpanch's Model Village", August 2004.

Patil, Shrilekha Prakash, "What a Sarpanch Can Do", *Daily Sakal* ,13th November, 2002.

Thakkar ,Usha and Gawankar, Rohini, "Reservation and the Empowerment of Women: The Emerging Issues" in Poonacha Veena (ed), *Women, Empowerment and Political Participation* , SNDT Women's University, Mumbai, 1997.

5

Factors Influencing Women's Participation in Panchayati Raj Institutions

Archana Kamble (Jagatkar) and Sarjerao Salunkhe

The 73rd Constitutional Amendment Act (1992), on panchayats, was assented to by the President of India on 20 April 1993 and it was brought into effect on 24 April 1993. The Act is being viewed as "a landmark in the Constitutional history of the country" (Saran, 1993: 6), "a revolutionary decision" (Sawhney, 1994: 7), "a good beginning and well-come step" (Kaushik, 1993: 13-15) and having "revolutionary implications" (Thakkar and Gawankar, 1997: 87).

Before implementation of reservation of 33 per cent seats for women in Panchayati Raj Institutions (PRIs) as provided by the 73rd Constitutional Amendment Act, women were not having sufficient access to power positions in these vitally important bodies of local governance. Earlier, only few women were getting entry into these institutions mostly through co-option or nominations. As one study (Hazel, 1983) has revealed, during earlier period, women belonging to upper castes, wives of big landlords, and women from politically influential families were occupying seats in Zilla Parishads (ZPs) and Panchayat Samitis (PSs). Now, with the implementation of reservation of 33 per cent seats for women, women belonging to almost all caste categories have been given an opportunity to occupy political space in these institutions, and that too, through direct elections. For the first time, in the history of PRIs in India, a large number of women from rural areas are being pulled out from their kitchen to actively participate in the public political field. This has been viewed as a beginning of a "silent revolution" (Mathew, 1995: 35).

The policy of political empowerment of women aims at eliciting their active participation in decision-making process in these institutions. However, the goal of political empowerment of women does not end up only with their induction into the power positions in PRIs. After getting elected for positions in these institutions, their real role begins. These are the bodies where decisions are taken democratically. Regular meetings are convened for this purpose. Village, block and district level problems are identified and discussed. Rural development programmes – of both central and state governments – are implemented through these institutions. Therefore, achievement of goal of rural development depends on the efficiency of PRIs. How efficient are the members in PRIs, is therefore important.

All members in the PRIs are expected to contribute to the development of village, taluka and district concerned. This they can do by using rights and powers that they have been given by virtue of being members in these bodies. Therefore, elected members' involvement and active participation in decision-making in PRIs is of crucial importance. In this context, the studies focusing on the variables that influence women's participation in PRIs deserve special significance.

Based on an exploratory empirical study, the present paper aims to explore answers to some questions such as "Do emerging women leaders attend the meetings held in the PRIs?" If not, "what are the major reasons?" If yes, "how regularly do they attend these meetings?" Similarly, "Do emerging women leaders take active part in discussions in the meetings held in the PRIs?" If not, "What are the major reasons?" and "what are the factors that influence their active participation in the discussions in the meetings convened in PRIs?"

The Study and Methodology

This empirical study has been carried out in the Latur district of Maharashtra. The selection of the Latur district was purposive. Keeping in view the exploratory nature of the study, it was decided to adopt mixed sampling design for the present investigation. In case of women leaders elected in 1997 election, it was decided to select (i) all women leaders working at the Zilla Parishad and Panchayat Samiti level in the Latur district (census study); (ii) while selecting women leaders from Village Panchayats, it was decided to adopt proportionate stratified systematic sampling with a random start, first, for selection of 5 per cent sample of Village Panchayats from all the seven Panchayat Samitis in the district, and then to select all women leaders belonging to these sampled Village Panchayats. Besides, it was decided to select women leaders elected in 1992-93, by adopting accidental sampling technique. This was thought necessary for getting valuable data relating to the experiences of women leaders who had already completed their full term.

Thus selected, the actual sample for the present study includes 23 women leaders from Zilla Parishad, 42 women leaders from Panchayat Samitis and 110 women leaders from Village Panchayats, making a total of 175 women leaders elected in two consecutive elections held in 1992-93 and 1997. The sample consists of two categories of respondents: (i) purposively selected 26 women leaders elected during the elections held in the year 1992-93 (4 from ZP, 4 from PSs and 18 from VPs); and (ii) 149 women leaders who were elected during the elections held in 1997 (19 from ZP, 38 from PSs and 92 from VPs). Table 1 below gives details regarding sample of women leaders selected for the study:

Table 1

Sample of Women Leaders Selected for the Study

Tier	*Sample of leaders elected in the year 1992-93*	*Sample of women leaders elected in the year 1996-97*	*Total*
ZP	04	19	23
PSs	04	38	42
GPs	18	92	110
Total	26	149	175

Personal interviews with structured schedule and informal interviews coupled with field observations were the tools used for collection of primary data. The data collection work was carried out during the months of January and February 1998. A collective profile of all the 175 women leaders in PRIs is presented. Data are not analysed separately for the respondents belonging to the three tiers of Panchayat Raj.

The Data, Observations and Discussion

As stated earlier, the policy of empowerment of women aims at eliciting their participation in decision-making process in PRIs. In order to effectively perform their role, the women leaders are expected to attend the meetings, participate in discussions and express their views and opinions in order to effectively influence the policy decisions. The first minimum expectation is that they should attend the meetings in PRIs. Attending the meetings in these bodies could be considered as a pre-condition to exercise influence on the process of decision-making. Regularity in attending the meetings could be considered as an indicator of women's involvement in decision-making, while their participation in the discussions in PRI meetings could be treated as an indicator of their active participation in decision-making. Against this background, the data regarding women leaders' responses regarding their attendance in the PRI meetings, regularity of their attendance and their participation in discussions in these meetings are presented, analysed and discussed below.

Women Leaders' Involvement in Decision-Making: Regularity in Attending the PRI Meetings

With the help of questions in the schedule, the data regarding number of meetings convened and number of meetings attended by the respondents were collected. On the basis of this data, the percentage of meetings attended by the respondents was calculated. For the convenience of analysis and meaningful interpretation, the data are classified into four categories: 'poor', 'low', 'moderate' and 'high'. 'Poor' category represents respondents attending unto 25 per cent meetings; 'low' category represents respondents attending 26 to 50 per cent meetings, 'moderate' category represents respondents attending 51 to 75 per cent meetings and 'high' category represents respondents attending 76 to 100 per cent meetings. It is important to note here that some of respondents who remained 'silent' on the question, "How many meetings you have attended?" are clubbed into the 'poor' category. The reason for doing this is that, the researcher on the basis of observation of their facial expression felt that they must have attended very few meetings. The data regarding the respondents' regularity in attending the PRI meetings are presented in Table 2 below:

Table 2

Respondents Classified According to Their Regularity in Attending the PRI Meetings

Percentage of meeting attendance	*Regularity in attending the meetings*	*Women leaders in PRIs*	
Percentage category	*Category label*	*Frequency*	*Per cent*
Upto 25 per cent	Poor	53	(30.3)
26 to 50 per cent	Low	51	(29.1)
51 to 75 per cent	Moderate	51	(29.1)
76 to 100 per cent	High	20	(11.5)
	Total	175	(100.0)

Looking at the overall meeting attendance of the respondents, the data reveal that, although the respondents whose meeting attendance was 'poor' (upto 25% attendance) represents single largest category (53 or 30.3%) among the respondents, in case of majority of the respondents (69.7%), the meeting attendance varied between 26 to 100 per cent. Again, although a very few (11.5%) respondents belonged to the category of having 'high' meeting attendance (75 to 100%), the proportion of those having 'low' and 'moderate' meeting attendance was relatively higher (29.1% each). Let us now look at the difficulties the women leaders have reported in regularly attending the PRI meetings. The data on this aspect are presented in the Table 3 below:

Table 3

Women Leaders in PRIs: Difficulties in Regularly Attending Meetings

Difficulties in attending the meetings regularly	*Women leaders in PRIs*	
	Frequency	*Per cent*
Household responsibilities	90	(51.4)
Family members do not allow	38	(21.7)
Inconvenience	27	(15.5)
No difficulties	20	(11.4)
Total	175	(100.0)

When the researcher probed into the difficulties encountered by the respondents in regularity attending the meetings, majority (90 or 51.4%) of the respondents reported that, mainly due to the family responsibilities/household burdens and personal difficulties such as illness, they could not attend meetings regularly. Gowda (1998: 676-77) has also noted similar difficulties. It is significant to note that, as many as 38 (21.7%) respondents have said that their family members did not allow them to attend the meetings, therefore, they could not maintain regularity in attending the meetings. Among others, there were 27 (15.4%) respondents who told that, it was not convenient for them to attend the ZP meetings arranged at district headquarters. Only 20 (11.4%) respondents told that they did not encounter any difficulty in attending the meetings regularly.

As per the established division of labour based on the sex, women have been given the tasks, which can be performed, in and around the home. Apart from the physiological burdens of pregnancy and childbirth, they are given tasks such as child rearing, fetching of water, preparation of food, serving food to all the members of the family, washing clothes, cleaning the house, managing the household activities and looking after the guests etc. Rural women, in addition to all the above activities, are also involved in agricultural activities. In case of poor families, women also work as daily wage labourers. The data of the present study needs to be interpreted in the context of this culturally determined division of labour. Their new role as community leaders in PRIs is an additional responsibility for them. Thus, the traditional division of labour based on the sex puts limitations on women's attendance at the meetings in PRIs.

Again, it is very significant to note that, as many as 38 (21.7%) of the respondents were unable to maintain the regularity in attending the meetings mainly because their family members were not allowing them to do so. This opposition comes from both the male as well as female members of their families. Some of the respondents were frank enough to tell that, their husbands do not allow them to attend the meetings; they pressurise them to remain absent, while in case of few other respondents, opposition comes not from their husbands but mainly from their mothers-in-law. Reportedly, their mothers-in-law feel that it is not proper for women to attend the meetings and mix with other male members. This is an indirect reflection of the fact that the patriarchal cultural norms and values, which control female sexuality and mobility, put limitations on women's attendance at the meetings in PRIs.

Women Leaders' Participation in Decision-Making: Participation in Discussions in the Meetings

Unless we understand whether the women leaders actively participate in the discussions in the meetings, we cannot hope to understands the extent of their actual participation in decision-making in PRIs. Therefore, let us now look at the data relating to the extent of women's participation in the discussions in the PRI meetings, reasons for non-participation, if they do so, and variables associated with/influencing their participation in discussions in PRI meetings.

(i) Do women leaders participate in discussions in the meetings?

In order to understand whether respondents participate in the decision-making in PRIs, a question was asked, "Do you take active part in discussions in the meetings?" The respondents' answers to this question are classified and presented in Table 4.

Table 4
Respondents Classified According to their Participation in Discussions in PRIs

Response categories	*Do respondents actively participate in the PRI meetings?*	
	Frequency	*Per cent*
Yes	108	(61.7)
No	61	(34.9)
No response	06	(3.4)
Total	175	(100.0)

The data in Table 4 shows that the majority (108 or 61.7%) of the respondents have replied in the affirmative (they participate in discussions in the meetings) whereas another 61 or 34.9 per cent respondents have said that they do not participate in discussions in the PRI meetings. The remaining (6 or 3.4%) respondents did not give any response.

(ii) Reasons for women's non-participation in the discussions in the PRI meetings

The researcher also wanted to know the reasons why some of the respondents were not participating in the discussions in the PRI meetings. Therefore, a supplementary question was asked, "why you do not take active part in the discussions in the meetings?" This elicited various responses from the respondents. Some of the noteworthy responses are: "due to our illiteracy ignorance and lack of experience, we do not know how to talk in the meetings"; "we are attending such meetings for the first time in our life, therefore, we are still learning"; "we do not have courage and confidence to talk"; "how can we talk in front of the male members?" These were the most frequently reported reasons for their non-participation in the discussions.

Some of the respondents belonging to the various reserved categories told that, the members belonging to higher castes discourage the women members belonging to SCs while they talk in the meetings. Therefore, sometimes, these women feel insulted. The analysis of above responses revealed that illiteracy, ignorance, lack of experience of working in PRIs, lack of confidence, impact of traditional cultural norms, gender and caste-biased attitudes of male members are some of the major reasons which prohibit some women from actively participating in the discussions in PRI meetings. Some other scholars have also reported similar reasons for non-participation of women in PRIs in the discussions (Thakkar and Gawankar, 1997: 87-99; Iyengar, 1998: 101-8).

Variables Influencing Women Leaders' Participation in Discussions in the Meetings

In order to explore and examine the relationship of respondents' participation in discussions in the meetings with some other variables such as age, education, occupation, average annual family income, caste category/community background, family political background, the data on earlier variable have been cross-tabulated with that of later variables. The data have been presented and the findings have been discussed below in this section.

(i) Age and participation in discussions

The data regarding age group categories of the respondents and their participation in discussions in PRI meetings are cross-tabulated and presented below in Table 5:

Table 5

Participation in Discussions by Age Group

Age group (in years)	*Do respondents take active part in discussions in the meetings in PRIs?*			*Total*
	Yes	*No*	*No response*	
Young (21 to 25)	41 (69.5)	15 (25.4)	3 (5.1)	59 (33.7)
Middle (36 to 50)	59 (56.2)	43 (41.0)	3 (27.3)	106(60.0)
Old (above 50)	8 (72.7)	3 (27.3)	-	11 (6.3)
Total	108 (61.7)	61 (34.9)	6 (3.4)	175 (100.0)

Figures in parentheses show percentages.

The data clearly show that, an overwhelming majority (72.7%) of the respondents belonging to 'old age' group actively participating in the discussions, followed by those belonging to 'young age' group (69.5%). The more active participation from 'old' respondents could be attributed to their 'maturity level' and in case of 'young' respondents, it can be attributed to their 'activeness' characteristic of their age.

(ii) Education and participation in discussions

The data regarding respondents' educational status and their participation in discussions in the PRI meetings are cross-tabulated and presented below in Table 6:

Table 6
Participation in Decision-Making by Educational Status

Educational status	*Do respondents take active part in discussions in the meetings in PRIs?*			*Total*
	Yes	*No*	*No response*	
1 to 5th	20 (69.0)	08 (27.6)	01 (3.4)	29 (16.6)
6 to 10th	45 (84.9)	05 (9.4)	03 (5.7)	53 (30.3)
11 to 12th	03(100.0)	-	-	03 (1.7)
Graduate and above	13 (92.9)	-	01 (7.1)	14 (8.0)
Illiterate	27 (35.5)	48 (63.2)	01 (1.3)	76 (43.4)
Total	108 (61.7)	61 (34.9)	6 (3.4)	175(100.0)

Figures in parentheses show percentages.

It can be easily noticed from the data presented above that:

(a) The proportion of respondents who actively participate in the discussions in PRI meetings is significantly high among those having higher education levels (i.e., higher secondary level 100% and graduation and above 92.9%).

(b) The proportion of respondents who do not actively participate in discussions in the PRI meetings is significantly high (48 or 63.2%) among the illiterates.

(c) Having higher the educational level of the respondents have increased the scope of their taking active participation in discussions.

The data thus reveal the existence of a certain pattern of relationship between educational status and active participation in discussions in PRI meetings. One can, therefore, generalise that there is positive association between higher levels of education and the higher levels of participation in discussions.

(iii) Occupation and participation in discussions

The cross-tabulated data on two variables, namely, respondents' occupational category and active participation in discussions are presented below in Table 7:

Table 7

Participation in Discussions by Occupational Categories

Occupational category	*Do the respondents take active part in discussions in the meetings in PRIs?*			*Total*
	Yes	*No*	*No response*	
Salaried job	3(100.0)	-	-	3 (1.7)
Self-employment	7 (100.0)	-	-	7 (4.0)
Profession	1 (100.0)	–	-	1 (0.6)
Labourer	1 (25.0)	3 (75.0)	-	4 (2.3)
Business	2 (66.7)	-	1 (33.3)	3 (1.7)
Housewives	94 (59.9)	58 (36.9)	5 (3.2)	157(89.7)
Total	108 (61.7)	61 (34.9)	6 (3.4)	175 (100.0)

Figures in parentheses show percentages.

Table 7 shows that the occupational distribution of the respondents is highly skewed. Nearly 90 per cent respondents are housewives. Therefore, it is very difficult to look for any significant relationship based on the comparison among respondents belonging to various occupational categories and their participation in discussion in PRI meetings that can be generalised. Nonetheless, the data does indicate that there is some relationship between certain types of occupations and likelihood of active participation in discussions. Let us note some important observations.

First, it can be seen from Table 7 that all the respondents involved in 'salaried jobs', 'self-employment' and 'profession' were actively participating in discussions in PRI meetings. Secondly, majority of those involved in business (66.7%) and nearly 60 per cent of the housewives have also reported that they were participating in the discussions. The third notable observation is that majority (75%) of the respondents belonging to the labourer category do not take active part in discussions.

Why there is greater active participation from the women leaders involved in profession, salaried jobs, self-employment and business as compared to those who are only housewives? Women respondents involved in above-mentioned occupations get in touch with number of other people. They get relatively better exposure to the world outside their house. Frequent contacts and interaction with other people lead to the development of better expression power and communication skills among these women. Equipped with these skills in expression and communication, it must be rather easy for them to participate more effectively in discussion in panchayat meetings in which they participate. Whereas, some of those who are only housewives and lack exposure to the world outside their family, may be finding it rather difficult to actively participate in the discussions.

(iv) Income and participation in discussions

The data regarding two variables, i.e., 'respondents' income' and their 'participation in discussions' are cross-tabulated and presented in Table 8. The data reveals that, active participation in PRI meetings was reported by an overwhelming majority (87.5%) of the respondents who belong to highest income category (above Rs. 1 lakh). As against this, majority (52.9%) of the respondents belonging to lowest income category (up to Rs. 11,000) do not participate in the discussions in PRI meetings. Again, one can clearly observe that, the proportion of respondents who participate in discussion in PRI meetings increases with increasing level of family income (observed steady increase in proportion from lowest income group, i.e., 47.1% to 51.6% to 67.5% to 87.5%). The proportion of the respondents who do not participate in discussions in PRI meetings decreases as the income level increases (observe percentage decrease from 52.9 to 43.5 to 31.3). Thus, there is positive relationship between high income level and active participation in discussions in PRI meetings.

Table 8

Participation in Discussions by Average Annual Family Income

Average annual family income (in Rs.)	*Do the respondents take active part in discussions in the meetings in PRIs?*			*Total*
	Yes	*No*	*No response*	
Upto 11,000	8 (47.1)	9 (52.9)	-	17 (9.7)
11,001 to 50,000	32 (51.6)	27 (43.5)	3 (4.9)	62 (35.4)
50,001 to 1 Lakh	54 (67.5)	25 (31.3)	1 (1.2)	80 (4.7)
Above 1 Lakh	14 (87.5)	-	2 (12.5)	16 (9.2)
Total	108 (61.7)	61 (34.9)	6 (3.4)	175 (100.0)

Figures in parentheses show percentages.

The relationship between income level and active participation in discussions is more of indirect nature than direct. The sound economic background creates a better social position in the community. This heightened social status originating from better economic position might be facilitating the development of self-confidence, which might be leading to take active part in the decision-making process. As against this, poor people have relatively lower social status, which might be discouraging them, from actively participating in the discussions.

(v) Caste-category/community background and participation in discussions

The cross-tabulated data on 'caste category/community background' and 'participation in discussions' are presented in Table 9:

Table 9

Participation in Discussions by Caste Category/Community Background

Caste category/ community	*Do the respondents take active part in discussion in the meetings in PRIs?*			*Total*
	Yes	*No*	*No response*	
General	52 (62.7)	27 (32.5)	4 (4.8)	83 (47.4)
OBCs	21 (53.8)	18 (46.2)	-	39(22.3)
SCs	27 (69.2)	09 (25.61)	2 (5.2)	38 (22.31)
STs	-	1 (100)	-	1 (0.6)
NTs	4 (66.7)	2 (33.3)	-	6 (3.4)
VJNTs	4 (50.0)	4 (50.0)	-	8 (4.6)
Total	108 (61.7)	61 (34.9)	6 (3.4)	175(100.0)

Figures in parentheses show percentages.

The data reveals that an overwhelming majority of the respondents belonging to SC category (69.2%) have reported active participation in discussions in PRI meetings, followed by NTs (66.7%), general (62.7%), OBCs (53.8%) and VJNTs (50%). The only respondent belonging to ST category has reported that he does not take active part in discussions in PRI meetings.

The trend, which can be observed from above table, makes it clear that majority women leaders belonging to SC category most actively participate in discussions in PRI meetings. One interpretation would be that SCs have experienced unjust treatment from the members belonging to higher castes over the years. The SCs constitute one of repressed and exploited categories in Indian society. Due to the constitutional provisions, social legislation and improvement in educational levels, SCs are now showing signs of improvement. It is a general observation that SC women enjoy relatively better freedom to participate in spheres outside their homes. Uptil now SC women were not given political space. Due to reservation of seats in PRIs for SC women, for the first time, they have got an opportunity to participate in the PRIs. The feeling of relative deprivation among SC women, might be, perhaps, the factor responsible for their active participation in the PRI meetings. At the time of interviews, the researcher found that, as compared to others, SC women were more free and vocal while responding to the questions in the interview schedule. The absence of active participation in PRI meetings in case of STs and relatively less active participation of members of VJNTs can be attributed to their marginalised socio-economic and political position in the village communities.

A further cross-tabulation of data relating to specific castes within different caste categories revealed that, from amongst the castes belonging to open category, hundred per cent respondents belonging to Brahmin and Yelam castes have reported active participation in decision-making. Whereas Lingayat and Maratha women leaders were found at the second and third rank respectively as reflected in the frequency distribution. From amongst the various castes belonging to the SC category, an overwhelming majority of the respondents belonging to Mahar caste have reported active participation in discussions in PRI meetings. Similarly from amongst the tribals, majority of the respondents belonging to 'Bhamata Rajput' tribe have reported active participation in discussions.

(vi) Influential family political background and participation in discussions

The data regarding respondents' 'family political background' and 'participation in discussions' are cross-tabulated and presented in Table 10. Accordingly, an overwhelming majority of the respondents, who had influential family political background (73.1%), have reported active participation in discussions in PRI meetings. Thus, there is positive relationship between influential family political background and women's participation in decision-making. However, distribution of respondents with respect to the family political background is highly skewed in favour of the respondents having no such influential family political background (85.1%). Therefore, it is rather difficult to make any generalisation regarding the relationship between these two variables.

Table 10
Participation in Decision-Making by Family Political Background

Categories of respondents	*Do the respondents take active part in discussions in the meetings in PRIs?*			*Total*
	Yes	*No*	*No response*	
Respondents having influential family political background	19 (73.1)	3 (11.5)	4 (15.4)	26 (14.9)
Respondents with no influential family political background	89 (59.7)	58 (38.9)	2 (1.4)	149(85.1)
Total	108 (61.7)	61(34.9)	6 (3.4)	175(100.0)

Figures in parentheses show percentages.

Summary and Conclusions

In this paper, an attempt has been made to understand women leaders' participation in Panchayati Raj in terms of their regularity in meeting attendance and their actual participation in discussions in the meetings of PRIs. Looking at the overall meeting attendance of the respondents, the data reveals that, although the respondents whose meeting attendance was 'poor' (upto 25% attendance) represent the single largest category among the respondents, in case of the majority of the respondents, the meeting attendance was better and varied between 26 to 100 per cent.

An enquiry into the difficulties encountered by the respondents in regularly attending the meetings revealed that the majority of the respondents was unable to attend the meetings regularly mainly due to the family responsibilities/household burdens. Thus, mainly, the traditional divisional division of labour based on the sex puts limitations on women's attendance at the meetings in PRIs. Further, it is the patriarchal cultural norms and values, which control female sexuality and mobility, and put limitations on women's attendance at the meetings in PRIs.

Majority of the respondents have reported that they took active part in the discussions in the PRI meetings, as and when they attend these meetings. The analysis of the responses regarding reasons for non-participation in PRI meetings revealed that illiteracy, ignorance, lack of experience of working in PRIs, lack of confidence, impact of traditional cultural norms, gender and caste-biased attitudes are some of the major reasons, which prohibit some women from actively participating in the discussions in PRI meetings.

The exploration of the relationship between some variables such as age, education, occupation, family income, caste/ community background and family political background on the one hand and respondents' participation in discussions in the PRI meetings on the other revealed that variables such as 'old age' and 'younger age', 'higher levels of education', 'exposure to the world outside house', 'higher levels of income' and 'influential family political background' are positively associated with respondents' active participation in the discussions in PRI meetings.

References

Gowda, S. Govinda, 1998, "Women in Panchayat Raj Institutions: A Case Study in Karnataka", *Journal of Rural Development*, Vol. 17(4), pp. 669-79.

Hazel, D'Lima, 1983, *Women in Local Government*, Concept Publishing Company, New Delhi.

Iyengar, Chandra, 1997, "Women in Politics: The Maharashtra Experience", in *Women Empowerment and Political Participation,* by Poonacha Veena (ed.), S. N. D. T., Mumbai.

Kamble, Archana, 2001, "Women Leadership in Panchayati Raj: A Sociological Study", Unpublished Ph. D. Thesis, Shivaji University, Kolhapur.

Kaushik, Sushila, 1993, "Empowering Women for Politics", in *Women and Panchayati Raj*, Har-Aanand Publications, New Delhi, p. 9.

Mathew, George, 1995, "Will Reservation Ensure Participation?", *Social Welfare,* August-September, p. 35.

Panda, Snehalatha, 1997, "Political Empowerment of Women: A Case of Orissa", *Journal of Rural Development,* Vol. 16(4), pp. 663-72.

Saran, S.V., 1993, "Women in Panchayats", *Yojana,* September, 15, p.6.

Sawhney, Inder, 1994, "Action Plan for Women Launched", *Times of India,* 12th December, p.3.

Thakkar, Usha and Gawankar, Rohini, 1997, "Reservation and the Empowerment of Women: The Emerging Issues", in *Women Empowerment and Political Participation*, by Veena Poonacha (ed.), S.N.D.T., Mumbai, p. 8, 87.

6

Can the Modern and the Traditional Panchayats Co-Exist in Schedule V Areas?

R. Siva Prasad

The welfare of the citizens is the responsibility of the state and no nation-state can ignore this fact. It is obviously more important for any government to ensure that the basic needs of the poor and backward groups/communities are met and their living conditions are improved. This is all the more important in case of developing nations like India. The Government of India, since independence, has consciously made efforts to establish a more egalitarian and just society. In this regard, it has rightly made a number of provisions in the Constitution of India to protect the interests of the Scheduled Castes, Scheduled Tribes, backward classes, women, minorities and other weaker sections. It also made efforts to ensure people's participation in different levels of democratic institutions, local governance, development programmes and to a certain extent in micro-level planning and their implementation. Time and again, it has introduced number of amendments in the Constitution and brought in new Acts to meet the exigencies more effectively. Recent PESA (Act No. 40 of 1996) is one such effort to ensure local self-governance in Schedule V areas of the country. This paper attempts to analyse the spirit of the Act and its actual implementation.

I

Traditionally, tribal communities were having their own systems of governance, justice and customary practices governing their own lives, resources and economies. Since the British rule, different policies adopted by the governments have only deprived them of right to their livelihoods, access to the resources and managing their affairs. The introduction of statutory panchayats has further contested/weakened the tribal institutions and unity.

The successive forest policies, be they of British or that of independent India, have only aggravated their misery and brought them into direct conflict with the non-tribal communities as well as among themselves (Guha, 1989; Sastry, 1984; Kulkarni, 2000; Raghavaiah, 1979; Sen, 1979; Singh, 1982, 1983 and 1984). Many tribal movements, which reiterate this, made the tribals into natural rebels. The intrusion of non-tribal contractors, businesspersons and petty vendors into tribal hinterlands have added to the plundering of the tribal natural wealth and deprived them of their livelihoods. It has resulted into new tensions and conflicts. It is in this background the Government of India had introduced the PESA (Act No. 40 of 1996) as an extension to the 73rd amendment to the Constitution for strengthening the process of democratic decentralisation.

This Act is the product of a long struggle of the tribal communities and their leaders that led to the constitution of Bhuria Committee. The Bhuria Committee suggested revolutionary changes in the management and governance of Schedule V areas, in line with Schedule VI areas. It suggested adoption of the pattern of Autonomous District Councils (ADCs) of Schedule VI areas into the administration of the Schedule V areas. It forced the governments to consult Gram Sabha as mandatory in case of land acquisitions for different development purposes, for managing the natural resources, and minor forest resources (MFPs)/non-timber forest produces (NTFPs), etc. However, the Central Act reduced it to mere consultation. The States' Acts further diluted this (Kumar, 1999: 6-8). In spite of all this, it still meets, to a certain extent, the aspirations of the tribal communities.

The PESA Act emphasises that the states' legislations should be "in consonance with the customary law, social and religious practices and traditional management practices of community resources". However, the tenor of the Act 40 of 1996 does not anywhere match with the ground-level reality. In fact, in quite a few instances, the situation is contrary to what was stated in the Act. This brings to the fore the question of compatibility of the traditional tribal systems of governance, political and judicial institutions with the structures introduced by the government.

It is presumed that with the introduction of statutory political institutions, formal law and order machinery, modern infrastructural facilities, and initiating several development programmes, the traditional institutions of the tribals have more or less waned out. However, in reality, the traditional institutions like the tribal councils still effectively deal with resolution of disputes and regulate their socio-cultural life. In fact, in many a case, the tribals prefer them to the modern systems (Siva Prasad, 2002). However, it is true that if any society's organic structure is disturbed, it causes ripples in its functioning thus, threatening its very survival.

What is worse is that we have taken it as a matter of our right, deliberately or otherwise, to reform these 'ancient and archaic' communities and bring them into the 'mainstream' of the nation. What we still do not realise is, in spite of our colonial past, that the destruction of knowledge system of any community or imposition of an alien system on them is nothing but subjugating them to our dictates and creating disharmony and confusion in them. This leads to loss of culture, desperation, unrest and anxiety among them. Thus, instead of solving any of the problems, we are creating new problems. Hence, the answer lies in letting these people govern their affairs. Thus, there is a need to look at the compatibility of the PESA Act with the customary law, social and religious practices, and traditional management practices of community resources of the tribal communities.

Though the tribal societies are diverse in nature, in linguistic and cultural sense, there appears a greater similarity among different tribal communities living in Schedule V areas with regard to patterns of family, marriage, inheritance, succession, traditional councils and dispute resolution mechanisms. While we notice the similarities in social structure, what interests us in the present paper is the similarity with regard to political structures. There is a co-existence of traditional dispute resolving mechanisms along side the modern statutory political structures.

In this regard, there is a need to understand the structure and functioning of traditional councils among the tribes of Schedule V areas in order to understand the levels of compatibility with the statutory panchayats specified under the Act of 1996. In quite a few of them it is quite well structured with different functionaries performing different duties.

II

Tribal communities have greater respect to human dignity, democracy, values of the society, etc. They live in harmony with the nature and all their activities are geared to the seasonal aspects of nature. Their respect to nature is reflected in their rituals. They value morals and despise intrigue, cunningness, cheating and dishonesty. Their notion of family, marriage, property, rituals and beliefs relating to the institutions, etc., is so distinctly different from the dominant non-tribal cultures.

Most important thing that we need to learn from them is the way they resolve their differences and how the entire community responds in resolving the disputes and the attitude of the people involved in the disputes proper. Their respect to the dispute-solving mechanisms (traditional councils), authority of the village elders, involvement in all important functions of the village activities, etc., indicate the organic unity of the tribal societies. Thus, tribal societies are the finest examples of a more healthy, normative-based, and community-oriented democratic systems.

The traditional councils continue to regulate their social, cultural and, to some extent, economic life and act like a watchdog. It is pertinent to note that the maintenance of the traditional mechanisms of dispute resolution has a greater linkage with the continuance of the social and cultural structures of the tribes. Disobeying the traditional council means ex-communication and this will place an individual/family outside the domain of the community/village. Fear of excommunication makes a tribal adhere to the customs and norms of the community. The quantum of fines is always a deterrent to disobey the norm. In a way, poverty keeps people away from disobeying the customs, as they cannot afford to pay the fine.

It is essential to understand that it is just impossible for a tribal to live outside the ambit of his society/community. Community is a very effective group and an individual cannot live without it. Maintaining the norms of the community becomes a necessity to ensure the cohesion of a community. Hence, a law-regulating agency gains significance in every society. It is an integral part of the community/society and disarming it implies the destabilisation of the community.

The system of justice and village management in tribal societies in Schedule V areas involves the village head, the priest, messenger, and other elders. It thus has both secular and religious force to enforce the judgements and to exercise the authority to govern the affairs of the village. The traditional panchayat also tries to compromise or resolve the cases at the village level rather than approaching statutory law enforcing agencies. In a few cases there are supra-village organisations, be it at the level of entire tribe or at the level of few villages forming into a confederation (Siva Prasad, 2002).

It is important to note that in almost all the tribes, both within and across the states, the traditional councils are in operation (Rao, 2000; Singh, 2000). Their functioning varies based on the composition of their settlement. In a settlement where only one particular tribe resides, the traditional panchayats function very effectively. In contrast, in villages, where there are other tribes or castes present the traditional councils tend to be less effective. In some cases, the heterogeneous villages have joint councils to deal with the inter-tribal or tribe caste disputes (Siva Prasad, 2002).

III

Disputes and conflicts are part of any society or culture. Disputes arise when people violate the norms or when there is a shift in the lifestyle, which leads to a conflict between the traditional and modern value systems. Societies, which have organic unity, always have mechanisms to resolve the disputes/conflicts. In most of the traditional tribal/rural societies these disputes resolution mechanisms are usually institutionalised. These are equivalent to modern-day law courts. The purpose of the institutionalised mechanism is to control deviance and to maintain norms in a society.

The process of dispute resolution in the Schedule V areas across the states has a striking similarity, as is the case with the structure and function of the dispute resolution institutions. The similarity is seen in terms of the process of taking up the case; constituting the council to meet the requirements of the case; process of cross-examining the witnesses; using ordeals to establish the crime; referring to the judgements given earlier to arrive at judgement, process of consultation, negotiation and pronouncing the judgement. All these are done in a more transparent manner (Siva Prasad, 2002).

We find different levels of dispute-resolving mechanisms/structures among different tribes. If any of the contending parties is unhappy with the judgement of the local traditional council, it has a right to appeal to the higher levels of the councils. There are higher courts of appeal for a tribal in most of the tribal communities. In quite a few tribes, the tribal councils/federations that have jurisdiction over several villages continue to be still active, though they are relatively less effective than what they were in the past. However, defiance or non-compliance to the judgement and disrespect to the council or to the *Panch* (members of the council, equivalent to jury) usually leads to ex-communication and ostracisation. While in all the tribes the procedures of imposing punishment or penalty are quite similar, the process of reincorporating the deviant(s) is also significantly the same. In most of the cases, it is always a negotiation of justice between contending parties through the medium of traditional councils. There is a wider participation of villagers and it is really a democracy of justice deliverance with the least delay in time.

Tribals have a different way of looking at the offenders or deviants and their attitude is to be more considerate to the offender if he confesses before the elders to his committing the crime or offence. But their resolve becomes stronger against those offenders who belittle the elders or refuse to attend the traditional *panchayat*. Many a time they have a novel way of punishing the deviant. They neither punish the person physically nor by imposition of any penalty, but he is made to offer public apology to the victim. Thus, for them, self-esteem is a higher value than physical punishment or monetary penalty.

In general, the traditional councils deal with the distribution of lands under *podu/jhum* (shifting) cultivation as they are communally controlled. Disputes pertaining to individual lands are also dealt with, if the intervention of the traditional council is sought. The main functions of the traditional panchayat observed in the Schedule V areas are: (1) settlement of disputes among individuals, families, and sometimes even between villages; (2) administration of justice, (3) maintenance of peace and security in the village; and (4) promotion of general welfare (Siva Prasad, 2002).

There is a belief that the tribals being illiterate cannot govern themselves and they need to be administered by the outsiders–be they officials or external elite. We forget the fact that for generations they have managed their resources, social, legal and economic affairs more efficiently and in harmony with the surrounding environment than what is being done in the name of 'democratic governance' by the more 'learned and educated'.

The traditional tribal panchayats main efforts are to maintain harmony, integration and tranquillity in the communities, in particular, and society at large, in general. Overall, the emphasis is on compromising and reincorporating the deviants into the mainstream tribal culture and society. Their processes involve wide range of consultation, deliberations, cross-examining witnesses, impartiality in pronouncing judgements, trying to arrive at some kind of compromise, etc. Their objective is not to convict and punish but to reincorporate the deviants into the life of the community. Only in extreme cases they resort to ex-communication. Even while penalising the persons their economic capabilities are also taken into consideration. In most of the cases, it is always a negotiation of justice between contending parties through the medium of traditional councils. In all this, there is a wider participation of villagers and it is really a democracy of justice deliverance with the least delay in time. No wonder, why the tribals prefer this to formal legal machineries.

IV

The leadership in most of the tribal societies in Schedule V areas is vested in the person who established the settlement and those other elder clan members, who had moved along with him, became members of the traditional council. Their heirs succeed these positions and in their absence, they go to close patri-kin members (Siva Prasad, 2002). These leaders have greater control over their members, who are closely related to one another, and have been maintaining a sort of harmony and integration, which is regarded as most important for the welfare of the village community. What we observe today is the downplaying of the traditional councils due to the introduction of the new institutional mechanisms that have come into existence challenging the traditional mechanisms' sway over the people.

Different studies have shown that there are no conflicts noticed between the traditional and modern panchayats in tribal villages in Schedule V areas. In fact, there are no areas of conflict between the election-based statutory panchayat and traditional *Kula Panchayat*, because the duties of both the panchayats are distinct. Singh (2002) chronicles the development of Nyaya Panchayats, and statutory panchayats in the tribal areas. He points out that, "The relationship of the two is generally understood by people. The tribals' customary laws are mainly concerned with ordering sex and marriage, and dealing with witchcraft, kinship, inheritance and related matters. It is tribals' own affairs. The two institutions co-exist. The tribal councils often try to adjust to the Statutory Gram Panchayat" (ibid.: 20). The traditional council is interested in preserving the traditional customs and norms of the society. It is still the most effective instrument of social control. Political, ritual and, to some extent, economic life of the village is still controlled by this council.

It is found that the villages that are situated close to the roads or urban centres and which are heterogeneous have shown some tendencies of drifting away from the traditional councils. However, even here, there is a semblance of traditional councils still in operation and some of the functions of the traditional council are taken over by the modern statutory panchayats. It is observed that wherever the traditional panchayats are functioning well, the statutory panchayats remained dormant. In fact, in these villages the traditional panchayats have even got involved in deciding the beneficiary selection for different development schemes of the government (Siva Prasad, 2002).

A discussion at this juncture about the Act No. 40 of 1996 (see Annexure 5) is essential. The Act states that, "a State legislation on the Panchayats that may be made shall be in consonance with the customary law, social and religious practices and traditional management practices of community resources". The Act further specifies that, "every Gram Sabha shall be competent to safeguard and preserve the traditions and customs of the people, their cultural identity, community resources and the customary mode of dispute resolution". In fact, the Act is very firm about the role of Gram Sabha in many aspects dealing with village management, including its resources, development, planning, fund utilisation, etc. Though a Gram Sabha is defined clearly, the Act is not clear about who should conduct the meetings of Gram Sabha and who should head it, etc.? It leaves the matter to state legislations. In states like Andhra Pradesh, the Gram Sabha is presided over by the sarpanch/upa-sarpanch, who are the statutory authority. This would go against the spirit of the Act and might lead to conflict in many a case.

This leads to a question as to how a Gram Sabha can perform the stipulated job when it does not any longer work under the traditional authority. It was the traditional authority, which has been safeguarding and preserving "*the traditions and customs of the people, their cultural identity, community resources and the customary mode of dispute resolution*" (Act 40 of 1996, emphasis added).

The above problem has serious implications for the tribals in Schedule V areas. Since the Act intends to safeguard and preserve their customs, practices, etc., there is need to legally recognise the role of customary institutions/authority at the village/Gram Sabha level. This implies the traditional village leadership should be given due recognition, particularly in matters of dispute resolution, at the Gram Sabha level in the Act. This would definitely ensure the balance between the traditional panchayat and the statutory panchayat. This would also ensure a proper development of tribal areas in harmony with their customs, practices, environment, etc., and with the nation at large. There is an urgent need to translate the intent of the Act into reality by bringing in legislation to give the traditional institutions of the tribals a legal status for their effective functioning. Let us remember that they have a right to lead their life the way their culture permits, as we have a right to ours and we have no right to impose our notions of justice, governance, etc., on them.

V

The traditional councils and dispute resolution mechanisms are still a force to reckon with and they need to be strengthen. There are many areas where we find a lot of commonality in their structural and functional aspects, though we find many local variations. All the tribals have different customs and normative structures and there is no reason why they cannot have their own judicial processes with different levels of appeal. There is a need to think more in terms of a decentralised legal and administrative system than a centralised one, as it exists today. When many functions of administration are being transferred to the statutory panchayats, it is also illogical to think that the judicial process should be centralised.

Tribal societies are culturally and socially very rich and they live in harmony with the nature and people. In comparison to the dominant non-tribal societies, the tribal communities are highly democratic, more egalitarian and, more than anything, human. Let us not think that our judicial and governance processes, which are not even ours, are any better than other processes. They also have equal amount of biases, if not more. Without understanding the culture and society of the tribal communities, if we thrust any system on them, we will have to share the responsibility for their disastrous consequences. Enough harm has already been done and it may be near to impossible to rectify our past mistakes and we should not continue to repeat the same mistakes repeatedly. Let us not treat the tribal societies as guinea pigs for our social experiments and adventures and they should be allowed to steer their future, as we have our claims to it.

What is important to note is that the tribal lives in the midst of his community and an estranged tribal cannot have a peaceful living. In addition, it is not desirable to impose alien system of control, management, etc., in the name of development. The disasters of the so-called 'development' are there clearly before us as frightening examples of disaster. We need to have a more pluralistic, transparent and confidence building systems of management of various things, including justice, rather than centralisation of every aspect of life in the garb of 'nationalism'. The problem that we have before us today in the tribal societies, also true with the other rural areas, are due to excessive indulgence of the state in the local governance. There is an air of domination and feeling of superiority in our approaches and today there is need for a change in our philosophy of governance, planning and development. Otherwise, we will be doing irreparable injustice to the communities that have for centuries lived in harmony with their surrounding environment and other people.

References

Kumar, Girish, 1999, *Tribal Panchayats in Andhra Pradesh: A Study of Post-1996 Act Status* (sponsored by Ministry of Rural Development, GoI, New Delhi). Hyderabad: NIRD (unpublished report).

Guha, R., 1989, *Unquiet Woods*, New Delhi: Oxford University Press.

Kulkarni, S., 2000, The Plight of the Tribal, *Seminar,* August 2000.

Kushawa, R., 1977, *Working of Nyaya Panchayats in India*, Delhi: Young Asia.

Mohan Rao, K., 2000, Traditional Tribal Panchayats, *Yojana*, April 2000.

Natarajan, L., 1979, The Santhal Insurrection: 1855-56. in A.R. Desai (ed.) *Peasant Struggle*, New Delhi: Oxford University Press.

Ragavaiah, V., 1979, Background of Tribal Struggles in India. In A.R. Desai (ed.), *Peasant Struggles in India, New Delhi: Oxford University Press.*

Sastry, V.N.V.K., 1984, Two Rajgond Uprisings in Forty Years: A Conflict Analysis, *Man and Life*, Vol. 10, Nos. 1-2, pp. 62-76.

Sen, Sunil. 1979, Tebhaga Chai. In A.R. Desai (ed.), *Peasant Struggles in India*, Delhi: Oxford University Press.

Singh, K.S. (ed.), 1982, *Tribal Movements in India*, Vol I, New Delhi: Manohar.

— (ed.) 1983, *Tribal Movements in India*, Vol II, New Delhi: Manohar.

— 1984, Introduction. In W.G. Archer, *Tribal Law and Justice: A Report on the Santhal,* New Delhi: Concept Publishing Company.

— 1984, Introduction. In *Tribal Ethnography, Customary Law and Change,* New Delhi: Concept Publishing Company.

— 1994, *The Scheduled Tribes, People of India,* National Series, Vol. III, New Delhi: Oxford University Press.

— 2000, Tribal Customary Laws: Policy Implications. In *Yojana*, April 2000.

Siva Prasad, R., 2002, *Customary Modes of Dispute Resolution in Schedule V Areas of Andhra Pradesh, Madhya Pradesh and Orissa.* UNDP-NIRD Project Report submitted to National Institute of Rural Development, Hyderabad (unpublished).

7

Decentralisation, Panchayati Raj and the Rights of Marginalised Groups in India

A Case for Civil Society

Gaurang R. Sahay

Like most of the modern nation-states, India too has adopted the model of decentralisation to realise the principles of equality, fraternity and prosperity (see Crook and Manor, 1998: 1). At the heart of this socio-political development, there are many multi-faceted yet interconnected themes and issues. This paper is primarily concerned with one of them: decentralisation brings about a system of governance that protects and facilitates human rights, particularly the rights of weaker and marginalised groups such as Scheduled Castes (SCs), Scheduled Tribes (STs) and women. By contextualising the process of decentralisation in the various initiatives of the state, primarily the 73rd Constitutional Amendment, this paper, on the basis of important studies and reports, tries to reflect on the human rights of marginalised groups against the background of decentralised local governance, namely, the Panchayati Raj system. In so doing, it argues for a serious and determined intervention of the institutions of civil society – non-government organisations and competitive political parties – in the process of decentralisation to make the provisions of the 73rd amendment, particularly the ones related with human rights of weaker and marginalised sections of our society, a ground reality.

Decentralisation: Meaning and Importance

Decentralisation is generally defined as a process whereby administrative authority, public resources and responsibilities are devolved and delegated from central or state government agencies to lower level institutions such as village panchayats, municipalities and non-government organisations. Such a process develops a people-centred system of governance that enables hitherto powerless individuals and groups to play significant roles in the implementation of programmes and policies and mobilisation, allocation and distribution of public resources so that they become basic engine of development and not merely its beneficiaries. Its main purpose is to bring accountability in governance ensuring economic and social justice (see White, 1959, Laski, 1960: 61; Crook, and Manor, 1998; Rondinelli et al., 1989; Meenakshisundram, 1999: 56-57; Kothari, 1999: 48).

Scholars belonging to different disciplines have made several arguments favouring decentralisation as a model of development, empowerment and social justice (see Smith 1985; Ostrom et al., 1993; Dreze and Sen, 1996; Evans, 1996; Crook and Manor, 1998; Pomeroy and Berkes, 1997; Agrawal and Gibson, 1999; Kothari, 1999: Manor, 1999; Blair, 2000; Lal, 2000: de Souza, 2000; Crook and Sverrisson, 2001). Some of the significant ones are following:

- First, decentralisation overcomes the problems of centralised planning by adopting a paradigm of development that reflects on the real needs and preferences of the concerned community particularly its vulnerable and marginalised sections.
- Second, it facilitates greater participation in the local politico-economic affairs that improves the quality and effectiveness of government sponsored schemes and services particularly those ones which are aimed at empowering poor and marginalised groups.
- Third, it develops communicative understanding and cooperation between public officials and citizens that help in creating an atmosphere conducive for sustainable development

including the management and proper utilisation of common property resources.

- Fourth, it formalises and enhances the authority of citizens over public officials so that the latter ones do not find enough opportunities and power to indulge into 'rent-seeking' activities.
- Fifth, it can lead to the formation of a new forward-looking self-identity among different sections of society that help in breaking down the iniquitous and hierarchical social order and its ramifications.
- Sixth, it generates conditions for the realisation of specific demands and needs of different regions and groups with minimal chances of public complain and religious, ethnic and minority upsurges.
- Lastly, it facilitates democratic values for resolving fundamental and specific social and economic problems faced by diverse groups and communities in a complex, tradition-bound and culturally and economically diversified society like India.

Decentralisation and Panchayati Raj in India: A Historical Outline

The history of decentralisation in India, in one sense or another, goes back to the colonial period. To quote Lieten and Srivastava, "It started with Ripon Revolution in 1882 which aimed at involving the 'intelligent class of public spirited man' in the management of rural areas under British rule. In the following years, district boards and taluk boards were set up with nominated members to look after health, roads and education" (1999: 16). Decentralisation received a boost with the constitution of Royal Commission on Decentralisation in 1907. The Commission proposed that decentralised governance should start from the village rather than the district. The process went further ahead with the Montague-Chelmsford Reforms that made local self-government a 'transferred subject' under the scheme of 'dyarchy'. Following the recommendations of commissions and reports eight provinces and six native states passed acts and laws by 1926. However, S.N. Jha rightly observes that "these schemes of decentralisation were clearly administrative, governed by the requirements of the centralised colonial state" (1999: 16). Therefore, the placement or position of local self-government in the centralised structure was always inconclusive. The district board and village council were totally dependent on centralised bureaucracy for power and resources; hence, their role as the local unit of administration and rural development remained non-functional. In fact, on the contrary, such a set-up helped the colonial government by containing the upsurge of the local people to a certain extent (Maddick, 1970: 14-21; Morris-Jones, 1971: 156; Zamora, 1990: 20-24; Khanna, 1994: 5).

Decentralisation, in real sense of the term, started in India when it became an independent democratic nation-state and began realising in concrete terms the principles of modernity project. Various different programmes and institutional schemes were introduced under the name of decentralisation to achieve this goal. One of such programmes is known as the system of Panchayati Raj.

In the beginning, the Panchayati Raj system was introduced as an institutional arrangement to bring about development in the villages through the participation of local people. Its introduction largely followed the recommendations of Balwantrai Mehta Committee Report, which was constituted by the Government of India on the request of National Development Council to make an overall assessment of the Community Development Programme (CDP). The Committee observed that the failure of the CDP was due to the conspicuous absence of people's participation from development projects. In order to secure their participation, the Committee recommended the introduction of some institutional arrangement. It resulted into the creation and introduction of a three-tier Panchayati Raj system consisting of 'Gram Panchayat' at the base, 'Panchayat Samiti' in the middle at block or taluka level and 'Zilla Parishad' at the top or district level. The Committee recommended that the Panchayati Raj Institutions would henceforth be vested with "the entire charge of all development works within its jurisdiction" (Mehta, 1957: 28). The institution to which power should be devolved was thought to be the 'Samiti', an area overlapping with the previous National Extension Block. Thus, from 1957 onwards began a new experiment in the sphere of decentralisation. By 1959, all the states had passed Acts and by mid-1960s panchayats were set up in all the parts of the country. In this system, Panchayat Samiti became the principal or primary unit of development activities.

After the implementation of the Panchayati Raj system, it was soon realised that, despite the centre of government attention and concerted effort, the system failed miserably in bringing about positive changes in the villages. In fact, the institutions, particularly Village Panchayats, "more often than not were captured by autocratic and invariably corrupt leaders from among the male village elite" (Jha, 1999: 22). It benefited the better-off segments and resulted in the subordination of social justice as democratically defined (Berrman, 1979:39). After realising this fact, the government decided not to involve PRIs in implementing the land reforms in the Chief Ministers' Conference (1969).

The Panchayati Raj system was left in hibernation until the formation of the Janata Party government in 1977. This government was dead against centralisation and was inspired by the ideals of Jayprakash Narayan in particular. Hence, it constituted a committee headed by Asok Mehta to assess the functioning of the Panchayati Raj system and to suggest measures to make it functional. The Committee noted that the system should not be viewed as a God that had failed; it had many achievements to its credit and its problems can be overcome by making some changes in the institutional arrangements and by introducing some policy measures. It opined that the system could not perform as expected vis-à-vis rural development because development programmes were routed through the official state bureaucracy and finances remained inelastic. The Committee made some suggestions to revitalise the system. It proposed a two-tier model of decentralisation to be handed down from the state government to the Zilla Parishad and then on to the Mandal which would fall somewhere in between the block and the village. It suggested that, in order to increase accountability and to facilitate the linkages with higher-level political processes, political parties should be allowed to participate in panchayat elections. It also made a specific plan for the active participation and involvement of women and other weaker sections such as SCs and STs in PRIs through reservation of seats and posts.

The recommendations of the Asok Mehta Committee were not implemented because the Janata Party government collapsed in 1980, just after being in power for three years. The new Congress government appointed G.V.K. Rao Committee in 1985 and L.M. Singhvi Committee in 1986 to review the situations and make recommendations. The Rao Committee recommended that the district should be the basic unit of policy planning and programme implementation and also favoured holding of regular elections to the panchayats. It also made some suggestions for radical changes in the planning process for block level and village level activities. The Singhvi Committee suggested for reorganisation of villages for creating viable village panchayats. It recommended for devolving more financial resources to panchayats to make them more viable. The committee viewed that a proper functioning of panchayats is needed for the democratic operations of the nation-state.

Thus, all of the committees in their reports listed prominently three reasons for the failure of the Panchayati Raj system in achieving the objective of decentralisation: states did not devolve enough substantive power to the PRIs, bureaucracy did not cooperate with PRIs, and the traditional local elite groups manipulated the PRIs in their own interests. Such assessments made the Government of India think in the direction of giving the panchayats a constitutional status. The process began with the 64th Amendment Bill, which was introduced in parliament in 1989 and culminated into the 73rd amendment to the Constitution, which was passed with near unanimity in both houses of parliament in December 1992. The Amendment was ratified by most of the states and came into effect from April 24, 1993. The 73rd amendment gave village, block and district level panchayats a constitutional status under Indian law. The more important provisions of the amendment are the following:

1. There will be a three-tier Panchayati Raj system, with elected bodies at village, block and district levels, in every state. However, states with populations less than 2 million are not required to introduce block-level panchayats if they decide to do so.

2. There will be Gram Sabha in the form of a deliberative body constituting all eligible voters at the village level within a village area. It is meant to dish up as a primary mechanism for transparency and accountability by reviewing the annual statement of accounts, reports of the preceding financial year and views on development programmes for the following year, and by participating in the identification of beneficiaries for some government schemes.
3. There will be direct elections to five-year terms for all members at all levels of the panchayats. The election of the chairperson at the intermediate and district level will be through indirect elections. In case of dissolution, election will be held within six months of the date of dissolution.
4. One-third of all seats at all level will be reserved for women, and reservations for SCs and STs at all level will be proportional to their populations at each level. The office of chairperson of the panchayats will also be subject of this provision.
5. States will have option regarding the reservation of seats for other backward caste (OBC) groups at all the three levels.
6. There will be a State Election Commission to supervise, organise and oversee elections at all levels.
7. There will be a State Finance Commission to review and revise the financial position of the panchayats on five-year intervals, and to make recommendations to the state government vis-à-vis funds.
8. In order to enhance the credibility of panchayats as institutions of self-governance, state government can authorise panchayats to prepare plans for economic development with social justice for their respective areas and to levy and collect some local taxes.
9. The 'Eleventh Schedule' added through the 73rd amendment identifies 29 areas over which panchayats can legitimately have jurisdiction. Many of these, such as agriculture, minor irrigation, animal husbandry, fisheries, social forestry, small-scale industries, and implementation of land reforms, focus on the sectors of livelihood within the rural economy.

Others, such as rural housing, rural electrification, and transportation and communication linkages, are primarily concerned with the provision and maintenance of rural infrastructure. Some cover the provision of key rural services, such as health, sanitation and primary, secondary and vocational education. In addition, some others govern the provision of targeted welfare benefits such as the public distribution system, and benefits for SCs and STs, women and children and the handicapped.

Thus, it can be said that the 73rd amendment covers many areas that would enable the panchayats to perk up the lives and well-being of poor, vulnerable and marginalised groups. Furthermore, it holds specific provisions that promise the participation of traditionally excluded groups, such as women, SCs and STs, and transparency for local institutions such as the Gram Panchayats and the Gram Sabha. S. Jha has rightly opined that "the 73rd and 74th Amendments... are designed to promote self-governance through statutory recognition of local bodies. The latter are expected to move away from their traditional role of simply executing the programmes handed down to them by higher levels of government and to formulate and implement their own programmes of economic development and social justice" (Jha 2000: 103).

After the insertion of 73rd amendment in Part IX of the Constitution, the Government of India made it mandatory for all states to implement it within a year. Following 73rd amendment, all the states passed their own 'conformity legislation' that outlines the rights, duties and procedures of panchayats at village, district and intermediate levels. For the first time, panchayats with a high degree of uniformity in terms of structure, composition, powers and functions have taken shape throughout the country. Now, there are approximately 600 District Panchayats, 6,000 Block or Taluka Panchayats and 250,000 Village Panchayats covering 72.2 per cent of India's population. Almost all states have held at least one round of elections since 1993 in accordance with the provisions of Act. Voter participation in those elections has been exceptionally high (Alsop et al., 2000).

The 73rd Amendment and Marginalised Groups: Expectations and Outcomes

The 73rd amendment comprises several provisions that protect and cultivate human rights in general and the rights of poor and marginalised groups (SCs, STs, OBCs) and women in particular by counterbalancing the existing structural patterns of inequality and discrimination in rural India. The provisions, such as reservation of seats and the post of chairperson for women, SCs and STs, Gram Sabha as a constitutional deliberative body, and empowering states to reserve seats in panchayats for other backward caste groups, ensure the participation of poor and marginalised groups into the schemes of governance and development.

Nevertheless, a number of studies show that, like earlier attempts at decentralisation, the 73rd amendment has also not fully lived up to its expectations (see Lieten and Srivastava, 1999; Jha 1999; Vyasulu and Vyasulu, 1999; de Souza, 2000; Behar and Kumar, 2002; Mathew, 2001; Nambiar, 2001; Deshpande and Murthy, 2002). There has not been noticeable structural change in rural social formation. The traditional dominant or elite groups, supported by the traditional iniquitous and exploitative land and caste relations in the villages, have continued to maintain their control over the panchayats in one way or another.

The continued dominance of traditional dominant groups in rural India and the constitutional provisions of the 73rd amendment have intensified the antagonistic or conflict-ridden rural situation, which result into, more often than not, the violations of human rights on mass scale including violence, bloodshed and loss of life. Widespread violence preceded and followed the panchayat elections in most of the states and many seats were won without being contested. This shows that the tussle of power exists not just between state and panchayats, but also between the traditional dominant power structure and emerging new leadership from the marginalised groups at the grassroots. The dominant groups vehemently oppose any attempt by subordinate or weaker sections, particularly SCs and STs, to exercise their constitutional rights by participating in the process of voting, campaigning, attending meetings, running for office, lobbying for their own representatives, etc., independently and differently. That is why, in the recent past, panchayat elections at many places in most of the states resulted into killings of the villagers belonging to the weaker sections, particularly SCs and STs. The classic case is that of Melavalavu, a village in Madurai district of Tamil Nadu. When Melavalavu was declared a panchayat reserved for SCs in October 1996, the dominant castes felt bitter about this and created a state of condition in which the polls could not be held. The second effort to hold elections was also thwarted by violence and booth capturing. Finally, the election was held on 30 December 1996 with the involvement of non-dominant castes, particularly SCs. The upper castes continued their unbending resistance and forcibly stopped the SC sarpanch and upa-sarpanch to enter the panchayat office. Finally, on 30 June 1997, the sarpanch and upa-sarpanch along with their three accompanying persons were murdered in broad daylight. Their only crime was that they participated in the election process and stood for the posts against the wills of the dominant caste groups (Mathew, 1997). This trend has not stopped. There are many reports of suppression of constitutional rights of the weaker and lower castes by dominant castes in the last panchayat elections in Tamil Nadu. The *Frontline* (26 October 2001) has reported that elections could not be held in four Gram Panchayats reserved for Scheduled Castes. It happened because the dominant caste people in these villages boycotted the elections and did not allow Scheduled Caste people to file nomination papers for different posts. In the areas where Scheduled Castes participated in the elections by defying the wishes of the dominant castes and filed nomination papers for different posts, they were humiliated and kept in a terror situation. These apart, there have been cases of SC voters being prevented from voting in many panchayats and their houses and colonies were attacked to intimidate them. At some places the dominant castes put up mannequin SC candidates in the elections who can be easily manipulated and wheedled to carry out their whims and fancies (also see Institute of Social Sciences, 2001: 3).

Similar kinds of human rights violations have occurred in most of the other states. The northern states have witnessed more conflict of interests and serious human rights violations during and after the panchayat elections. In the recent panchayat elections in Bihar, over 96 people including a magistrate and several candidates, were killed during the polling and more than 40 candidates were murdered in different districts between notification of polling and filing of nominations (Institute of Social Sciences, 2001). Scheduled Castes were more at the receiving end. At many places, the panchayat elections proved nightmarish for them. In this whole affair, administration including the police force has sided with the traditional dominant groups. Mathew (2003) writes that after the panchayat elections in Madhya Pradesh there was a report of beating up of a Scheduled Caste member by the police at a meeting where the District Magistrate was present. When this case was brought to notice of the Human Rights Commission, the District Magistrate visited the villages and instructed the villagers not to appear as witness in favour of the Scheduled Caste member. The people became too alarmed to comment on the issue.

Even after duly getting elected to the PRIs, the Scheduled Castes and other marginalised castes representatives are not getting the power and status they deserve. According to a survey done by P. Sainath, a noted journalist and social worker, in several panchayats in Tikamgarh of Bundelkhand region of Madhya Pradesh the Scheduled Caste sarpanchas are continuously ousted by a variety of methods like rigged suspension, manipulated vote of confidence and two-child norm (Popkin, 1979; Behar and Kumar, 2004: 86). This apart, there is a plenty of instances where they sit on the ground during the course of the panchayat meetings while the upper dominant caste members sit on the chairs. In such a situation they simply follow the decisions and wishes of the upper dominant castes. Even, when upper caste groups commit atrocities against the lower castes, the latter do not have a supportive redress mechanism. Lower and weaker caste people are being subjected to unabated atrocities particularly through the connivance and collusion of the state administration and the local police. In many instances, cases are not even registered against the perpetrators by the police

(Mathew, 2003). Therefore, the fact-finding report of the collective of concerned writers and intellectuals of Tamil Nadu on the caste riots in Rajapalayam area of Kamarajar district (1997) has recommended that at least one-third of the officials of various ranks in both revenue and police departments must be from the affected sections.

Scheduled Tribes (STs) have faced more or less similar situation. Mathew (2003) writes that a tribal woman sarpanch was stripped naked by the dominant people while unfurling the national flag on 15 August 1998 (Independence Day) in a district of Rajasthan. In another case, a tribal woman sarpanch in Madhya Pradesh was stripped naked in a *Gram Sabha* meeting because she was not agreeing to follow the wishes of a leader of the dominant caste. Such violations of the human rights of STs during and after the panchayat elections have also taken place in many other states, even in the scheduled or tribal areas, in spite of powerful legislations for decentralised governance. Just like the SC representatives, the panchayat representatives belonging to Scheduled Tribes are also not treated with dignity by other non-tribal panchayat officials and dominant group members. Elected tribal members of the panchayats, more often than not, go through traumatic experience if they dare to challenge the authority of the higher officials and dominant individuals.

STs are also denied their basic human rights in many other different ways. A more blatant human rights violation took place when the state government denied reservation to Scheduled Tribes just 48 hours before the announcement of Village Panchayat elections in Gujarat. The Gujarat government, through a notification on 23 November 2000, nullified the provisions for reservation of seats for STs in the Village Panchayats in the Fifth Schedule areas where the population of STs was less than 25 per cent of the total population of a Village Panchayat. In the original Act there was a sub-clause providing reservation of panchayat seats for STs and SCs in proportion of their population to the total population of the village.

The 73rd amendment created a condition for a fair political representation of women in the PRIs. It provided the much-needed opportunity for women to participate actively in the decision-making processes of their locality. In this new era of Panchayati Raj, there are now more than one million women elected representatives in all the three tiers of Panchayati Raj. Their importance and contributions in running the panchayats efficiently have been widely reported and duly recognised. Some of the awardees have done excellent work in raising women's economic status, campaigning against child marriage and child labour, building health centres, strengthening primary schools and self-help groups and so on.

Like SCs and STs, many of our women panchayat representatives, particularly those ones belonging to the poor and marginalised castes or classes, have experienced serious and violent backlashes from various quarters of our dominant patriarchal system. There are stories from all over the country of the violations of their rights despite the constitutional provisions and their overwhelming numbers (approximately one million) in the panchayat institutions. Mathew (2003) observes that, after more than a year of the panchayat elections in Madhya Pradesh, a lady sarpanch was being stripped naked in Raigarh district, another lady sarpanch was being gang raped in Chhatarpur district and an upa-sarpanch was tortured, and a Scheduled Caste member was beaten up in Raisen and East Nimar respectively. A woman councillor, Leelavathy, of Villapuram in Tamil Nadu was murdered in broad daylight because she made water facility available in her area against the wishes of those powerful people who were involved in corrupt practices and making a lot of black money by providing water to the needy people (Sivaraman, 1997).

The basic rights of women are also being curtailed by manipulating the constitutional provisions empowering women through proxy rule. A group of *sarpanch patis* (husbands of women *sarpanchas*) has emerged on the scene. They are managing the affairs of the panchayat and use their sarpanch wives as their rubber stamp. A study in the state of Karnataka has shown that many women elected to the local bodies or panchayats are either substitute for husbands and fathers or puppets of the dominant groups who conveniently use the resources of panchayats for their vested interests (Mathew, 2003). This has led to the mockery of the elected women representatives by various names.

The above citation of facts on the violations of human rights is not meant to deny the truth that the 73rd amendment, compared to the earlier attempts of decentralisation, has brought more positive developments in rural India. The studies and assessments by Alsop et al. (2000), Harriss (2000 and 2001), Corbridge and Harriss (2001), Crook and Manor (1998), and Ghatak and Ghatak (2002) clearly demonstrate that the 73rd amendment has led to some real improvements in democratic participation, accountability and governance vis-à-vis rural development and social justice. Despite the odds, traditionally, subordinate groups, such as women, SCs and agricultural labourers have been able to make their presence felt in the panchayat institutions. They are not so afraid of involving themselves into 'proactive' forms of participation, such as campaigning during elections, signing a petition, attending non-official meetings, joining a protest and contacting representatives. The villagers, cutting across caste and class lines, take part in the local elections every five years and assert their right to vote. The emergent system has definitely taken a leap forward in guaranteeing a life of dignity and respect to the weaker and marginalised groups at the village level by pursuing the ideals of social justice. In his review of PRIs, Mathew writes: "Since the new phase of decentralisation, there is evidence that some of the worst forms of exclusion that plagued the rural society in India are no longer practiced in a number of states. Elected members sit together and discuss issues in formal and informal meetings. A symbolic participation of all in the village, including Scheduled Castes and Scheduled Tribes and women does take place at least as a constitutional requirement. This is due to the slow but sure changes in the larger political landscape in India" (2003: 161).

The Citizens Report on Governance and Development by Social Watch India has also detailed some positive implications of the 73rd amendment. It says that, considerable number of women have been elected on unreserved seats and demonstrated their leadership and ability. It seems southern states are fairing better in promoting women leadership. The states like Kerala, Karnataka, Andhra

Pradesh, Tamil Nadu, West Bengal, Madhya Pradesh and some other states have elected women representatives much above the minimum of 33 per cent prescribed limit.

Karnataka, in fact, has 6.8 per cent above the prescribed reservation of 33 per cent representation for women in panchayat bodies. This proves that many women representatives have been elected on unreserved seats. There are many examples across the nation of meaningful leadership provided by the female sarpanchas. Mithi Beri Gram Panchayat in Uttaranchal, Jamunia in Madhya Pradesh and many others have women leadership on unreserved seats who are striving to bring equitable justice to the marginalised groups, specifically the women, in their panchayats. Similarly, the elected Scheduled Caste leadership is far more confident today as compared to earlier years. Equality and equity between Scheduled Castes and non-Scheduled Castes are slowly emerging and caste feelings are not as openly expressed as before (cited in Popkin, 1979; Behar and Kumar, 2004: 86). The Citizen Report has also cited some of the cases of women leaders belonging to Scheduled Castes in favour of the emergent not so unequal situation in rural India. It cites the case of Mohini Devi Megwal as a noteworthy representative of Scheduled Caste women sarpanchas who fought her way back to office through constitutional forum of election after being unceremoniously removed by the panchayat members led by her bête noire, Iswar Ram, because she dared to defy the corrupt traditional power set up in the village. Kala, a Scheduled Caste woman leader, was elected sarpanch of Noothulapuram Gram Panchayat in Tamil Nadu. Her exposure to the outside world and official contacts with district officials enhanced her leadership qualities and capacities for development work particularly in Scheduled Caste hamlets.

Concluding Remarks

However, the prevailing situation in rural India clearly asks for serious thinking and programmes to realise the provisions of the 73rd amendment. In this context, I would like to propose that civil society, particularly its two institutions, non-government organisations (NGOs) and political parties, could play significant roles in making the 73rd amendment a ground reality.

Civil society is generally defined as "the population of groups formed for collective purposes primarily outside of the state and market place" (Rooy, 1998: 30) or as "an intermediate associational realm between the state and family populated by organisations which are separate from the state and are formed voluntarily by members of society" (White, 1994: 379; Harriss, 2001). Taking the ideas, particularly from Alexis de Tocqueville's account of associationalism in the United States, it is believed that voluntarism, community or collective spirit and independent organisational structure and existence constitute essential features of civil society. According to Beteille (2000: Ch.8; 2001: 286-307), civil society is an open and secular historical formation that mediates between citizens on the one hand and state on the other in a modern democratic social formation. In this process of mediation, freedom is advanced and fraternity is realised with economic development and social justice (Gupta, 2001: Ch. 5). It is open in the sense that it is independent of race, caste, creed, ethnicity, gender and other primordial collectivities and secular in the sense that religious or non-secular rules and authorities do not regulate its internal arrangements. Since civil society is situated beyond household and consists of people cutting across social divisions such as caste, kinship group and gender, etc., it brings about horizontal relationships, mutual trust and reciprocity among them, which form the basis of social work and services. It makes a differentiation between organisations that are organised on principles of hierarchy and control and the ones that are based on the principles of equality and freedom before aligning with the later ones. Therefore, it is generally believed that civil society or its various institutions, such as NGOs, trade unions, farmers' associations, political parties, etc., are a good and desirable structural development with many positive values and is capable of balancing the act of state and market by reducing and controlling their power of governance and through social work and services.

The proposal for a serious intervention of civil society in the process of decentralisation is supported by some significant studies.

Drawing on evidence from China and Nigeria, Meenakshisundaram (1999: 66-67) argues that accountability and functioning of the PRIs are highly dependent on the existence of 'mass participation' at the local level which can be made possible by the participation of civil society organisations in this process. Reflecting on findings from Bolivia, Honduras, India (Karnataka), Mali, Ukraine and Philippines, Blair (2000: 27) argues that civil society organisations have fostered strong accountability vis-à-vis decentralised governance in peripheral rural areas. An important assertion here is that accountability is strengthened when people outside the state apparatus organise to ensure that public officials are acting in accordance with formal and informal norms of performance.

This apart, civil society organisations can empower poor and marginal groups in society so that they can participate in the process of decentralisation at equal level (Crook and Manor, 1998; Tendler, 1997). NGOs, for instance, have been empowering poor people by connecting them with a wider circle of allies, with whom they can mount a more effective political lobby (Bratton, 1990; Clark, 1991; Johnson, 2001; White and Runge, 1995). Second, and related to this, they can absorb some of the costs of engaging in political action (e.g., transportation, communication and so forth). Third, and somewhat less tangibly, they can encourage what Popkin (1979: 243) has described as "new conceptions of identity and self-worth". This they can do by encouraging poor people to engage in collective action (White and Runge, 1995) or by transmitting information about constitutional rights, potential allies and other political opportunities.

Drawing on both national and international experiences, various scholars have highlighted the roles of political parties or a party system in making the decentralisation successful. Crook and Manor (1998), Blair (2000) and Echeverri-Gent (1992) argue that the political parties do it by encouraging a culture of accountability in local political institutions and processes. According to Manor (1999: 74-76), a multi-party system can help to organise 'opposing forces' into clearly recognisable groups, stimulating public criticism and debate. The experience in West Bengal suggests that political parties do challenge the interests of dominant and exploitative groups by striking an ideal balance between local governance and a central executive. They do it more when they develop and pursue a programme that is ideologically committed to the principles of equity and justice (see Crook and Sverrisson, 2001; Echeverri-Gent, 1992; Ghatak and Ghatak, 2002; Kohli 1987). The experience of West Bengal may not be replicated in other political settings or it may not be a 'model' for the rest of the country. Nevertheless, it does shed some light on the important ways in which a party system constituting competitive political parties can empower poor and politically marginal groups in the society.

References

Agrawal, A. and C.C. Gibson. 1999. Enchantment and Disenchantment: The Role of Community in Natural Resource Conservation, *World Development* 27, 6: 629-49.

Alsop, R., A. Krishna and D. Sjoblom. 2000. 'Are Gram Panchayats Inclusive? Report of a Study Conducted in Rajasthan and Madhya Pradesh', Background Paper No. 3 of the World Bank's unpublished Project Work *Overview of Rural Decentralisation in India,* Volume 3.

Behar, A. and Y. Kumar. 2002. *Process of Decentralisation in Madhya Pradesh: Panchayati Raj to Gram Swaraj (1995-2000).* London: Overseas Development Institute.

Berrman, G. D. 1979. *Caste and Other Inequities: Essays on Inequality.* Meerut: Folklore Institute.

Beteille, A. 2000. *Antinomies of Society*, New Delhi: Oxford University Press.

—. 2001. Civil Society and the Good Society, *Sociological Bulletin*, 50, 2: 286-07.

Blair, H. 2000. Participation and Accountability at the Periphery: Democratic Local Governance in Six Countries, *World Development,* 28, 1: 21-39.

Bratton, M. 1990. Non-governmental Organisations in Africa: Can They Influence Policy? *Development and Change,* 21, 1: 87-118.

Clark, J. 1991. *Democratizing Development: The Role of Voluntary Organisations.* London: Earthscan.

Corbridge, S. and J. Harriss. 2001. *Reinventing India: Liberalisation, Hindu Nationalism and Popular Democracy*. Delhi: Oxford University Press.

Crook, R.C. and J. Manor. 1998. *Democracy and Decentralisation in South Asia and West Africa*. Cambridge: Cambridge University Press.

Crook, R.C. and A.S. Sverrisson. 2001. Decentralisation and Poverty Alleviation in Developing Countries: A Comparative Analysis or, is West Bengal Unique? *IDS Working Paper 130*. Brighton: Institute of Development Studies.

Deshpande, S.V. and G. B. V. Murthy. 2002. Pressures from Below: Decentralised Governance in Karnataka, *Economic and Political Weekly*, 4 May: 1766-67.

de Souza, P.R. 2000. Multi-State Study of *Panchayati Raj* Legislation and Administrative Reform. Background Paper No. 1 in World Bank unpublished Project Work *Overview of Rural Decentralisation in India*, Volume 3.

Drèze, J. and A. Sen. 1996. *India: Economic Development and Social Opportunity*. Delhi: Oxford University Press.

Echeverri-Gent, J. 1992. Public Participation and Poverty Alleviation: the Experience of Reform Communists in India's West Bengal, *World Development*, 20, 10: 1401-22.

Evans, P. 1996. Introduction: Development Strategies across the Public-Private Divide, *World Development*, 24, 6: 1033-37.

Frontline. 2001. October 26: 34-35

Ghatak, M. and M. Ghatak. 2002. Recent Reforms in the Panchayat System in West Bengal: Towards Greater Participatory Governance? *Economic and Political Weekly*, 5 January: 45-58.

Gupta, D. 2001. *Culture, Space and the Nation-State: From Sentiment to Structure*. New Delhi: Sage Publications.

Harriss, J. 2000. How much Difference does Politics Make? Regime Differences across Indian States and Rural Poverty Reduction. *Destin Working Paper No. 00-01*, Development Studies Institute, London School of Economics.

—. 2001. Social Capital Construction and the Consolidation of Civil Society in Rural Areas. *Destin Working Paper No. 00-16*, Development Studies Institute, London School of Economics.

Institute of Social Sciences. 2001. *Panchayati Raj Update* VIII, 10 October: 3.

Jha, S.N. 1999. Introduction. In S.N. Jha and P.C. Mathur, eds., *Decentralisation and Local Politics: Readings in Indian Government and Politics*, London: Sage Publications, pp. 13-44.

Jha, S. 2000. Fiscal Decentralisation in India: Strengths, Limitations and Prospects for Panchayati Raj Institutions. Background Paper No. 2, World Bank unpublished Project Work *Overview of Rural Decentralisation in India,* Volume 3.

Johnson, C. 2001. Community Formation and Fisheries Conservation in Southern Thailand, *Development and Change,* 32, 5: 951-74.

Khanna, B.S. 1994. *Panchayati Raj in India: National Perspective and State Studies.* New Delhi: Deep & Deep.

Kohli, A. 1987. *The State and Poverty in India: The Politics of Reform.* Cambridge: Cambridge University Press.

Kothari, R. 1999. Issues in Decentralized Governance. In S. N. Jha and P. C. Mathur (eds.), *Decentralisation and Local Politics: Readings in Indian Government and Politics,* New Delhi: Sage Publications, pp. 45-53.

Lal, D. 2000. *The Poverty of Development Economics.* Delhi: Oxford University Press.

Laski, H. 1960. *A Grammar of Politics.* London: George Allen and Unwin.

Lieten, G.K. and R. Srivastava. 1999. *Unequal Partners: Power Relations, Devolution and Development in Uttar Pradesh.* New Delhi: Sage Publications.

Maddick, H. 1970. *Panchayati Raj: A Study of Rural Local Government.* New Delhi: Orient Longman.

Manor, J. 1999. *The Political Economy of Democratic Decentralisation.* Washington DC: World Bank.

Mathew, G. 1997. The Making of Melavalavu. *The Hindu,* September 30.

—. 2001. Maharasthra's Gram Sevak Raj. *The Hindu,* August 13.

—. 2003. Panchayati Raj institutions and Human Rights in India, *Economic and Political Weekly,* 11 January: 155-62.

Meenakshisundaram, S.S. 1999. Decentralisation in Developing Countries. In S.N. Jha and P.C. Mathur (eds.), 1999. *Decentralisation and Local Politics: Readings in Indian Government and Politics,* London: Sage Publications, pp. 54-69.

Mehta, B. 1957. The Panchayat Samiti at the Block Level as the Basic Unit of Panchayati Raj, *The Indian Journal of Public Administration,* VIII, 4: 22-45.

Morris-Jones, W. H. 1971. *The Government and Politics of India.* London: Hutchinson University Library.

Nambiar, M. 2001. Making the Gram Sabha Work, *Economic and Political Weekly*, 18 August: 3114-17.

Ostrom, E., L. Schroeder and S. Wynne. 1993. *Institutional Incentives and Sustainable Development: Infrastructure Policies in Perspective*. Oxford: Westview Press

Pomeroy, R.S. and F. Berkes. 1997. Two to Tango: the Role of Government in Fisheries Comanagement, *Marine Policy*, 21, 5: 465-80.

Rondinelli, D., J. S. McCullough and R.W. Johnson. 1989. Analyzing Decentralisation Policies in Developing Countries: A Political Economy Framework, *Development and Change*, 20, 1: 57-87.

Rooy, V. A. 1998. *Civil Society and the Aid Industry*. London: Earthscan.

Popkin, S. 1979. *The Rational Peasant: The Political Economy of Rural Society in Vietnam*. Berkeley: University of California Press.

Sivaraman, M. 1997. Blow to Goodness, *The Hindu*, May 18.

Smith, B. C. 1985. *Decentralisation: The Territorial Dimension of the State*. London: George Allen and Unwin.

Tendler, J. 1997. *Good Government in the Tropics*. London: Johns Hopkins University Press.

The Hindu. 2001. December 14.

Vyasulu, P and V. Vyasulu. 1999. Women in Panchayati Raj: Grassroots Democracy in India, Experience from Malgudi, *Economic and Political Weekly*, 25 December: 3677-86.

White, G. 1994. Civil Society, Democratisation and Development (1): Clearing the Analytical Ground, *Democratisation*, 1, 3: 378-89.

White, T.A. and C.F. Runge. 1995. The Emergence and Evolution of Collective Action: Lessons from Watershed Managementm, *World Development*, 23, 10: 1683-98.

White, L. D. 1959. Decentralisation, *Encyclopaedia of Social Sciences*, Vol. 5, New York: Macmillan.

Zamora, M. D. 1990. *The Panchayat Tradition: A North Indian Village Council in Transition, 1947-1962*. New Delhi: Reliance Publishing House.

8

Development through People's Empowerment

Lessons from Rural Maharashtra

B.B. Mohanty

To facilitate the people's participation in community development programmes, Panchayati Raj was introduced in the country in the 1960s based on the recommendations of Balwantrai Mehta Committee's report. After an initial period of optimism, it apparently failed to generate people's participation in local development. Given their inferior position in the rural society, the members of lower castes, tribes and women were hardly able to participate in local decision-making process owing to the dominance of the privileged groups. In the early seventies, keeping in view the rising poverty and disparity levels, there was a shift in the implementation of developmental programmes with more focus on target-oriented poverty alleviation programmes instead of community development programmes. As a consequence, Panchayati Raj became least important as the developmental programmes were mostly planned and implemented without consulting the local community. Besides, lack of funds, irregular elections, bureaucratic apathy and domination of these institutions by the dominant elites in the countryside led to the atrophy of the system (Jain, 1985; Pai, 2001). A second round of experimentation beginning in 1977 based on the Ashok Mehta Committee's report, which shifted the focus from development per se to local government by greater devolution of power, achieved a modicum success in a limited number of states.

To generate participatory grassroots democracy and people-centred development, Panchayati Raj was restructured again in 1992 through the enforcement of 73rd Constitutional Amendment Act. The Act explicitly made certain provisions mandatory and few others were left to the discretion of the state governments as the states have some distinct characteristics. The salient features of the new Panchayati Raj Act are: (a) establishment of gram sabha and three tiers of panchayats at the village, block and district levels, (b) regular elections every five years, (c) reservation of not less than one-third seats for women as members and chair-persons at the three levels, (d) reservation of seats for Scheduled Castes, Scheduled Tribes and Other Backward Communities, (e) constitution of State Finance Commission to make recommendations as regards the financial powers of the panchayats, and (f) establishment of District Planning Committee to prepare the draft development plan for the district as a whole. In pursuance of the 73rd constitutional amendment each state made necessary changes in the structure of its Panchayati Raj Institutions (PRIs). Though the impact of this new Panchayati Raj system on the quality of rural development is not clear across the states, the early studies have indicated some success stories (Lieten, 1996; Vyasulu and Vyasulu, 1999; Pai, 2000). However, in many cases, the practical results have been held back by the antecedent social inequalities, educational backwardness and other barriers inherited from the past (Mathew and Nayak, 1996; Dreze and Sen, 2002; Lieten and Srivastav, 1996). However, the findings of these studies may not fit neatly into the situation in Maharashtra where the initial conditions of Panchayati Raj and the socio-economic and historical features are different. Against this background the present paper attempts to provide an overview of Panchayati Raj system and its likely impact on the village development in Maharashtra.

Though the institution of panchayat is as old as the state, the formal laws regulating the rural local government came into force only during the later part of the British rule with the establishment of the District Local Fund Committees under the Bombay Act III of

1869. These committees consisted mostly of the officials and government, nominated landholders. Following the principle of local self-government of Lord Ripon, the Bombay Local Boards Act, 1884 came into force which made provisions for the district and taluka local boards headed by the collector and the sub-divisional officers respectively. Subsequently, the Bombay Local Boards Act, 1923 introduced the provision of direct election of the members of the district local boards. Consequent upon the inclusion of the subject of local government in the Provincial Legislative List, the Bombay Act XXIII of 1938 was passed to make local bodies truly representative. It abolished the taluka local boards and reserved seats on a population basis for scheduled castes and non-Muslim minorities. The attempt to resuscitate the Village Panchayat was first made through the formation of Sanitary Committee under the Bombay Village Sanitation Act, 1889. The panchayat was constituted as an elected body under the Bombay Village Panchayat Act, 1920. It confined the voting rights to only adult male members. Based on Hatch Committee's suggestions, the Bombay Village Act was enacted in 1933, which enfranchised all the adult villagers. With the formation of the new government of Bombay Province, the Act was amended and the Bombay Village Panchayat (Amendment) Act, 1939 came into force. Following the reorganisation of states in 1956, a comprehensive legislation for the village panchayat was passed known as the Bombay Village Panchayat Act, 1958. It made provisions for the constitution of gram sabhas, district village panchayat mandals and nyaya panchayats.

After the formation of the unilingual state of Maharashtra on 1st May, 1960, the then Chief Minister Y.B. Chavan advocated the creation of a democratic socialist state with the help of PRIs. In pursuance of the recommendations of Balwantrai Mehta Committee, the state government appointed the V.P. Naik Committee in 1960. The latter opted for a three-tier structure like that of the Mehta Committee. But, unlike the Mehta Committee, it suggested that the zilla parishads be all-powerful in the hierarchical structure of panchayats. It recommended the devolution of power of taxation and disbursement of development funds to the zilla parishads. Thereafter, the Maharashtra Zilla Parishad and

Panchayat Samiti Act, 1961 was enacted. Village panchayats had already been in existence under the Bombay Village Panchayats Act, 1958. Thus, the three-tier Panchayati Raj system in the state comprising the village panchayat at the lower level, panchayat samiti at the middle level, and zilla parishad at the highest level was introduced. As recommended by the Naik Committee, the government also appointed Panchayati Raj Evaluation Committees to periodically to review the functioning of panchayats. The notable among them are the Bongirwar Committee of 1970 and Patil Committee of 1984. Maharashtra is considered one of the few states which has satisfactorily implemented the Panchayati Raj system in the wake of Balwantrai Mehta Committee report of 1957 (Mathew, 1994).

In compliance with the 73rd constitutional amendment, the Maharashtra Zilla Parishads and Panchayat Samitis (Amendment) Act, 1993 was enacted. As many provisions of the 73rd constitutional amendment were similar to the recommendations made by the Patil Committee earlier, only minor changes have been made like enhancement of the provisions of reservations for women (up to 33 per cent) and introduced reservation for the backward classes (27 per cent) on a rotation basis, etc. In pursuance of the Provisions of Panchayats (Extension to Scheduled Areas) Act, passed by the parliament in 1996, the Maharashtra Zilla Parishads and Panchayat Samitis (Extension to the Scheduled Areas and Amendments) Act was passed in 1997.

Based on the recommendations of the Bongirwar Committee and Patil Committee, most district level schemes have been transferred to the zilla parishads. Their activities as envisaged by the 73rd amendment are given in the Schedules I and II of the Zilla Parishad Act and the Schedule I of the Village Panchayat Act. As many as 234 schemes have been transferred fully to the zilla parishads, which include those relating to education, public health, family welfare, water supply and sanitation, etc. The zilla parishads can also undertake the execution of government development works and schemes on an agency basis under the Zilla Parishad and Panchayat Samiti Act. Forty-four schemes have been transferred to the zilla parishads on an agency basis for which 3 per cent and now raised to

5 per cent agency charges are given to them for implementing these schemes which cover employment guarantee, natural calamities, arts and culture, rural development programme, medical and health, general education, family planning, crop development, MLA fund, and social security and welfare. Most of the schemes dealing with development programmes at the district level such as agriculture, animal husbandry, primary and secondary education, drinking water supply, health and sanitation, primary health centres, women and child development, biogas and improved *chulhas* have also been transferred to the Panchayati Raj bodies. A recent estimate shows that schemes and programmes worth of Rs. 2,000 crores per annum were with these bodies in 2001.

However, many schemes are only partially transferred to the Panchayati Raj bodies. The line departments and DRDA continue to have major control over the planning and implementation of the schemes. The PRIs mostly act as the delivery units. Since the inception of the zilla parishads in 1962, many rural development programmes with substantial financial outlays such as IRDP, NREP, DPADP, social forestry, literacy programme, horticultural development programme, diary development, EGS and tribal sub-plan have been introduced by the central and state governments. But they were not entrusted to zilla parishads. Instead, a separate society (DRDA) under the Societies Act has been established for implementing them.

Comprehensive data are not available to assess the impact of the people's empowerment through the revival of PRIs on the quality of rural development particularly in post-73rd amendment period. Given historical background of the rural local governance in the state, one would expect exemplary development in the rural areas in terms of literacy and education, reduction in the incidence of poverty, supply of drinking water and infrastructural facilities, etc. Though in terms of primary education, power supply and communication and few other items, the state has done a fair job so far, it lags far behind many other states as well as national average in several important indicators. It is believed that Maharashtra's better performance in the field of primary education is mainly due to the effective role of PRIs because the primary and secondary public education in the state is entrusted to them. As per the 2001 census, Maharashtra is second to Kerala with the literacy rate of 77.27 per cent. As per the 1991 census, every village is provided drinking water and 96 per cent of the villages have been electrified. Over 58 per cent of the rural households have electricity as against the all-India average of only 31 per cent. However, as regards the safe drinking water, only 54 per cent households have this facility as compared to the all-India average of 56 per cent. To go by the estimate of the Planning Commission the incidence of poverty in Maharashtra was as high as 45 per cent in 1983 and it came down to only to 41 per cent in 1987-88 and 38 per cent in 1993-94. At all points of time it was more in the state than the national average. But by 1999-2000, it has come down to 24 per cent, which is less than that of national average (27%). However, the poverty ratio continues to be more in the state compared to many other progressive states like Gujarat, Andhra Pradesh and Karnataka.

Viewed from a different perspective, the PRIs have succeeded in bringing qualitative changes in the rural society in terms of stimulating popular participation and local leadership. It has been noted by a number of studies (Inamdar, 1970; Sirsikar, 1995; Mandlekar, 1991; World Bank, 2000).

The participation of women, which was unheard of in the rural local governance in the state, emerged after the introduction of the three-tier Panchayati Raj system. Way back in 1963 an all-women panchayat was formed in Nimbut village of Pune district. In 1984, another village of the same district came up with another all-women panchayat. As many as 13 women attempted to challenge the male dominance in local governance by contesting gram panchayat elections in 1984 in two villages of Satara district. Further, in 1989, eight and in 1992 two panchayats came up with all women representatives in the districts of Pune, Ahmednagar, Amravati, Jalgaon Yavatmal, Solapur and Wardha.

As a result of the provision of reservation, the participation of the members of the hitherto excluded groups in local decision-making process has increased noticeably in the post-73rd amendment period. According to the election results of 1997 and 2002 (see Table 1), over 33 per cent of the elected representatives

Table 1

Panchayati Raj Institutions and their Elected Representatives in Maharashtra

Level	*1997*					*As on February 2002*				
	No.	*Total elected members*	*Per cent of SCs*	*Per cent of STs*	*Per cent of women*	*No.*	*Total elected members*	*Per cent of SCs*	*Per cent of STs*	*Per cent of women*
Gram Panchayats	27619	303545	13.43	5.58	33.33	28553	232644	11.53	13.68	33.33
Panchayat Samitis	319	3524	16.61	12.85	33.31	349	3902	11.46	13.53	36.06
Zilla Parishads	29	1762	11.69	13.17	33.31	33	1951	11.53	13.68	33.73

Source: Department of Rural Development and Water Conservation, Government. of Maharashtra, Mumbai.

were women. In 2002, their representation at the panchayat samiti level has gone up to 36 per cent. According to the Maharashtra Human Development Report (2002) over 22 per cent of the chairpersons of standing committees of zilla parishads, 40 per cent of chairpersons of panchayat samitis and 29 per cent of sarpanchas of gram panchayats were women as on 1st April, 2001. Similarly, the number of representatives belonging to the scheduled castes and scheduled tribes was also significant. The percantage of tribal representatives, which was relatively less in 1997 at the gram panchayat level, has increased to 14 per cent, i.e., more than the proportion of their population (9%). It indicates that these groups were also elected from the unreserved seats. Looking at the distribution of sarpanchas (see Table 2) it is found that the number of sarpanchas belonging to the scheduled castes, scheduled tribes and women has increased noticeably across the districts as compared to the pre-73rd amendment period. The proportion of tribal sarpanchas has gone up to 66 per cent in Nandurbar district, followed by 46 per cent in Gadchiroli and 37 per cent in Thane.

Besides, in March 2000, over one thousand elected women representatives from different parts of the state assembled for two days at Saigata village in Chandrapur district to look back on the five years of women's participation in PRIs and take decisions to strengthen their role in the future. They announced Mahaila Rajasatta Andolan and urged the women to contest for unreserved seats to increase their strength in local governance. "*Vote Hamara, Raj Hamara, Leke Rahenge, Leke Rahange*" (vote is ours, governance is ours, we will get it) was the prime slogan of the Saigata convention. As a result, 145 organisations are working together in as many as 129 talukas covering 30 districts. In fact, this movement in the state has given ample scope for women to share their experience of local governance. Following a government directive and consistent efforts by several voluntary organisations, the national flag was hoisted by women sarpanchas on the 26th of January 2003 (54th Republic Day) and women gram sabhas were also held across the state. According to a survey, the PRIs in Maharashtra have inspired more trust in women than men, unlike the national average

Table 2

District-wise Distributions of Sarpanchas in Maharashtra

District	*Woman*		*SC*		*ST*	
	1992-93	*1999-2000*	*1992-93*	*1999-2000*	*1992-93*	*1999-2000*
Thane	1.16	13.73	0.58	2.83	33.18	37.04
Raigad	2.94	33.99	1.54	1.36	2.52	8.28
Ratnagiri	0.75	26.81	3.77	6.41	0.15	0.59
Sindhudurg	0.73	33.02	0.00	5.15	0.00	0.47
Nashik	2.08	16.64	1.31	5.15	29.14	28.66
Dhule	1.23	26.14	0.62	3.11	37.03	NA
Nandurbar	NA	12.45	NA	2.74	NA	66.24
Jalgaon	2.08	33.42	0.72	6.37	4.60	9.60
Ahmednagar	1.96	30.59	0.89	7.94	6.05	26.96
Pune	1.05	27.11	0.53	7.56	4.89	5.11
Satara	0.99	20.41	0.76	8.91	0.00	1.36
Sangli	0.90	23.83	0.15	9.36	0.45	16.31
Solapur	0.78	5.66	0.59	25.82	0.00	11.50
Kolhapur	1.69	29.41	1.46	9.41	0.00	9.80
Aurangabad	0.00	33.33	2.23	12.03	0.00	4.93
Jalna	1.97	37.10	2.62	8.22	1.53	1.16
Parbhani	2.27	29.06	4.10	13.53	8.30	4.03
Hingoli	NA	28.60	NA	10.48	NA	13.68
Beed	2.74	28.47	1.90	14.09	0.00	0.39
Nanded	2.16	21.51	2.24	9.20	2.31	13.72
Osmanabad	1.86	35.06	0.37	17.69	0.19	1.62
Latur	2.55	28.17	1.42	14.08	0.99	1.54
Buldhana	1.82	25.81	4.85	7.29	3.52	4.98
Akola	2.48	20.60	4.03	6.80	2.28	6.60
Washim	NA	30.30	NA	19.13	NA	7.74
Amravati	2.88	12.95	5.64	11.51	13.28	9.23
Yavatmal	2.35	31.01	1.48	7.81	15.57	18.12
Wardha	2.45	27.24	5.93	12.45	9.61	13.04
Nagpur	2.56	28.13	6.84	9.64	6.98	11.72
Bhandara	1.47	34.95	6.49	12.66	4.08	11.10
Chandrapur	0.87	33.54	3.22	14.20	7.93	20.07
Gadchiroli	1.29	28.19	4.51	3.52	43.22	46.04
State	1.74	26.14	2.29	9.59	8.50	12.77

Source: Directorate of Economics and Statistics, Mumbai.

as well as many other regions (Mitra, 2001). In fact, the increasing participation of the hitherto excluded groups is not only due to the reservation provisions for them, it may also be attributed to the impact of their strong movements against the privileged groups. The movements led by Phule and Ambedkar, followed by the organised activities of the lower castes, as also the Bhil and Koli tribals movements in Dhule, Gadchiroli and Thane districts, encouraged the dalits and tribals to assert their rights. The same could be said about the womenfolk in general.

The representation of hitherto excluded groups has not only enhanced their participation in local decision-making process but also motivated many of them to undertake innovative measures for local development. The success stories of some villages as reported in the successive issues of *Panchayati Raj Update* (Institute of Social Sciences) provide firm evidence in this regard. In a village called Methikheda in Yavatmal district, which is having an all-women panchayat, the women established the practice of having water taps and pipes repaired within 24 hours and extended water supply to the marginal communities. Besides, they also played a crucial role in the removal of the corrupt gram sevak. In Brahmanghar also women contributed labour to repair the road to the village school so that children could go to school without difficulty. In yet another village Arjunwada, the woman sarpanch and deputy sarpanch undertook somewhat new kind of development activities like construction of water tank, pipeline and road in the backward dalit locality. They have also formed two women Self-Help Groups (SHGs). The dalit women sarpanch succeeded in providing toilet to each household in Malawadi, which has emerged as an example for other villages. Similarly, in Paniv, a village in Solapur district, the woman sarpanch through SHGs has come out with a milk cooperative society. It has enhanced the economic position of many households and thereby strengthened the confidence of the womenfolk. In Vinter, in Jalgaon district, where people had encroached on 52 acres of common land, the women reclaimed the land and turned into a community orchard. In another village, where no teacher had been appointed to the school and endless paper work did not help, 22 women marched to the Block Development Office and left only when a teacher was appointed.

However, in many cases, the elected representatives of the hitherto excluded groups were also unable to challenge the dominance of the privileged groups. The assertive women members are harassed because of the dominant male prejudice. This is more so in the case of dalit women representatives. The all-women panchayat at Gokawadi in Pune district was reported to be under the control of the male members and women were the representatives only for name sake. The *purush mandali* managed the panchayat affairs (*Indian Express*, 8 March 2001). It is well known that the illiterate woman sarpanch of Panjawadi Panchayat (Nasik district) unknowingly put her thumb impression on her resignation letter prepared by the panchayat officials. Recently, it was reported that a dalit women sarpanch of Maratha-dominated Pethvadaz village in Nanded district was humiliated and opposed by the upper caste upa-sarpanch and his associates. In a number of cases the women contested elections to retain the seat for the male members of their families and these women representatives often acted as proxy for men. Besides, the local level bureaucrats, particularly the gram sevaks, also find it easier to dominate a scheduled caste or tribe woman sarpanch. It was reported that the sarpanch of Tirht Gram Panchayat of Osmanabad district, who was a scheduled caste woman, was bypassed by the gram sevak in many panchayat affairs (Mathew, 2001). Apart from this, in many cases, the elected representatives of the privileged groups have succeeded in removing the sarpanchas, presidents of ZPs and PSs belonging to the reserved categories by using the provision of no confidence motion against them. A study lately undertaken in Tuljapur block of Osmanbad district shows that of the 22 sarpanchas removed by the no-confidence motion, 19 belong to the reserved category (Jare and Kumar, 2001). Sometime back, the woman president of the Wardha zilla parishad was also removed through a no-confidence motion. However, the recent amendment that the motion against a woman sarpanch can be passed by a majority of not less than 75 per cent of the members may strengthen the position of women sarpanchas. Notwithstanding this, the inclusion of hitherto excluded communities has generated a kind of awareness among them on local governance and contributed for their empowerment. Some micro-level studies provide firm evidence in this regard (Omvedt, 1990; Baviskar, 2002; Patil, 2002).

The widespread participation of women and members of the scheduled castes and scheduled tribes has helped them to be the beneficiaries of various rural development schemes. In fact, the beneficiaries of Swarnajayanti Gram Swarozgar Yojana (SGSY), which is the single self-employment programme for the rural poor, is considerably higher among these groups compared to their demographic strength in most districts and regions. The number of women beneficiaries has gone up to 68 per cent in the state as whole and it is over 80 per cent in many districts. Similarly, in the case of Indira Awas Yojana, the numbers of scheduled caste and scheduled tribe beneficiaries are also higher in relation to the proportion of their population across the districts (see Table 3).

Table 3

Distribution of Beneficiaries of IAY and SGSY in Maharashtra (percentage to total number)

Districts/Region	*Population (1991)*		*IAY beneficiaries (2002-03)*		*SGSY beneficiaries (2002)*		
	SC	*ST*	*SC*	*ST*	*SC*	*ST*	*Woman*
Thane	5.18	18.12	5.39	59.58	3.79	63.12	59.18
Raigad	2.79	12.82	15.63	35.94	4.28	56.62	60.29
Ratnagiri	1.77	0.96	64.91	12.28	14.09	0.00	29.82
Sindhudurg	5.10	0.47	81.48	0.00	14.64	0.00	46.79
Konkan Region	4.15	12.47	10.39	55.15	8.73	32.50	48.03
Nashik	8.48	24.18	13.18	52.72	14.90	45.17	54.19
Dhule	5.30	40.87	5.52	88.76	2.77	71.43	60.05
Jalgaon	9.25	9.84	26.71	27.36	26.96	21.57	64.51
Northern Region	7.90	23.82	11.19	69.33	16.09	43.45	59.14
Ahemadnagar	12.41	7.12	41.13	18.30	6.40	8.18	53.10
Pune	11.41	3.91	39.29	21.43	23.69	15.29	76.01

Contd...

Contd...

Satara	9.50	0.75	62.82	0.00	23.61	0.00	53.11
Sangli	12.56	0.49	55.56	0.00	28.93	0.00	96.62
Solapur	15.41	1.50	59.69	0.00	47.41	1.29	77.41
Kolhapur	12.75	0.49	65.60	0.00	49.32	0.00	58.14
Western Region	12.33	2.77	52.28	8.22	30.58	3.64	68.36
Aurangabad	13.79	3.77	35.69	20.82	30.30	6.61	79.34
Jalna	12.93	2.07	N.A	N.A	27.82	2.45	72.50
Parbhani	11.02	5.26	48.22	1.52	41.63	9.01	62.66
Beed	13.41	1.13	60.00	0.00	13.33	0.00	30.00
Nanded	18.15	11.48	42.22	21.11	40.26	6.99	77.50
Osmanabad	16.34	1.76	56.52	4.35	23.96	2.08	69.79
Latur	19.06	2.24	N.A	N.A	39.50	1.25	73.35
Marathwada Region	14.92	4.53	47.06	9.84	33.51	4.60	72.07
Buldhana	11.49	5.06	50.44	9.97	26.29	4.76	47.42
Akola	11.95	7.03	N.A	N.A	41.21	12.36	58.00
Amaravati	17.48	14.38	27.62	34.76	35.08	33.11	89.28
Yavatmal	10.92	21.46	27.64	38.91	16.86	37.25	78.38
Wardha	14.05	15.59	29.92	29.55	30.08	23.25	80.81
Nagpur	18.84	13.92	29.32	30.96	27.93	20.88	44.28
Bhandara	16.87	14.70	N.A	N.A	42.18	20.75	71.05
Chandrapur	16.90	19.70	24.91	35.23	22.33	29.97	86.74
Gadchiroli	12.20	38.70	15.46	43.46	16.61	19.84	79.03
Vidarbha Region	15.02	14.95	26.60	34.50	29.56	24.25	72.26
State	11.09	9.11	26.74	38.33	26.75	20.98	67.76

Source: Project Formulation and IRDP Cell, Department of Rural Development and Water Conservation, Government of Maharashtra, Mumbai.

The example at Ralegaon Siddhi proves that socio-economic development at the local level can be achieved by activating the panchayat through the people's initiatives and participation. The village has witnessed remarkable development during the last 25 years. Ralegaon Siddhi, like many other Indian villages, was stricken by poverty, unemployment, illiteracy and social discrimination. There was hardly one acre of irrigated land per family and the agricultural production was inadequate to sustain the village population for the whole year. Men were migrating to cities in search of livelihood. The village panchayat was monopolised by the privileged groups. The socio-economic transformation in the village began in 1975, under the leadership of Anna Hazare, who mobilised people for village development through gram sabha. The gram sabha emerged as the important forum for collective decision-making in the village and it nominated the sarpanch and other officials through general consensus. The women and the members of the scheduled castes came to the forefront of the gram sabha. The success of the watershed development programmes, which changed the economic profile of the village by tremendously enhancing the irrigation facilities and thereby the agricultural output, is mainly due to the people's participation in the decision-making process of the gram sabha. Now, the village has two percolation tanks, 30 nullah bunds, about 90 wells and 10 borewells that are viable all through the year. There are 17 SHGs, a grain bank and several cooperative and registered societies to monitor the various developmental activities in the village. Matters related to the ban on Nasbandi (sterilisation), Nashabandi (ban on alcohol), Kurhadbandi (ban on tree felling) and Kuranbandi (ban on grazing) were decided in the gram sabha. The meetings of the latter were held periodically to discuss the issues relating to the welfare of the village and a final decision was taken. The gram panchayat in the village is answerable to the gram sabha just as the cabinet is answerable to the state assembly. In short, the gram sabha acts as the decision-making wing and the gram panchayat as the executive wing. Members of backward classes and women take part in the decision-making process in the gram sabha. The village had all-women members in the panchayat in 1990-1995 and the present sarpanch is a dalit. It shows that the government can only provide financial and technical assistance up to a certain limit, but the people of a locality as also their leadership ultimately shape the quality of development. The success stories of Ralegaon Siddhi are gradually spreading across the state and beyond. In 1992 the Government of Maharashtra started the Model Village Project to spread the success to other villages. The replication of Ralegaon Siddhi is in progress in 75 villages of 10 districts of the state with the help of 29 NGOs.

Similarly, Hiwarebazar panchayat of Ahmadnagar district has emerged as another success story of the gram sabha. The village has undertaken several development projects effectively with the active involvement of its people from all sections. The gram sabha prepares the development plan for the village, which serves as the guideline for the panchayat. The noticeable economic development of the village in the recent years has often been cited in the media reports. The same could be said about another small drought-prone village called Nimbavi in Ahmednagar district. The health project in Jamkhed taluka initiated by a doctor couple – Rajnikant Arole and Mabelle Arole – with the support of local resources and personnel also provides an example of participatory development.

Besides, Maharashtra has been a torchbearer in promoting voluntary organisations because of sustained services rendered by a large number of eminent social workers and their dedicated followers. Efforts have been made through PRIs to encourage their participation in local development relating to education, health, welfare of weaker sections, etc. The involvement of these organisations helps not only in improving the people's participation in local governance but also gives direction to the leadership of PRIs to work for the development more effectively. Recently, the Pune zilla parishad entrusted the entire responsibility of managing the public health activities in a number of villages of the hilly areas to an NGO named Savadham Trust. Similarly, another NGO – Hamcha Arogya Hamcha Hath – is undertaking the work of health services in the tribal district of Gadchiroli. It may be mentioned that an NGO – Resource Support Centre for Development (RSCD) along with its regional network partners – has addressed many of the women representatives in PRIs to take active part in the decision-making process.

On the whole, the PRIs have imparted a new strength to the entire process of planning and implementation. They helped in the emergence of rural leadership, which contributed for the improvement of quality of life. These institutions have generated a kind of awareness among the hitherto excluded groups on many aspects of local governance. Participation in the election process, becoming representatives, attending meetings and expressing viewpoints at various levels shows signs of changes in lives of the members of these groups. However, the Panchayati Raj system in the state has to be geared up further to catch up with states like West Bengal which are cited as the progressive states in terms of people's mobilisation and participation at the local level (Lieten, 1996; Crook and Manor, 1998). Devolution of more power to the gram sabha with greater accountability and transparency at all levels could enhance the people's participation and empowerment. As indicated by the State Planning Board, in its approach papers to the Tenth Five-Year Plan, the gram sabhas have to be empowered to prioritise the projects for their villages and also to monitor their implementation. The panchayats should be endowed with adequate responsibilities and necessary powers in the area of financial administration so as to ensure greater autonomy in the decision-making process at their levels.

References

Baviskar, B.S., 2002. Empowering the Powerless: Panchayati Raj in Maharashtra, A Case Study. Paper presented in a workshop at Institute of Social Sciences, New Delhi, on 12-13 September.

Crrok, R.C, and Manor, J., 1998. *Democracy and Decentralisation in South Asia and West Africa: Participation Accountability and Performance*, Cambridge University Press, Cambridge.

Dreze, Jean and Sen, Amartya, 2002. *India Development and Participation*, Oxford University Press, New Delhi

Government of Maharashtra,1961. *Report of the Committee on Democratic Decentralisation* (V. P Naik Committee), Bombay.

Government of Maharashtra,1971. *Report of the Evaluation Committee on Panchayati Raj* (L.N. Bongirwar Committee), Bombay.

Government of Maharashtra, 1986. *Panchayati Raj Evaluation Committee Report* (P.B. Patil Committee), Bombay.

Inamdar, N.R 1970. *Functioning of Village Panchayats*, Popular Prakashan, Bombay.

Institute of Social Sciences, 2000, *Status of Panchayati Raj in India*, Concept Publishing Company, New Delhi.

Institute of Social Sciences, *Panchayati Raj Update*, various issues, New Delhi.

Jain, L.C., 1985. *Grass without Roots*, Sage Publications, New Delhi.

Jare, Ramesh and Kumar, Santosh, 2001. *Motion of No-Confidence Against sarpanchas in Tuljapur Taluka: A Study Report,* Rural Campus, Tata Institute of Social Sciences, Mumbai.

Lieten, G. K., 1996. *Development, Devolution and Democracy Village Discourse in West Bengal,* Sage Publications, New Delhi.

Lieten, G. K. and Srivastav, R., 1999. *Unequal Partners: Power Relations, Devolution and Development in Uttar Pradesh*, New Delhi: Sage Publications.

Mandlekar, V.B., 1991. *Panchayati Raj in Maharashtra*, Ph.D thesis submitted to the University of Bombay, Bombay.

Mathew, George, 1994. *Panchayati Raj From Legislation to Movement*, Concept Publishing Company, New Delhi.

— 2001. Maharashtra's Gram Sevak Raj, *The Hindu*, August 13.

Mathew, George and Nayak, Ramesh, 1996. Panchayats at Work, What it means for the Oppressed? *Economic and Political Weekly*, Vol. 31, No. 27, pp. 1765-71.

Mitra, Subrata K.,2001. Making Local Government Work: Local Elites, Panchayati Raj and Governance in India', in Atul Kohli (ed.), *The Success of India's Democracy*, Cambridge: Cambridge University Press.

Omvedt, Gail, 1990. Women, Zilla Parishads and Panchayat Raj Chandwad to Vitner, *Economic and Political Weekly*, Vol. 25, No. 31, pp. 1687- 90.

Pai, Sudha, 2000. New Social and Political Movements of Dalits: A Study of Meerut District, *Contributions to Indian Sociology*, Vol. 34, No. 2, pp. 191-218.

Pai, Sudha, 2001. Social Capital, Panchayats and Grass Roots Democracy Politics of Dalit Assertion in Uttar Pradesh, *Economic and Political Weekly*, Vol, 36, No. 8, pp. 645-54.

Patil, R.B., 2002. *Panchayati Raj in Kolhapur District (Maharashtra*), Paper presented in a workshop at Institute of Social Sciences, New Delhi, on 12-13 September.

Sirsikar, V.M., 1995. *Politics of Modern Maharashtra*, Orient Longman, Bombay.

Vyasulu, Poornima and Vyasulu, Vinod, 1999. Women in Panchayati Raj Grass Roots Democracy in Malgudi, *Economic and Political Weekly*, Vol.34, No.52 pp.3677-86.

World Bank, 2000. *Overview of Rural Decentralisation in India*, Vol. II, Washington D.C.

9

Empowerment of PRI Representatives

Framework and Realities

Aureliano Fernandes

The passage of the 73rd Constitutional Amendment Act in 1992 was a landmark in democratic evolution since it gave formal constitutional recognition to local self-governance units. Most significantly, it brought in a participatory dimension to village democracy by reserving one-third of the total seats filled by direct election for women. Additionally, one-third of the total seats of chairpersons and vice chairpersons of Panchayati Raj Institutions (PRIs) were also to be reserved for women. Since 1993 an estimated one million Indian women hold political office at three tiers of Gram Panchayat, Block Panchayat and District Panchayat.

Framework for Empowerment in Goa

Goa has an unique history of local self-government institutions dating back to ancient times, called 'Communidades' or communities,[1] which functioned as autonomous units of village administration concomitant with the ancient system of village governments in India.

After its liberation on 19 December 1961 from the Portuguese colonial rule and its integration into the Indian Union, Goa was directly induced into the Panchayati Raj system[2] leapfrogging the community development programme, which was implemented in the rest of the country. The village panchayat elections preceded the elections to Goa's Legislative Assembly of Daman and Diu and envisaged the development of rural areas and transfer of power to the people. The Goa model of Panchayati Raj was simply a single tier system with only village panchayats, probably due to its small size (3,701 sq. kms).

In all, 180 village panchayats were constituted including those of Daman and Diu under the Regulation of 1962. Though successive governments in Goa have ritually held elections to the panchayat bodies every five years, the Panchayat Raj system has failed to empower the villages as self-sustaining units and to inject social and economic transformation. The ruling parties as well as the opposition displayed a complete lack of political will to empower the panchayats politically and financially.

The Goa Panchayati Raj Act, 1994

The conformity legislation to the 73rd Constitutional Amendment Act, the Goa Panchayati Raj Act (GPRA) (1994) established a two-tier structure, retaining the Village Panchayats at the local level and adding Zilla Panchayats at the district level (GoG, 2001).

Village Panchayats

The post-GPRA demographic composition of panchayats in Goa ranges from 5-member wards for a population of 1,500-2,000 to 11-member wards for a population of more than 8,000.[3]

Presently, there are 190 village panchayats with about 1,470 members, all directly elected. The Director of Panchayats divides each panchayat area into wards equal to the number of members with reservations for Other Backward Classes (OBCs) and Scheduled Castes (SCs), in proportion to their total population in that panchayat. There is a provision for reserving seats for SC women also. One-third of the total number of seats in a panchayat are reserved for women. One-third of the total posts of sarpanch and deputy sarpanch are also reserved for women. These are allocated by rotation. There is no reservation for Scheduled Tribes (STs) in Goa since there is no such population in the state.

The total number of seats reserved for women in Village Panchayats in the two districts of Goa is shown below in Table 1:

Table 1
Panchayat Wards/Members/Reserved Seats in Goa

Districts	*Panchayats*	*Wards/ Members*	*Reserved for women*	*Reserved for OBCs*
North Goa	121	917	305 (approx)	31
South Goa	69	553	169	46
Total	190	1470	474	77

Source: Fernandes, 2003, updated in 2004.

Zilla Panchayats

Goa's two districts merit just two Zilla Panchayats with North Goa Zilla Panchayat consisting of 30 elected members and South Goa Zilla Panchayat consisting of 20 elected members. Additionally every Zilla Panchayat has MPs, MLAs and chairpersons of panchayats from each taluka elected according to a ratio, as ex-officio members.[4]

The term of the members of the Zilla Panchayat other than the elected members shall be co-terminus with the term of members of parliament or members of the State Legislative Assembly or chairpersons of the panchayat as the case may be.

Table 2
Composition of the Zilla Panchayats in Goa

Zilla Panchayats	*Elected represen tatives*	*Reserved for women*	*MPs*	*MLAs*	*Indirectly elected from Sar-panchas*	*Total*
North Goa	30	10	1 Lok Sabha	06	11	58
South Goa	20	07	1 Lok Sabha	05	06	39
			1 Rajya Sabha			01
Total	50	17	03	11	17	98

Source: Fernandes, 2003a.

Reservations

One-third of the total seats of the Zilla Panchayats are reserved for women. No seats are reserved for SCs, STs or OBCs in Goa at the Zilla Panchayat level. One seat of chairperson and one seat of deputy chairperson of the Zilla Panchayat are also reserved for women in rotation.

Examining Empowerment

The United Nations High Commissioner for Human Rights has defined empowerment as the process "of giving people the power, capacities, capabilities and access needed to change their own lives, improve their own communities and influence their own destinies". It is a process which enables a person to understand the workings of power so that she/he can deal with questions of existing power and exercise control over the sources of power.

Traditionally, empowerment has had two meanings–investing authority in a role or person. This implies accepting personal responsibility and is traced to the US Constitution. It means that the person's mandate is clear and he/she knows what performance is expected of him/her.

The second meaning is enablement. It means enabling men and women to hold legitimate positions of authority and to influence others, or in other words, to become leaders. It also means they can choose to take charge of their destinies. It is difficult to understand empowerment without understanding of power. Power generally means power *over,* meaning authority or power *to* which means enablement (Maccoby, 1999). Empowerment as power *is* also used to mean productive power to create new possibilities without domination. In its power *with* connotation, it means the ability of a collective or group to work together to achieve which is impossible as an individual. Empowerment is, therefore, a process and a goal (Woronuik, 1999).

Has the 73rd Amendment or GPRA Empowered Representatives?

The 73rd amendment no doubt lays the foundation for empowering representatives and local communities, but due to federal constraints it is not able to breakthrough states' intransigence not to devolve powers to the grassroots. Though all states passed the conformity legislation a year after the passage of the 73rd Constitutional Amendment, most states have not devolved substantial powers to the sub-state level.[5]

This is mainly due to the perception of the state by the ruling elite, and the state bureaucracy that they alone know best, what is good for the state. They refuse to put faith in the capabilities of rural communities to better understand and solve their problems and their ability to decide on issues and problems that confront and concern them.[6]

Although the GPRA was passed in 1994, elections to panchayats in Goa were held three years hence. For six years after the passage of GPRA there was only a single-tier system, which existed since 1962, until Zilla Parishad elections were held when the state was under President's rule. The Election Commission and Finance Commission were appointed five years later in 1999. Ten years after GPRA the status of PRIs in Goa remained substantially unchanged. There is failure of operation as well as administrative devolution. The state governments (of both the Congress and the BJP) have failed to devolve even a single power of the 29 subjects that have been allocated to panchayats in the Schedule XI. Similarly, none of the 25 powers have been devolved to the Zilla Panchayats.

This goes against the fundamental notion of United Nations High Commissioner for Human Rights' definition of empowerment which implies the process "of giving people the power" to determine the present and the future of the village communities, resources and the power to govern themselves. Failure to devolve powers results in failure to provide them the opportunity to develop their capacities and capabilities to make their own decisions and develop skills to deal with their day-to-day situations. Failure to devolve powers to PRIs denies access needed to change their own lives, improve their own communities and influence their own destinies.

Panchayats have been saddled with residual powers and functions well short of the legitimisation of 'self-government' envisaged by the 73rd Constitutional Amendment Act. The most critical issue has been the non-devolution of financial allocations to PRIs in Goa. Although the State Finance Commission (SFC) was constituted in 1999 and had submitted its report suggesting allocation of 27 per cent of the state's own tax revenue and share of central tax for activities transferred under non-plan and 13 per cent of annual state plan, excluding earmarked negotiated loan component and project-specific central assistance, for activities transferred under plan expenditure, it was not accepted by various governments (Fernandes, 2003b: 2875). The second SFC, which was due in 2004, has not been appointed so far.

GPRA and Women's Empowerment

Women constitute 48.98 per cent of the total population (1,343,998) in Goa. The decadal growth of women in the 2001 census has been 14.50 per cent compared to 15.27 per cent for men. The sex ratio has shown a decline from 967 per 1,000 in 1991 to 960 in 2001. The literacy level for women is 75 per cent compared to 88.88 per cent among men and 82.32 per cent overall (CSI, 2001).

Traditionally, the position of women in Goa has been 'better' than in most states given the colonial background of 450 years of Portuguese rule. Under the Portuguese Uniform Civil Code women had not only equal share in the parents' property but also an equal civil status. Liberal access to Portuguese education, and uninhibited freedom of movement and accessibility to employment gave women a relatively respectable position in society.

Various post-liberation state governments did not have to make excessive efforts to raise the position of women but deliver services equitably for welfare of women in Goa. Central and state welfare schemes have been implemented with little misappropriation if any, and generally reached to the women and weaker sections in rural Goa.

Political Empowerment

Empowerment has various dimensions — personal, collective, national, global, economic, political and social. The 73rd amendment and the GPRA have provided the basis for political empowerment through representation. The total number of seats reserved for women in North Goa panchayats are approximately 305, while in South Goa are 169. Women have 17 seats reserved for them in the Zilla Panchayats: 10 in North Goa and 7 in South Goa. Besides, one-third of the seats of sarpanchas and deputy sarpanchas, and one seat each of chairperson and deputy chairperson are also reserved for women. Besides the regular quota, five women have also been elected from the general category wards, in 1997.

The representation of women in panchayat bodies may not be adequate given the high level of literacy and economic independence of women. Most families, especially in the now 50 per cent urban Goa, are nuclear families where most women are working mothers. But nowhere is there a fear in the minds of women to participate at any meetings. There are no instances of violence against women for political participation. Socially too, they hold an egalitarian position with men. The 73rd amendment has reinforced the role of women and women themselves come out to contest, win elections and participate in the development of the villages in Goa.

Similarly, the weaker sections generally do not encounter gross injustice or public humiliation in Goa, for participating in panchayat elections or exercising their rights as members of PRIs. Their position is relatively better in Goa. Thirty-one seats in North Goa and 46 seats in South Goa have been reserved in the panchayats for OBCs to facilitate their political empowerment.

The debate on empowerment of women emerges from the situation of under-representation of women in elective offices in India. In Goa too, at the state level, there have been on an average one or two women MLAs. One woman who was a minister of state in 1973 and went on to become the Chief Minister in the same year. Presently, in the 2002-2007 terms, there is a lone woman MLA in the Goa Assembly.

Quotas and reservations by themselves do not lead to empowerment of women as opined by women academicians themselves. They may lead to recognition but may not lead to redistribution thus limiting the transformative potential of the PRIs. Quotas do not allow to challenge hierarchies. Quotas help the elites rather than grassroots women to participate in PRIs. In Goa, it is largely the middle class women, with sufficient education, who have entered PRIs after the enactment of the 73rd amendment. A cross-section of them are teachers, some having small businesses and some are housewives. But, there is also a section of women, especially from rural Goa, who come from marginalised sections. To this section of women the collective dimension of empowerment seems to operate since they can support each other and work together to make sufficient impact.

Women in Goa have also undergone personal empowerment. Though self-confidence and dignity alone do not result in empowerment, self-confidence and capacity undo the effects of internalised oppression.

Empowerment may mean different things to different women even in a homogeneous society such as Goa. It is not something that is done to people; women need to be agents of their own empowerment. Outside organisations can create conditions and support the process in that direction.

Obstacles to Empowerment

Obstacles to empowerment exist at the level of state, PRI representatives themselves and at the level of civil society. The fundamental cause of why panchayats in Goa have failed to empower elected representatives, including women, is due to non-devolution of powers by the state government. Other obstacles to empowerment are described as under:

Consultative Role to Gram Sabha

The 73rd amendment gives merely a consultative role to the gram sabha in most matters. The state legislations too, for want of commitment to local self-government, have not empowered gram sabhas to pass mandatorily approve budgets. The panchayat members and secretaries do not discuss the budget before gram sabhas since the last gram sabha before the budget is held in January while the budget is prepared in February.[7] In case the gram sabha objects to certain expenditure, disagrees with the administrative report or NOCs given by panchayats, there is no way people can object, more so women.

Failure to Effectively Mobilise People

While the panchayat members canvass with commitments during or prior to elections, this kind zeal is not seen in the case of mobilisation for gram sabha meetings. There is an urgent need for panchas to mobilise the people to facilitate their empowerment. Women representatives should be at the forefront of such mobilisation, since women's attendance at gram sabhas is abysmally low.

Indifferent Attendance at Gram Sabhas

The attendance at gram sabhas in Goa varies from 0.33 per cent (15 to 25 people) in Chodan Madel Panchayat of North Goa to a high of about 3.33 per cent in Candolim Panchayat, also of North Goa. The level of attendance shoots up to about 16 per cent (1,000 people) when the issue pertaining to merger of panchayats with municipality comes up.[8]

Empowerment is contextual. In Goa, since the average standard of living is high, with a per capita income of about Rs.45,000, panchayats are seen as "poor man's burden". For want of devolution of substantial powers to panchayats, they appear to be only doling out schemes to the poor. Hence, the upper-middle class or sometimes even the middle class do not attend gram sabhas.

PRIs as Site of Contestations

Village rivalries are reflected at the gram sabha meetings. Caste, class, gender, neighbourhood and personal fissures lead to disruptive behaviour at the gram sabha. So, citizens, especially women, choose to stay away from meetings.[9] In some panchayats sarpanchas themselves have connived to invite unruly elements to shout down opposing or dissenting panchas, as was the case in Socorro Panchayat of North Goa. Such behaviour does not allow for oppressed people to gain control over their lives and discourages their involvement in local government affairs to the detriment of the entire community.

Proxy Rule by Men

Given the higher level of education of Goan women, in most cases, women who are sarpanchas are able to manage the affairs of the panchayat independently without interference from male member(s) of their family. However, there are few cases of husbands attending and conducting panchayat executive council meetings, gram sabha meetings and even intervening in panchayat projects. This does not allow women to grapple with the dynamics of power.

Women and men begin from different positions in mobilising power. In one case, a woman sarpanch elected for the 1997-2002 term to the Anjuna Consua Panchayat of North Goa, knew nothing about wooing and tackling voters since her husband had canvassed on her behalf while she was in Mumbai. This woman is a practising advocate in the district court, in Goa.

Secondly, proxy rule by men does not allow women to execute the gender perspective in most issues such as health care, sanitation, and execution of other community projects.

Thirdly, most women who have come to power in PRIs seem to be from the family where a male has been a sarpanch or panch and cannot contest from that ward when it is reserved for women. Women should be able to challenge existing power relations and gain greater control over the sources of power on their own.

Power and Decision-Making

There is a feeling, which may be empirically true, that women spend panchayat budgets differently from men. Our research revealed that given the fact that the VP secretary is invariably a male, the fact that the panchayat budgets in Goa are meagre, running into a few lakhs, a woman sarpanch does not spend money differently from a male sarpanch. In other words, gender does not make a difference to village governance.

This underlines the fact that besides quotas, other relevant changes have to be effected to make gendered intervention in panchayats more transformative. The 73rd amendment could, in its revised avatar, mandate that one-third seats of secretaries be reserved for women, since they effectively know the rules, make most decisions, finalise budgets and execute projects.

In discussions at training programmes or gram sabhas, women representatives do not discuss solely women's issues or even issues that purely appeal to women. Women in Goan PRIs discuss issues pertaining to safety of people with regard to installation of mobile towers in a village, illegal constructions, playgrounds and mainly about the secretary's highhandedness in not allowing them access to panchayat records, despite the Right to Information Act prevalent in Goa.

Patriarchy and PRIs

Most women, even in a progressive state such as Goa, do not hold properties in their name, although the Uniform Civil Code entitles them to equal share parental property. However, most women either voluntarily give up these rights in favour of their brothers or are pressurised to do so. The result is that they do not have control over economic resources.

Women's needs are not considered when community prioritises expenditure. Hence, women need access to economic resources to enable them to improve their status and that of the fraternity. It is questioned that how can a woman representative oppose another elected male member if she works in his fields? This is part of the empowerment that has to be understood in everyday context. Social and economic power is translated into political power. The 73rd amendment, in its radical dimension, should, when revised, challenge these structures.

Tasks Ahead

Globalisation and conformity structures within nation-states negatively impact women, marginalising them and violating their human rights. Women must explore ways to empower themselves to fight imbalance in society, and to participate equally in the ongoing process of development. When women feel they can operate in society on the same terms as men, then, we can affirm women as empowered.

Empowerment has multiple connotations to different groups of women, and is variant to levels of societal development. The potential for empowerment varies, both according to region and economic position.

Quotas and reservations for women have gone much to co-opt women into circles of power and influence. Goan situation demands panchayat legislation and institutions to first tackle the issue of changing the content of power within its villages. Sensitising the bureaucracy, especially of departments dealing with rural development and police, through training programmes to develop gender sensitive skills, is another exigency.

Creating Economic Opportunities

Empowerment is meaningful when economic opportunities are created since there is a complementarity between economic opportunities and social conditions. Agriculture in Goa is on the decline, increasingly the population opts for white-collared jobs and Goa gets urbanised. There is need for human resource planning. Though Goa appears to have achieved the first stage of human development in terms of reach to the entire population, it is exigent to improve the quality of education and health services.

Drawing up an Agenda for Empowerment

There is an urgent need to devolve substantial powers and taxes to panchayats. There can be no empowerment without delegation of powers. There is need for partial devolution in model panchayats and then gradually devolve powers to all panchayats.

Role Definition

To engender meaningful rural development role definition of stakeholders — government, civil society, NGOs and profit organisation – is essential. NGO activity in some part of Goa is commendable especially in mobilising people to gram sabhas. Role of civil society and especially community-based organisations needs to be defined.

Research and Documentation on PRIs

There is insufficient raw data on PRIs in Goa. The sole repository of data is the Directorate of Panchayats. There is lack of systematic research, as the State Institute of Rural Development has no full-time director. The incumbent Member Secretary, who is also Director of DRDA (North Goa District), holds charge of Chief Officer of a municipality 33 kilometres away. The faculty conducting training is relatively junior and comprised of fresh postgraduates. Without the guidance of senior faculty, it would be too much to expect them to tailor training programmes to trigger the process of empowerment.

Networks

Network and inter-organisational linkages are critical to empowerment of all representatives. Of these women's networks are crucial and should use the new information and communication technologies to share experiences, support and devise strategies to strengthen the collective dimension of empowerment.

These networks can discuss leadership issues, functions for women, as well as strategies to enable women to assume powerful positions in society and develop personal self-esteem. Above all the networking with NGOs and universities should aim to change in the power relations between men and women, without which empowerment cannot be achieved.

Conclusion

In the light of the above-mentioned tasks, the 73rd Constitutional Amendment Act has to undergo a radical revision this time, not only ensuring recognition of gender but also basing redistribution on the basis of gender. Its goal should be to challenge patriarchal ideology to transform the structures and institutions that reinforce and perpetuate gender discrimination and social inequality and to enable poor women to gain access to and control both material and informational resources (Batliwala, 1994).

Notes

1. These Communidades or Communities have been variously referred to as Gauncarias or Gaonkaria, Camara Agraria (Agricultural Community) in Portuguese Correspondence and Legislation. The government was vested in the assembly of elders of each clan or *vangor*. Members of Communidades consisted of (i) *Zoneiros* (descendants of original gaonkars who received a *Zon* annual income of Communidade, (ii) *Acsaocar* (shareholders who received dividends), and (iii) *Gaonkar* (participants who registered their names at communidades and received certain amount of net income (Gune 1979). The primary activity of the Communidades consisted in leasing out their commonly held agricultural land, orchards, and ponds through auction. The income was utilised to fund common services for the village like those of priests, barer, construction and maintenance of markets, halls etc. This village government was allowed to exist alongside the Portuguese administrative machinery and regulated through empowering legislation.
2. The 1962 elections to the village panchayats under the Goa, Daman and Diu Village Regulations (1962) were the first ever democratic elections in the territory after 450 years of Portuguese colonial rule.
3. Demographic Constitution of Panchayats in Goa (1994):

For panchayats with a population of	*No. of wards/ members*	*Classification*
1500 upto 2000	5	D
2001 upto 5000	7	C
5001 upto 8000	9	B
More than 8000	11	A

4. The ex-officio members of the Zilla Panchayat include: Three members of Parliament who are registered as electors in the two districts, including one belonging to the Rajya Sabha. Members of the State Legislative Assembly as may be prescribed provided none of them are minister, Speaker or Deputy Speaker of the Legislative Assembly or Leader of Opposition and chairperson of panchayat in each taluka of the district elected from amongst themselves in the ratio of one such chairperson for a taluka having upto 15 panchayats and two such chairpersons for taluka, having more than 15 panchayats who shall be a member of Zilla Panchayat so long as he continues to be the chairperson of the panchayat.

5. A study of 15 select states revealed that where middle or top tiers were not constituted, states did not endow them with adequate functional responsibility even after the 73rd amendment. States which had constituted PRIs prior to amendment merely repeated the provisions of existing statutes in the new conformity legislations. Study was conducted in Gujarat, Maharashtra, Kerala, Goa, Punjab, Haryana, Orissa, Assam, Madhya Pradesh, Andhra Pradesh etc. by RC. Choudhury and K. Siva Subramaniam of National Institute of Rural Development, Hyderabad and sponsored by XI Finance Commission, Government of India, May 2001.
6. The obstinate refusal of the former secretary (rural development and panchayats), Government of Goa, Mr. C.V.S. Ramarao to accept that no powers can be given to even a limited number of panchayats at a Workshop on Devolution of Powers to Panchayats, held at the Goa Institute of Rural Development and Administration in 2000 is indicative of the tendency. Similar is the attitude of the political class as well.
7. Information gathered from VP Secretaries at the "VP secretaries Training Programme" 16th August to 16th November, 2000 organised by Goa Institute of Rural Development and Administration, Old Goa, Goa.
8. As seen in the case when Porvorim was to be merged with Corporation of the City of Panjim; and Taleigao Panchayat into Panjim and merger of Candolim panchayat with Calangute Panchayat to make a municipality.
9. This was disclosed by woman representative at the "Empowerment of Elected Women Representatives" training programme organised by Goa Institute of Rural Development and Administration, Old Goa at Nagoa Village Panchayat (South Goa) for women representatives of Mormugao and Salcete talukas of Western and South Goa, 30th December, 2004.

References

ANED 2001. Gender Policy. December (ECLOF BOLIVIA) www.eclof.org

Batliwala, Srilatha. The Meaning of Women's Empowerment: New Concepts for Action in Gita Sen, Adrieene Germaine and Lincoln C Chen (eds) *Population Policies Reconsidered*: Health, Employment and Rights. Boston: Harvard University Press.

Centre for Development Studies and Action (CDSA). 2001. *Directory of Panchayati Raj and Women in India*. New Delhi: CDSA and United Nations Development Fund for Women

Choudhury, R.C. and S.P. Jain. 1999. *Strengthening Village Democracy*. Hyderabad: National Institute of Rural Development.

CSI Census of India. 2001. www.censusindia.net/profile/goa.htm

Decentralisation and Empowerment of Rural Poor. www.fao.org

Fernandes, Aureliano. 2003a. Goa Training Assessment Report. Presented at the National Seminar on "Stocktaking of Training and Capacity Building of Women Elected to Panchayati Raj". Organised by Centre for Development Studies and Action, New Delhi and Friedrich Ebert Stiftung, New Delhi, at Mysore.

— 2003b. Aggrandiser Government and Local Governance in *Economic and Political Weekly*. (ed) Krishna Raj. Vol XXXVIII, No 27, July 5, 2003. pp 2873-2879.

GoG.2001. *The Goa Panchayati Raj Act*. 1994. second edition. Panaji: Government of Goa.

HeiDok - Political Representation and Empowerment : Women in the Institutions of Local Government in Orissa after the 73rd Amendment to the Indian Constitution. http://www.ub.uni-heidelberg.de/ archiv/4098

Human Development in South Asia. 1999. *The Crisis of Governance*. Karachi: Published for the Mahbub Ul Haq Human Development Centre by Oxford University Press.

IFUW - SAAP - Empowering Women. Geneva Switzerland. www.ifuw.org/index.htm

Jain, Devaki. 2000. *The Vocabulary of Women's Politics*. New Delhi Friedrich Ebert Stiftung.

Maccoby, Michael. 1999. *Rethinking Empowerment in Research Technology Management*, Volume 42. No. 4. September-October. cited at www.maccoby.com

Mathew George. 2004. The Silent Revolution. Www.indiatogether.org/ 2004/may/wom-panchayat.htm

Mishra, Alok. Some Problems in the Movement for the Affirmation of Indian Women. www.columbia.edu/cu/ipsg/eld/ eld_amishra.html -

Mohanty Bidyut. 1998. *Women and Political Empowerment*. New Delhi: Institute of Social Sciences.

Mohanty, Bidyut. Daughters of the 73rd Amendment. http://action.web.ca

National Policy For The Empowerment Of Women.2001. http://wcd.nic.in/ empwomen.htm

Rai, Shirin. Political Representation, Democratic Institutions and Women's Empowerment: The Quota debate in India. www.sain_glg.net

What difference a Constitutional Amendment makes. www.sticer.lse.ac.uk

Women's Empowerment. http://rural.nic.in

World Bank Development Report. 2000-2001. Attacking Poverty. Washington DC: World Bank

Woronuik, Beth. 1999. Women's Empowerment in the Context of Human Security. Working Paper for UN ACC Inter Agency Committee OECD/DAC Working Party on Women and Gender Equality. Thailand: ESCAP. www.ifuw.org.

Women's Political Presence and Empowerment: Women in the Institutions of Local Government in Orissa after the 73rd Amendment to the Indian Constitution www.eldis.org/static/DOC14163.htm.

10

Functioning of Panchayati Raj in Scheduled Areas of Gujarat

Satyakam Joshi

This paper is on and about governance in the Fifth Schedule areas of Gujarat. In the wake of Gujarat Panchayat (Extension to the Scheduled Area) Act (PESA), 1998, it has opened up the possibilities for tribal people to manage their survival resources, i.e., land, water and forest, monitor the development process, settle disputes, and manage their affairs of the village and protect their culture and traditions. More fundamentally, the law recognises for the first time that the higher institutions of governance are subsidiary to the basic unit, the elected representatives are accountable to the electorate and the people are the final arbiters of their life and destiny. In this respect, this Act is a significance departure from legislation in modern democracies and hence, needs to take stock of the implementation of this Act in last five years.

The provisions of the new Act are an integral part of the constitutional provisions concerning tribal affairs and self-government. The functioning of communities in the scheduled areas are automatically endowed with the formal recognition on December 24, 1996 with the assent of the President. Moreover, the community as Gram Sabha is also endowed with specific powers automatically. These powers include management of community resources, resolution of disputes, approval of plans and programmes and also mandatory consultation before the acquisition of land. Conferred with certain other powers on the Gram Sabha concerning vital matters such as ownership of minor forest produce, enforcement of prohibition, restoration of unlawfully alienated lands, control over moneylending and marketing, etc. has been made mandatory. The State Legislature shall make suitable laws accordingly within a period of one year. Any law of the state not in consonance with the provisions of this Act shall become invalid thereafter. Each of the scheduled states was given a period of one year to suitably amend their respective Panchayati Raj Acts in conformity with PESA. In December 1997 the Gujarat government has also passed the PESA with some modification. Now, eight years have passed since the enactment of the PESA, it is worth to examine its impact on tribal areas in general and tribal people in particular. In this context, it is pertinent to know how far Gram Sabhas and Gram Panchayats have been able to exercise control over government schemes? And, to what extent PESA is being implemented in the scheduled areas of Gujarat in its true spirit or in other words the beneficial effect of PESA in tribal societies?

The present paper is a part of a larger study on examining the functioning of panchayats in scheduled areas of Gujarat. The data is based on information collected through secondary and primary sources. The secondary sources include available data from various government departments, District, Taluka and Village Panchayats, and reports prepared by various governmental and non-governmental agencies. The primary data is collected by interviewing Village Panchayat members from selected villages and also government officials and village leaders. In order to achieve objectives of the study, we have selected eleven tribal villages from four tribal districts of Gujarat, viz., Dangs, Valsad, Surat and Narmada, where there is high concentration of tribal population and fall under the Fifth Schedule areas. The villages were selected on the basis of purposive sampling method. In total, we interviewed 89 elected Gram Panchayat members of the eleven tribal villages. Besides, we have also conducted an in-depth case study of all selected villages.

Before going into the details of assessing the PESA in the tribal areas of Gujarat, it is worth to know the present situation of tribals in the state.

Tribal Situation in Gujarat

Gujarat is the home of about 29 major tribal communities who are inhabited in its eleven districts. As per 1991 census, Gujarat has 14.92 per cent tribal population, i.e., 61,61,775. Tribal population occupied 15 per cent of total geographical area of the state. Out of this, 56.86 per cent is the forest area. Entire tribal belt of Gujarat can be divided into three zones, i.e., North Zone, Central Zone and South Zone. While the North Zone comprising of Sabarkntha and Banaskantha districts has 8 per cent of total tribal population of the state, the Central Zone comprising of Panchamahal, Dahod and Baroda districts accommodates 36 per cent of the total tribal population of the state and the South Zone comprising of Narmada, Bharuch, Surat, Navsari, Valsad and Dangs districts houses 53 per cent of total tribal population. Only 3 per cent of the tribal population is spread out in the rest of districts of Gujarat. Literacy rate amongst tribals is 36.45 per cent as per 1991 census. In 1961, only 11.60 per cent tribals were literate; within 30 years span, the number of literate tribals has gone up to 36.45 per cent only.

As per 1991 census, out of 57 backward blocks in the state, 22 fall under tribal areas. It should be noted here that only 14 per cent land in tribal areas is cultivable. Similarly, only 25 per cent of land in tribal areas is forest land. In other words, per capita availability of cultivated land in tribal area is only 0.15 per cent. There are 26.30 per cent (6,88,881) tribal families who are living below poverty line. Out of 5,884 tribal villages in the state, only 732 are having pipeline connection for drinking water. There are only 41.03 per cent tribal villages having drinking water facility. With regard to toilet facility the scenario is very grim and pathetic, as only 5.42 per cent tribal villages are having this facility, and in remaining villages the people have to defecate in the open. Irrigation is a major source for agriculture and its development but for tribal areas this facility is far from satisfactory, as only 18.89 per cent cultivated land is under irrigation. Twenty-three per cent tribal villages are covered under

Primary Health Centre (PHC) scheme, while 26.52 per cent villages are covered with Sub-Centres. Around 30 per cent villages do not have access to health facilities at all. More than 40 per cent of tribals are working as labourers in agriculture and allied sectors. In spite of so many government schemes for tribals, their conditions are far from satisfactory. Earlier, forest was the main source of their livelihood but after deforestation tribals have to migrate from their villages in search of employment. According to a government estimate, around 21 per cent of tribal families from Dangs, Dahod, Panchamahal, Narmada and Surat districts are migrating out every year for work. Conditions of primitive tribes like Kotvalias, Kolgas and Kathodis are very pathetic. There are 20,000 Kotavalias in South Gujarat, who completely live on bamboo works. They make bamboo items and sell them in the local market. Due to paper mills Kotvalias are not getting enough bamboos for work. Hence, they are facing acute survival problem. In the year 1997-98, as per the Gujarat Forest Department report, Kotvalias and Vasfodas were given only 3,734 metric tonnes bamboos as against 1,24,721 metric tonnes given to Central Pulp Mill for making paper. Such huge gap in the allotment of bamboos makes the poorest among the poor's life miserable. Besides, the bamboos given to Kotvalias were totally dry. Dry bamboos are not good for making bamboo products. Tribals' traditional rights over *jal, jamin and jungal* in their own areas have been systematically curtailed or taken away by the government and non-government agencies. Recent upsurge among tribals is the response towards the suppression of their traditional rights. The foremost problem the tribals of Gujarat confronted presently is of growing unemployment. Particularly, educated tribal youths are not getting jobs. More than 24 thousand tribal graduates in Gujarat are without job. Because of the government policy of reducing staff and to cut the non-plan expenditure, tribal youths are not getting jobs. There are no alternatives available for this vast section of tribal society. These educated tribal youths do try to get jobs in private sectors but because of the lack of linkages they do not succeed in private sectors. Keeping the above situation in mind, the functioning and implementation of PESA in tribal areas has to be seen.

Functioning and Implementation of PESA in Tribal Areas of Gujarat

In this section, we discuss the functioning of panchayats in tribal villages after introducing new Panchayat Act. For the study we have selected 11 tribal villages. The details are given below:

Table 1

Selected Villages, Talukas and Districts and Number of Village Panchayat Representatives Interviewed

Village	*Taluka*	*District*	*No. of Village Panchayat Representatives Interviewed*
Maipur	Vyara	Surat	08
Malotha	Vyara	Surat	08
Vadpada	Uchchal	Surat	10
Naranpur	Uchchal	Surat	12
Linga	Ahwa	Dangs	09
Motidabhas	Ahwa	Dangs	09
Khambhala	Ahwa	Dangs	07
Khutali	Kaprada	Valsad	07
Khadki	Dharampur	Valsad	08
Juna-Mozda	Dediapada	Narmada	03
Tavel	Sagbara	Narmada	08
		Total	89

Except Juna-Mozda, we interviewed cent per cent village panchayat representatives. In Juna-Mozda some of the panchayat representatives were working in urban areas, hence we could not interview them. Selected villages, talukas and districts are tribal-dominated areas and the Panchayat Extension to the Scheduled Areas Act (hereafter PESA) is enforced in these villages since 1998.

In order to review the implementation of PESA, we have asked a variety of questions to elected representatives, which include the knowledge of PESA, issues discussed in Gram Panchayat meetings as well as Gram Sabhas, types of difficulties faced by villagers, problem solution and roadblocks in implementation. We have also asked whether the Gram Panchayat and Gram Sabha meetings are held as per PESA's provisions and do they try to implement it in its true spirit or not. In this section, we will analyse the data in order to understand the level of implementation of PESA in the tribal villages of South Gujarat.

Issues Discussed in Gram Panchayat Meetings

When we asked what are the issues discussed in Gram Panchayat meetings, we got interesting response. All representatives said that developmental issues like road, electricity and drinking water are the main issues discussed in the meetings. While 92 per cent representatives also said that besides development issues in our meetings we do discuss issues of village school and check dam. Surprisingly, issue of cultivating reserve forest land was never discussed in any panchayat meeting. It should be noted here that cultivating reserve forest land in the tribal villages is the burning issue and conflict with the forest department on this issue is very prominent but this issue does not get place in the meetings. In other words, in the Village Panchayats meetings, issues concerning infrastructure facilities get primary concern of elected representatives. It also should be noted here that the functions of panchayats confine only to infrastructure facilities. Issues like unemployment, right over common property resources and villagers' economic development are not discussed at all. One of the representatives of Khutali puts this aspect candidly in following words: "So many people are telling us that Village Panchayat can bring positive change in the lives of villagers but our experience with the Village Panchayat suggests that Village Panchayat has its own limitations. It does not have financial resources and power to govern the village in true democratic spirit. The main function of Village Panchayat is restricted to village cleanliness, streetlights, collection of land revenue and housing tax. It gives income and caste certificates. Most of the village development schemes come from Zilla Panchayat or state government and the duty of the Village Panchayat is just to implement these schemes. Thus, Village Panchayat remains as mere implementing agency." Our data also reinforces this fact.

Level of Awareness among the Village Panchayat Representatives

With regard to representatives' awareness about their responsibilities and knowledge, our investigation reveals that representatives are very particular and conscious about attending meetings but there is a lack of knowledge with regard to various functions of panchayats. Representatives are totally unaware of the PESA and its provisions. They know nothing about their rights and responsibilities as enshrined in the Act. In fact, in most of the Taluka Panchayats too, members were ignorant about the Act. It is therefore not difficult to comprehend that why many vital development issues are not discussed in the meetings. One of the members of Naranpur Gram Panchayat told us: "We have been hearing from people that there is an Act for Village Panchayat power to villagers but so far we have not been informed or given proper guidance on what the Act is and how it has to be implemented. Even government officials did not informed us about this Act. Hence, we do not know anything about this Act." Similar situation was also

Table 2

Level of Awareness Among the Village Panchayat Representatives

Total No. of Respondents	*Name of the Village*	*Regular Attendances in the Meeting*	*Participation in the Meeting*	*Knowledge about PESA*	*Knowledge about Taxes Collected by Village Panchayat*
8	Maypur	87.50	62.50	12.50	75.00
8	Malotha	87.50	75.00	00.00	100.00
10	Vadpada	90.00	100.00	00.00	100.00
12	Naranpur	91.66	91.70	00.00	75.00
9	Linga	100.00	77.80	00.00	77.80
9	Motidabas	88.80	88.90	00.00	55.60
7	Khambhala	100.00	100.00	00.00	85.70
7	Khutali	100.00	100.00	00.00	100.00
8	Khadki	75.00	87.50	00.00	100.00
3	Juna-Mozda	100.00	100.00	00.00	100.00
8	Tavel	100.00	100.00	00.00	100.00

Note: Data given are in percentages.

prevailing amongst the Taluka Panchayat members. In September 2003 we had organised an orientation training programme on PESA and Fifth Schedule provisions in tribal areas for all tribal Taluka Panchayat representatives of Gujarat. We found that not a single member was aware about provisions of PESA and the Fifth Schedule. They were of the opinion that they are very much concerned about implementing the various provisions of the Act but do not have any information. District and Taluka Panchayat Development Officers were also found ignorant about the above Acts. Table 2 shows the level of awareness among the Village Panchayat representatives.

Implementation of Village Development Programmes

As we have seen earlier that the panchayats give priority to the development issues only. But, this is not always right. Apart from roads and drinking water facility, very little has been done across the villages in terms of school, community hall/panchayat hall, community development programmes and check dams. Even, the villages like Malotha, Linga, Motidabas and Khambhala have less than 50 per cent responses to confirm that roads have been laid, or repaired. The implementation of drinking water facility has been completely ignored in the villages like Malotha, Khutali, Khadki and Juna Mosda. Rest other villages too show poor implementation with hardly 50 per cent response in few villages. As mentioned earlier, the functions of panchayats are restricted to build or repair roads, providing water facility for all purposes and education facility only. Village Panchayat, as a unit of local self-governance, is hardly working. As per PESA's provisions Village Panchayat supposed to discuss various aspects of tribal problems like minor forest produce, regulation of liquor sale and moneylending, giving consent for establishing any industry nearby village, protecting tribal communities' customary rights, impose taxes on village common resources and to identify BPL families of the village, but none is discussed in panchayat meetings. Even representatives are not aware about these provisions. However, there is a widespread curiosity amongst the village representatives to know PESA provisions. For example, Dangs District Sarpanch Association (DSA) President and Sarpanch of Bhuri Khet, Sivram Gangode, an advocate, is very enthusiastic about implementing PESA in its true spirit to all villages of Dangs.

He has arranged PESA orientation trainings for sarpanchas of Dangs and campaigned for strict implementation of PESA during Gram Sabhas. He is of the view that "PESA provisions are very much beneficial to tribals but government officials and state do not have much interest in implementing it. The reason is, once PESA provisions are implemented, then, the villagers and Village Panchayat will get more powers, which will minimise the state's role, hence state does not want to implement it in true spirit."

Implementation of PESA

With regard to representatives' understanding about village problems, the maximum percentage of responses pertained to infrastructural difficulties faced by the villagers. It includes access to road, electricity and water for drinking as well as irrigation. This was followed by health, employment, transportation and education. It reveals that transportation problem and to some extent education are felt more in hilly terrains of Dangs and Dharampur. These problems are also voiced vehemently in Gram Sabhas of these villages. As mentioned elsewhere, the functions of Village Panchayats are restricted mainly to implementing and monitoring facilities like roads, transportation, education, and water. In almost all Gram Sabhas these were the main grievances expressed by the villagers. It is also found that villagers are passing resolutions after resolutions in each Gram Sabha to resolve these grievances but they hardly get resolved. Due to this apathetic attitude by government and elected representatives villagers have lost confidence in panchayats. This is also one of the reasons for poor attendance in Gram Sabhas. One of the village youth leader of Tavel told us: "In last four Gram Sabha meetings we have been passing the resolution for repairing village approach road and installing handpumps for drinking water but so far nothing has been done. Now, we have decided that we will boycott the next Gram Sabha meeting. Government officials are not interested in resolving our problems. Gram Sabha is a mere formality."

Reasons for Unresolved Difficulties

Most of the representatives could not figure out the reason for non-resolution of the difficulties faced by villagers. It is clear from our data that a little response (only 10.42%) was given to the lack of interest among villagers and their representatives towards the cause. Biased and undemocratic attitude of sarpanch was highlighted at Khutali and Vadapada. Thus representatives themselves too are little bothered about solving the problems of the village. Their low concern and indifferent attitude towards problem resolution would probably defeat the essence of whole process of decentralisation of governance. Here, the case of Khutali Village Panchayat is in point. Due to factionalism amongst panchayat representatives of Khutali Gram Panchayat, majority of representatives are against the sarpanch. Sarpanch does not enjoy confidence of panchayat members, hence development of village gets hampered. Because of sarpanch's biased and autocratic attitude panchayat representatives are not able to work pro-actively for village development. Our data also indicates that a large number of representatives are of the view that lack of interest among representatives is one of the reasons for not resolving village problems.

As per PESA Gram Sabha plays pivotal role in village development. Identification of BPL families, planning for village development and sanctioning budget are the main functions of Gram Sabhas but our enquires reveals that Gram Sabhas hardly perform these functions. As we have discussed elsewhere Gram Sabhas are poorly represented by villagers and only few relevant issues are discussed. As per our enquires, it is revealed that at Malotha, Vadpada and Naranpur only identification of BPL family is done by Gram Sabha. Taxation on weekly market is never done. However, commonly discussed issues are identification of BPL families, social customs and festivals as well as registration of births and deaths. However, the Gram Sabhas of Dangs and Dharampur again score high percentage in terms of their response to various issues concerning people. It was also noticed that despite low performance of panchayats in redressing their problems but people consider Gram Sabha as an important forum where they can openly ask for their betterment through administrative/political intervention. This awareness about the realisation of their right is praiseworthy. Gram Sabha as one of the important events for villagers where they can come together and discuss the village problems.

Though the people's gradual awareness is slowly taking roots, the dissemination of information by government about people's political rights is still to catch up among the grassroots political structure. Under the PESA, a lot of provisions have been made to safeguard socio-cultural and economic life of Scheduled Tribes. But, none of the Gram Panchayat in the selected villages knew about the Act set aside its provisions. Thus, the panchayats do not discuss these matters in their meeting. It is found that regulation on moneylending and taxes on public property used for private purpose do not figure at all whereas issues of minor forest produce and registration of liquor selling are seldom discussed. Malotha, Vadpada, Naranpur and Juna-Mozda seem to be most important about these provisions, hence, these issues do not find mention in their discussions.

Gram Sabha and PESA

As per PESA Gram Sabha (people's forum) shall perform the following functions:

(a) The Gram Sabha shall endeavour to safeguard and preserve the traditions and customs of the inhabitants of the village, their cultural identity, community resources and the customary mode of dispute resolution.

(b) The Gram Sabha shall approve the plans, programmes and projects for social and economic development before such plans, programmes and projects are taken up for implementation by the Village Panchayat.

(c) The Gram Sabha shall be responsible for the identification or selection of persons as beneficiaries under poverty alleviation and other programmes in the village.

Gram Sabha has always been an integral part of the concept of a village government or Gram Panchayat. Decision-making in a Gram Panchayat is valid only if the Gram Sabha endorses it. Therefore, the Gram Sabha is an institution of direct democracy rather than representative democracy introduced in more recent time. In order to understand the role of Gram Sabha in the light of devolution of powers and governance at grassroot level, we have attended 22 village Gram Sabha meetings.

Before going into the functioning of Gram Sabha meetings it should be noted here that as per the 73rd Constitution Amendment Act, it is villagers' prerogative to decide the date, venue, time and agenda of the Gram Sabha meeting. But, in last three years, in Gujarat, the state government decides this. Such act by the state government is totally undemocratic and not allowing villagers to discuss their problems on their terms and conditions. In other words, Gram Sabhas are merely acting like a ratifying body for the state government. Number of villagers did express their objection on this issue. In fact, the Dangs District Sarpanch Association has prepared a resolution which says that as per PESA it is the villagers' right to decide the date, time and agenda of the Gram Sabha meeting by themselves only and asked the villagers to pass this resolution in Gram Sabhas and the copy be sent to the District Development Officer and the Collector. Out of 70 Gram Panchayats of the Dangs 33 have passed such resolution and sent to the concerned authority. However, the government is not accepting this as a legal resolution. One of the activists working in Dangs – struggling hard to make the Gram Sabha and PESA to work – told us that "provisions of PESA are very beneficial to tribals and if properly implemented it will bring real SAWARAJ for tribals but unfortunately the state, the bureaucrats and the political leaders are not interested to implement it because it may challenge their dominance over tribals. Like rest of the other legislations made for people, this legislation also remains on paper unless there is a strong people movement to implement this Act in its true spirit. The another problem before properly implementing this Act is to challenge the provisions in court after putting this Act into practice so that it establishes the validity of the Act. We are planning to challenge it in the court."

Our observations on functioning of 22 Gram Sabhas recorded during the fieldwork are as under:

1. There was a lack of awareness amongst people about the role of Gram Sabha. Large-scale illiteracy, low awareness, inaccessibility to sources of information and an unsupportive

administrative environment – all contribute together to this problem. Sheer survival issues dominate the life of the tribals. Immediate issues of food insecurity leave little scope for any hullagulla on a relatively abstract subject such as self-governance. Seasonal migration is a fact of life in these villages, which reduces interest and participation of people in Gram Sabha meetings and activities.

2. Attendance in Gram Sabha meetings was found very low. Our inquiry reveal that on an average 25 to 30 per cent adult of the village attend the Gram Sabha. Often, the quorum is not met with as prescribed or the register is taken house to house to get signatures for the requisite quorum. Attendance and participation of villagers in Gram Sabha meetings was low in majority villages, except Bilpudi and Chikali, the most important reason for this was people were disillusioned by false claims by sarpanchas and government officials. A sense of disillusionment on the efficacy of the Gram Sabha was perceptible. People felt that decisions and recommendations made by the Gram Sabha did not carry any weight and were brushed aside by senior government officials.
3. Gram Sabha is serving as a forum where information about government schemes is disseminated. Though a few Gram Sabha take real interest in its deliberations, its importance is gradually recognised, as some of the villagers admitted that now they know what schemes are made for them, and how they can get them.
4. The issues discussed at Gram Sabha were more or less same in all the villages. In all Gram Sabhas mainly infrastructural and basic amenities issues like road, electricity, drinking water, forest land issues, employment and benefits from schemes were discussed. Matters related to monetary benefits gained ground over more significant issues of development and participatory governance.
5. Since villagers were not consulted in drawing up of the Gram Sabha agenda, there was a sense of apathy in their involvement in its affairs.

6. Duration of Gram Sabha is sometimes so short that it is difficult to discuss the problems of the village as this concern was also raised at one of the meetings. Officials too seem to be in hurry either to avoid further questions or to reach home early.
7. It was also noticed that resolutions passed by previous Gram Sabha are not resolved till the next Gram Sabha meets. When asked for action taken report by the villagers, the government officials tried to cover up the problem by giving various excuses. It was also found out that in the Gram Sabha meeting previous Gram Sabha meeting proceedings were not read out seriously so that villagers could not for implementation of the resolutions passed by them. Many villagers complained that in each Gram Sabha meeting the resolution passed earlier has not been executed and hence what is the use of Gram Sabha.
8. Dominance of Gram Sabha meetings by the government officials, sarpanch and others in the local power axis led to widespread indifference among people about the usefulness of the Gram Sabha meetings.
9. Accountability of the Gram Panchayat to the Gram Sabha was very weak. Voices were not raised against corruption since accountability was an unlikely possibility due to strong interpersonal relationships. Mechanism and procedures for making the Gram Panchayat and other bodies accountable and transparent to the Gram Sabha exist within the Panchayati Raj system. For example, the Gram Panchayat should get the approval of Gram Sabha in identifying beneficiaries for different government programmes; similarly, the Gram Panchayat budget needs to be presented to the Gram Sabha for approval. However, due to low awareness and weak participation, Gram Sabha is unable to exercise their rights.
10. Awareness among the people and representatives regarding their rights is very low. They do not know what they can ask for and what they can get. Discussion about forest produce, taxes and employment seldom takes place. Even the erring government functionaries like ANM, gram sevak and talati are seldom questioned for fear of their wrath.

11. Despite its lackluster functioning people still feel that it is an important platform where they can air their grievances and expect redressal of their problems. They acknowledge that development in some areas has made its presence and government machinery has responded towards it. This is a very positive sing and also brings hopes for tomorrow. Earlier, sarpanch used to implement governmental scheme as per his willingness. It has now changed; at least villagers can now question government and other officials.
12. With regards to the implementation of PESA, we found that in none of the Gram Sabhas it got discussed and debated. Villagers and panchayat representatives were ignorant about this Act. Wherever there is some awareness villagers are helpless to implement it due to government apathy and lack of will to implement it.

The above observations thus reveal that the enactment of new law has not empowered people as much as it was expected to. The issue of self-governance has not been realised and still they have not come out of the chamber of government bureaucracy. There also has been a flaw in Gujarat's Act. It has accorded greater power to Gram Panchayat and Taluka Panchayat than Gram Sabha, which itself is against the soul of PESA, 1996. Gram Sabha is merely acting like a ratifying body. It is not obligatory on part of Gram Panchayat to act as per the wishes of Gram Sabha. People themselves need to realise their role and assert. They need to have a feeling of oneness and Gram Sabha as their own informal meeting.

Conclusion

Our inquiry reveals that PESA in Gujarat has opened up the possibilities of self-rule in tribal villages. Tribals are slowly understanding the importance of PESA and becoming conscious about their rights and responsibilities. They do try to exercise their rights and compel the government officials to solve their problems. On the other hand, our study also reveals that PESA is not being implemented in its true spirit. Politicians and bureaucrats are apathetic to it. Gram Sabhas are not held as per PESA's provisions. There seems to be lack of information on the part of villagers and elected representatives of panchayats. Another problem that we noticed pertains to provisions which have been there in the PESA do not corroborate with the national laws pertaining to land acquisition, market regulation and moneylending. There is also an anomaly on the part of legislation, which has hampered its implementation. It should be noted that due to external forces like outside invasion, market penetration and differentiation of tribal communities on socio-economic line, there have been some roadblocks in implementing PESA in its true spirit. There is an urgent need to implement this Act but it will require political will and people's participation. The legislation is necessary but it is not enough. Spirit of legislation needs to be translated into practice.

References

Chaudhary, A.K., 1995. 'Panchayati Raj: Concern and Issues', *Viklpa*, 4(2): 11-18.

Dwivedi, O.P., 1998. 'Common Good and Good Governance', *The Indian Journal of Public Administration*, 17 (3).

Government of Gujarat, 2000. *Human Development Vision 2010*, Gandhinagar.

Government of Gujarat, 2000. *Socio-economic Review of Gujarat State-1999-2000*, Gandhinagar.

Jena, A.C., 1995. 'Panchayati Raj and Development: Analysis of Structural Features of Gujarat, West Bengal, Karnataka and Kerala', *Viklpa*, 4(2): 20-30.

Joshi, Satyakam, 1998. 'Bhuria Samiti Na Aheval No Amal Karvo Jaruri Che', *Naya Marg*, July 1.

–, 2002. *Panchayati Raj: Samajik Nayay Samiti onu Saskatikaran* (in Gujarati), Surat, Centre for Social Studies.

–, 2003. 'Panchayati Raj Leadership in Gujarat', *ISSI Querterly*, July-September.

–, 2003. 'Tribal Life of South Gujarat', Souvenir, West Zone Vice-Chancellor's Conference, South Gujarat University, Surat, 16-17 October.

–, 1999. 'Role of Forest Labour Co-operative Societies in Tribal Development' in Joshi, V.A. (ed.), *Tribal Situation in Western India*, Jaipur and New Delhi, Rawat Publications.

Khare, H., 1998. 'An Unending Struggle for Gujarat's Political Soul', *Seminar*, 470: 17-23.

Menon, P.S.K. and Sinha, Bakshi, 2003. *Panchayati Raj in Schedule Areas,* Concept Publishing Company, Delhi.

Nambiar, M., 2001. 'Making the Gram Sabha Work', *Economic and Political Weekly*, 26 (33).

Shah, Ganshyam and Joshi, Satyakam, et.al., 1997. *Panchayati Raj in Gujarat,* Surat: Centre for Social Studies (mimeo).

Shah, Ganshyam, 1998. 'Polarised Communities', *Seminar*, 470: 30-35.

11

Impact of Positive Discrimination on Leadership of Marginalised Sections in Rural Governance

Some Concerns

Santosh Kumar

In the Indian scenario, social exclusion is not a recent phenomenon. History bears witness to marginalisation and exclusion of social groups on the basis of caste, class, gender and religion. Most notables are the socially marginalised category of dalits (constitutionally categorised as Scheduled Castes). Access to and control over economic and social opportunities have relegated them to the category of social outsiders. The leadership in rural India, traditionally, has been associated with the landowning castes that were regarded as the community representatives of the village community. Though the dalit constitute about one-fourth of the Indian population, traditionally, they have been denied an adequate political space and a place in the decision-making process. Despite various measures, the inequities in terms of control and access to social and economic opportunities continued leading to sporadic incidents of dalit assertion and movements.

The socially marginalised were given a place in the state agenda after independence by way of inclusion of the right to equality in various Articles of the Constitution of India. However, the attempts were only on paper. The years of marginalisation of dalits (and women), in particular, seems to have driven them to the periphery of the political process. Beyond the periodic exercise of their voting rights, this socio-economically excluded and marginalised category has limited participation in the electoral and political process in the country. Though not out of conscious choice, dalits have been driven into an apolitical frame of mind, even when they are the most affected by the political decisions. It can be stated here that their under-representation in the political process, particularly at the grassroots level, is one of the reasons for the backwardness.

The 73rd Constitutional Amendment Act and subsequent State Acts guarantee reservations so as to lead to the empowerment of socially marginalised through an entry in the grassroots leadership. The reasons for providing representation are based on several assumptions, which include:

- shared perception of injustice, deprivation and oppression;
- shared experience of marginalisation *vis-a-vis* the power structure;
- collective empowerment through the representation and democratic process will give them voice, feeling of solidarity and democratic politics;
- with regular elections and constitutionally mandated Panchayats, the power concentration will change and issue-oriented groupings or interest groups will emerge; and
- affirmative action will build a critical mass of local leadership from such groups, who will be active participants in the strategic decision making process.

The present paper is based on an exploratory-empirical study, conducted to explore the theme of impact of affirmative action and positive discrimination for the marginalised in the leadership in a process of rural governance. Besides critically understanding the above stated assumptions, the study seeks to explore two major issues:

- whether the historical injustices can be removed through the affirmative action and positive discrimination, and

- whether in the context of the same, the leadership has been able to respond to the needs of their communities and what more action is needed for better functioning of the dalit leadership in grassroots political processes.

Conceptual Framework

The universal concept of social justice in human societies is based on matching of rewards to person's investment and cost or one's investment and contributions. In the traditional Indian socio-cultural context, acquired characteristics such as gender, age, caste and so on have been considered as legitimate characteristics as compared to the achievements criterion which is becoming a part of the modern secular societies. This has been referred to the theory of distributive justice.[1] The essence of such social justice lies with the way a society allocates its resources to its members. When such ways are perceived as unfair, they lead to negative outcomes. Hence, acceptance of the norms of distribution of resources is indicative of a harmonious state of affairs and lack of inter-group conflicts. Equality, on the other hand, refers to equal distribution, irrespective of the amount of contribution. This norm stands out as the highest norm. To allocate the resources equitably among the various groups, irrespective of superior-subordinate order, the equality norm is related to social justice.[2]

The basis of superior-subordinate relationship can be traced to the steeply hierarchical caste structure in which the lower castes have remained underprivileged and have been exploited by those at the top. These oppressed and exploited groups cannot compete with the advanced sections of the society and, hence, need protection. Dr. Ambedkar has emphasised that certain political rights alone do not constitute the basis of liberty, justice, equality, natural rights, and the rule of law. "To uplift the poor and underprivileged in a general process be devising system for their entry in to the realm of equality – the highest norms – has been the first priority of the democratic and secular government. Hence reservation policy."[3] This study has sought to explore, whether these historical social injustices can be removed through the reservation.

Backwardness may be expressed in terms of inadequate opportunities of self-development for groups or individuals, especially in economic life and in matters of health, housing and education. Reservation could be a device to eliminate backwardness arising out of the historical conditions of social injustice in which certain groups are located.[4] Reservation helps the struggling groups to re-gain the lost manhood and human rights. Social reformers have advocated social equality but not at the cost of others or at least at the cost of the national interest.[5] Contrarily, the elite, who is by and large from the higher castes, fills most of the top positions. Further, the move for privatisation on large scale, it is feared, will reduce even the small components of total employment (3%) in future and will further expose them (SCs) to the discrimination in the private sector.[6] In this way, the already underprivileged groups will be further marginalised with the process of privatisation under the new economic policies. An affirmative action through reservation may provide opportunities to discriminated groups to develop capabilities and skills for the emerging society. At the local level, in this reference, it is significant to understand, whether in the context of reservations the leadership has been able to respond to the needs of their communities and what more action need to be taken for better functioning of dalit leadership in panchayats.

Traditionally, the leadership in rural India has been closely linked with the control of economic assets and opportunities, and maintaining a balance in the village was in the hands of these so-called community leaders. On the extreme end were the landless agricultural labourers, majority of whom belonged to the dalit community. The term 'dalits' (Scheduled Castes) refers to a section of people who were formerly known as 'untouchables'. They belonged to the lowest rung in the Hindu social hierarchy and according to the religious laws, even simple physical contact with them signified a high degree of ritual pollution.[7] At the same time, the dalit caste itself is unequal in the sense that it is further sub-divided into various castes placed in a definite order of subordination, with majority of them observing some kind of untouchability in relation to each other.

The struggle for measures against untouchability started in the pre-independence era and after independence steps were taken to ensure equal rights and opportunities to dalits. Untouchability and its practice in any form were abolished by the Constitution of India.

Articles 14, 15, 16, 29 (2) and 46 of the Constitution of India sought to protect the weaker sections of the society from discrimination and violence by the powerful segments of the population. It was assumed that with the extension of democratic rights to socially disadvantaged groups, the development process would change. Nevertheless, the ideological model could not give the desired results due to complex realities and vested interest of some segments dominated over democratic agenda. Further, on the one hand, the growing inequity both in terms of control and access to economic and social opportunities, domination of non-dalits in decision-making process and growing atrocities against dalits led to dalit movements. On the other hand, it was found that these movements are mainly political in nature and address only macro-level issues related to dalits. The complexities resulting at grass roots rarely came into focus.

Presently, dalits comprise about 25 per cent of the Indian population.[8] Though they constitute a large section of the population of India, they still suffer from social oppression. Economically too, they are the poorest of the poor. The oppression varies from the crudest form of untouchability to the more subtle forms of discrimination, which is seen in urban areas. Though the central reservation policies have enabled dalits to enter the modern sectors of the economy, it has been observed that most of the dalit community members are still connected with land and the social distance between dalits and non-dalits has remained the same. It would be interesting to note here that though dalits constitute a large section of the population of India, only 1 per cent of the cultivable land is owned by them (while just 15 per cent of the Indian population own and control more than 65 per cent of the agricultural land). It has also been observed that where the dependency relations are more pronounced and have economic implications, atrocities on dalits have been greater.

The 73rd Constitutional Amendment Act, passed on 24th of April 1993, provided an opportunity for involving dalits in mainstream political, social and economic decision-making process. Article 243 (D) of the Constitution provides for reservation of Scheduled Castes (SCs) and Scheduled Tribes (STs) in every panchayat in proportion to their population in that area. At least one-third of the seats reserved shall be for women belonging to SC/ST communities. Following the provisions of 73rd Constitutional Amendment, the state governments amended their State Panchayati Raj Act and made provisions for reservation of seats for dalits.

As a sequel of implementation of constitutional provisions, a significant proportion of dalits entered the Panchayat system. However, after a decade of the implementation of these provisions, the questions to address would be how are the constitutional and legal opportunities getting translated on the ground and have they created an impact over social structure in general and dalits in particular? Definitely, reservation of seats has helped dalits in entering the mainstream democratic process but the issue here is how these leaders from marginalised community have functioned effectively during their five-year term in panchayats? What are the factors which support/hinder dalit leadership in panchayats?

Since the enactment of the 73rd Constitutional Amendment various organisations have been working for strengthening Panchayati Raj Institutions (PRIs). PRIs are viewed not just implementing agencies of development programmes but as institutions of local self-governance. One of the their important activities include enhancing active participation of dalit and women in the process of decision-making, which is possible through their zealous and enthusiastic involvement in grassroots governance. One of the common findings in functioning of these organisations is that, even today, dalit leaders at panchayat level have not been able to function independently and in general the upper castes still hold decision making powers. The atrocities on dalits and untouchability in various forms continue.

Scheduled Castes in Maharashtra

In 1981, the census enumerated 1,092 Scheduled Castes (SCs) in the country and 59 in Maharashtra. Of these 59, three castes, viz., Mahar, Mang and Chamar are numerically high constituting 83.16 per cent of the total SC population in the state.[9] They are still considered the major castes. There are five castes, namely, Bhangi,

Dhor, Lingader, Khatik and Holar that constitute 8.42 per cent of the total SC population, which can be clubbed as middle castes. All the remaining castes are numerically low and are hence clubbed together under the term 'minor castes'. Each caste in this category is represented by less than 1 per cent of the total SC population. There are as many as 1.45 per cent unspecified Scheduled Castes in the state.[10]

The state of Maharashtra, covering an area of 308 thousand square kilometres, is part of the peninsular India and the third largest state in terms of geographic area and population, which as per the census of 199 1stands at 78 million. The state is presently divided into thirty-three districts, but historically and in popular imagination it is constituted by five regions, distinct in terms of natural resources and socio-cultural history: Vidarbha, western Maharashtra, Marathwada, Konkan and North Maharashtra. Modern-day Maharashtra, as is well known, is the most industrially advanced state of the country. Capital-intensive industries have been engines of growth in Mumbai, Thane, Pune and Nashik regions. In Satara, Sangli, Ahmednagar and Kolhapur, agro-industries, essentially sugarcane-based, have defined the pattern of growth.[11]

High figures of economic growth, however, hide enormous urban-rural, caste-class, tribal-non-tribal and regional disparities. Poor and distorted agricultural growth, highly skewed patterns of industrialisation and urbanisation and sharp regional imbalances between the aforesaid five regions in overall economic development are also characteristic features of this economically 'advanced' state. Advance has excluded masses of labouring caste-communities that are overwhelmingly dependent on agriculture in the 'number one' industrial state.[12] Landless status, low productivity, drought. proneness of large number of talukas of the state, recurrent crop failures, water scarcity and low cultivable land have resulted in persistent levels of rural poverty. Acute seasonal and disguised unemployment for a majority of small and marginal farmers and agricultural labour has been major consequences of poor and inequitable growth.[13] Rural poverty levels in Maharashtra have been higher than other states and India.[14]

As regards atrocities on dalits in Maharashtra, over and above, the violence embedded inherently in the system of untouchability, the infliction of organised and systematic violence on its victims seems to occur in direct proportion to the intensity of challenges to its religious ritual basis. At the most basic level, atrocities signify violent outcomes of situations of social tensions and conflicts between the strong and the weak. In Maharashtra, the history of the atrocities on the dalits is perhaps as old as history of dalit movement, prompting Ambedkar to press for the inclusion of the caste issues on the political agenda of national liberation.[15] The Buddhists, who posed the boldest challenge so far to the Hindu social order and also attempted to envision and intervene in the formation of an alternative system, have been subject to the most frequent, systematic and horrendous of atrocities.[16]

Atrocities have noticeably increased and intensified as a backlash to continued struggles. At a different level, the exacerbation of atrocities has led to greater stringency in the original anti-untouchability law. While the stringency of law has served as deterrent and there exists a palpable public fear of the 'Atrocities Act', atrocities themselves have neither ceased, nor reduced in frequency or intensity. Terror, the quintessential weapon of feudal coercion, continues to be used with regularity and greater effect, to silence the oppressed in this capitalistic state.

The actual incidences of atrocities have been difficult to establish. It has numerous forms: physical assault, disfigurement, beating and lynching to death, rape, human sacrifice, social boycott, nude parades, destruction of property and crops, poisoning of wells and verbal abuses, etc.[17]

In general, the economic factors have been highlighted as crucial in the light of growing class contradictions in the agrarian structure. The common analysis is that caste atrocities usually reflect class conflicts. In some events, the economic factor is clearly primary, e.g., in struggle over land. A deeper examination, however, reveals that a complex of social, economic, political and religio-cultural factors are often at the root of modern-day violence against the dalits.[18] The Marathwada riots are a significant case in point. In overall context of a stagnant economy and caste-feudal value system, dalits' challenge and advance resulted in a virtual caste war. Both caste and patriarchal factors are at work in case of public sexual violence of dalit women. Apart from the patriarchal intent of violating their men's honour, such acts represent a direct derogation of low caste women's sexuality as more lax and therefore more easily transgressable.[19]

Dalit political mobilisation on a national level began in the late 1920s, when the then colonial government initiated a series of negotiations to provide political representation to the depressed (later scheduled) castes. As a result of this complex and at times bitter process, a negotiated formula was arrived at to guarantee 'reserved representation' in the parliament, the state legislatures, and the local self-government bodies, to bestow political power to the dalits. This compromise formula had two effects. On the one hand, it raised the political aspirations of the dalit leadership, and on the other increased the co-option of the articulated sections within the community into the system.[20]

The problems encountered by the dalits have remained unchanged, and have become more severe and acute. This has lent a factor of urgency to the situation, which deprives them not only of spaces, also of time. The lives and future of the dalits have come under a fierce assault, both physical and ideological. The tragedy of the situation has been with the middle class and the intelligentsia among the community, the beneficiaries of the policy of positive discrimination. They, unfortunately, rest content with some sort of sharing of powers from above without clinching the issues of powers at the grassroots.[21] In this context, the Constitutional Amendment Act, 1993 acquires added significance, which has opened the vistas for the participation of the deprived castes in a more meaningful way, and perhaps, give a new meaning to the dalit movement as well as participation in the political processes.

This analysis of dalits' situation suggests significance and limitations of dalit politics. The dominant reality of socio-economic backwardness, highly uneven dislocations in untouchability practice and the inability to stem the tide of rising atrocities indicate that whatever its presence, SC politics has not been strong enough to protect its political constituency. In attempting to throw further light on the nature, scope and substance, the coming section focuses directly on dalit politics in party and non-party political domains, concentrating on issues of participation, power and consciousness. Furthermore, a contextual approach enables us to show that macro social processes interacting with dalit political formations have largely shaped the restricted role and impact of the latter.

The Dalits Politics of Modern Maharashtra and Panchayati Raj Institutions

In attempting to throw further light on its nature, substance and scope, the paper focuses directly on the politics in party and non-party political domains, concentrating on issues of participation, power and consciousness. Furthermore, a contextual approach enables one to show that macro-social processes interacting with the dalit political formations have largely shaped the restricted role and impact of the latter.

The present section discusses the trajectory of dalit politics in the post-independence Maharashtra in the context of the new emergent political scenario that witnessed transfer of power to the Hindu majoritarian party combine, and also the recent processes and their implications, especially on the grassroots politics and processes of governance.

Social movements and politics of the dalits have had a deep and complex impact and generated a number of contradictory socio-political processes. Widespread politicisation, heightened political consciousness and a new collective political identity have brought the dalits from the periphery to the centre of the mainstream politics. This can especially be said in the context of the 73rd Constitutional Amendment. Replacing the Maratha-Brahmin conflict, the dalit-*Savarna* conflict has been a dominant socio-political reality in the post-independence modern Maharashtra, and has served as a potent force that has made possible social change.[22]

The social transformation, effected by political movement and power, has involved conflictual access to secularised avenues and domains, viz., education, occupation, and political office in the context of the rapidly emergent capitalist class society and modernist influences. Changing traditional status relations have changed relations between status and power. Secular power has helped challenge social power to a significant extent.[23]

Change, however, has varied between the various SCs and the regions of the state at the macro level. The major transformation has been from *asprishya* (socially degraded) village servant to exploited casual labourer in the work domain. Economically, the dalits remain assetless, whereas socially it is a mixed picture of forging egalitarianism, changing identities and situations of forced subservience. Politically, they are confronted with the paradox of heightened political activity and consciousness, and growing marginalisation. The modernising, secularising forces of capitalist economy have facilitated the embourgeoisment of the newly emergent middle class. The gains of democratisation of castes, positive discrimination and politicisation mainly accrued to this class and led to a sharp elite-mass polarisation within each of the major sub castes among dalits. The privileges of money, jobs, and higher education, have created formidable class interests and political conservatism.[24]

Some feel, the dalit politics is at low ebb today. In a radically changed contemporary context, characterised by an onslaught of global capitalism, caste-communally fractured and criminalised political culture and growing state repression of the voices of the affected poor, sporadic protests seem to have limited consequences.[25] As self-consciousness and self-awareness of smaller, lower caste communities is on the rise, capacity for the power negotiation is on the decline. Politics has built up identity but the overall situation has instilled feelings of powerlessness, particularly in the face of incessant violence and terror on the part of the dominant groups and growing state repression on the one hand and absence of radical mobilisation from below on the other.[26]

This macro-situational analysis must, however, be perused in the context of the political participation of the dalits at the grassroots level. The 73rd Constitutional Amendment and consequent State Acts guarantee reservations to lead to the empowerment of women and dalits through entry in grassroots leadership. By enabling these marginalised groups to use this democratic space, it aims to transform the existing oppressive social structures, policies and programmes.

Article 243 (D) makes provisions for the reservation of the SCs and STs in every panchayat in proportion to their population in that area. Not less than one-third of the total number of seats so reserved shall be for women belonging to the SCs/STs. Besides, not less than one-third of the total number of seats (including those reserved for the SC/ST women), to be filled by direct election, shall be reserved for the women and allotted by rotation so that within a time span of fifteen years, the whole state would have been covered in the reservation policy.[27] The office of the chairpersons, the Act further states, in the panchayats at the village or any other level shall be reserved for the SC/ST categories and women in such a manner as the state legislature may provide by law. As per the provisions of the Act, the present position in Maharashtra exhibits that the quantitative requirements have been met with.

Dalit Leadership in Panchayats: Some Concerns

Based on the findings, this study essentially explores the three questions, which are as follows:

1. Has positive discrimination helped/enabled the socio-economically marginalised cross their caste/class barriers at the grassroots level?
2. Which are the supporting and hindering factors for inclusion or exclusion of marginalised in the process of governance?
3. What needs to be done to overcome the constraints posed before the representatives of the socially marginalised for mainstreaming them in the process of governance and development in the rural institutions?

Broader Issues

Reservation and the caste barriers

As the findings and analysis indicate, the indispensability of the reservation for the marginalised has been felt and various arguments in favour of the same have been forwarded in most impressionable ways, such as, the reservation has been instrumental in eradicating backwardness and brought socially marginalised from the periphery to the core of decision-making for developmental work. Reservation has also eliminated purposefully created dependency syndrome among dalits and thus instilled confidence in them, although the process is gradual. Dalit leaders at the grassroots can better understand and represent the cause of dalits, hence reservation for them. Some respondents have stressed to bring attitudinal changes among dalits towards themselves by capacitating them to become efficient and effective as leaders. Reservation has also brought dalit population directly in the political process, and it has been a historical necessity. Thus, the institutional intervention in terms of the reservation policy.

When explored whether the said intervention has helped dalits in forgetting their castes, at least while participating in the institutions of local self-governance, the findings bring forward both the negative and affirmative points of views. Reservation has helped dalits in numerous ways. It has contributed to their economic betterment due to better access to schemes and implementation of the programmes meant for them, and provided them opportunities in decision-making and thus community as a whole has developed. Reservation has also given dalits a sense of security (social/ political) and thus overcome the caste barriers. Since the reservation has brought quantitative representation in place, qualitative representation has also been enhanced with mandatory training and capacity building programmes and processes for the dalits.

However, another view suggests that the caste backgrounds are the given reality, which would not change merely with instruments of reservation. These policies would just facilitate their enhanced entry in the processes of decision-making, but the psyche of the community at large has taken the reservation policy against the larger interest of the dalits. The reservation policy has certainly put the dalits in the leadership role in quantitative terms; the qualitative aspects would have to be monitored over a period of time. The respondents have suggested that it would take at least three generations to mainstream the dalits in the political process as has been desired and envisioned, and hence, it would too quick to conclude that the reservation has helped dalits cross caste barriers.

Since, the issue of reservation has been viewed in affirmative and negative terms, it would be necessary to see what are the factors that have helped dalits in the leadership role, and also the inhibiting factors that are destabilising them from their leadership positions.

Promoting/Supporting Factors for Dalits in Leadership Role

Reservation policy and knowledge of rules and regulations

As has been cited in various instances, the reservation provision as provided in the 73rd Constitutional Amendment Act, 1993 has been the main instrument in bringing forth the dalits into the political role on the one hand, and bringing into sharp focus the issue has generated for academic probing, on the other. Since the marginalised section is in the leadership role, they have been imparted with the inputs and skills into the functional aspects of the whole processes of PRIs, though the numerical strength of such representatives is quite low. However, knowledge of the rules and regulations of the PRIs has been major supporting factor for the dalits in the leadership role.

Promoting/Supporting Factors for Dalits in Leadership Role

- Support from spouse/family members/community in executing leadership role: 25%
- Reservation policy: 85%
- Literacy among dalits: 45%
- Political awareness among dalits, though in small proportion: 15%
- Numerical strength: 5%
- Knowledge of rules and regulations: 55%
- Gradual enhancement in the economic situation of dalits: 25%
- Support from bureaucracy: 11%
- Influence of media, education and exposure to the outside world: 25%
- Presence and support of voluntary community groups/organisations: 12%

Support from spouse/family members/community in executing leadership role

Today, the dalit in the leadership role does not feel isolated. The findings and the analysis suggest that moral and active physical support from the families and the community, especially in the case of the elected women representatives, has been another major supporting factor. Though, there have been instances of proxy representations for both dalit men as well as women, there is a concern felt for their part to be played well in the leadership, hence, there is a support seen. This factor has been manifested in numerous ways, from lending proactive support to being mentors to them in decision-making. The concern here is the thin line that divides lending the support and exercising the prerogatives of an elected leader by usurping the authority upon them.

Literacy and political awareness among dalits

As the study has brought out, the level of literacy among dalits has increased over the years; in quantitative terms, the number may be small. This factor has supported these elected representatives in the leadership, and has sharpened not only their acumen, but furthered their grasp of the social reality and enhanced their decision-making role. Another factor, which is a direct outcome of the Constitutional Amendment Act, is that the dalits are more aware of their political self. It is especially true in the context of Maharashtra, where there has been long tradition of dalit movements. They may not be politically very active, but their awareness on the political lines has been a support to their political agility in the PRI process.

Influence of exposure to the outside world and media

The compulsions of the modern times for social and economic enhancement have forced the dalit community to move out to the semi-urban/urban centres, which have exposed them to the newer visions and directions in their lives. These developments are of far-reaching consequences for their newly acquired political roles. The media too have played their role in a positive role in providing positive direction to them. There is an enhanced need to have a furtherance of the role of media in the political role of the dalits.

Presence and support of voluntary community groups/organisations

The present roles played by the NGOs/CBOs are essentially of guidance and capacity building of the leadership at the grassroots level. They are also playing an important role in sensitising the wider community in accepting dalits in the leadership role, and helping them resolve their own problems. Besides, the NGOs/CBOs are also extending functional help to the dalits. These external agencies are playing crucial role in bridging the gap between the dalit community on the one hand and government officials on the other hand. CBOs are more or less also involved in advocacy role for changes in the policies for welfare of the dalit community.

Expectations from the NGOs/CBOs are many – from setting up help-line desk to provide help to the dalit leadership in all respects, and involve in the advocacy role. At a functional level, these agencies are also expected to get involved in initiating income generation activities for the needy among the dalit community. Identification of potential leaders from the dalit community and preparing them for the future role is also thought essential, as also the spread of literacy and political education to these budding leaders. CBOs, suggests findings, must provide moral and proactive support to the dalit community.

Preparing political training module and imparting political literacy to the dalits is crucial contribution expected from the CBOs. They must capacitate dalits to understand the political dynamics at the village or higher levels. CBOs should launch campaigns for the dalit's rights, and take efforts to generate unity among dalits especially during elections. It is important for them to understand legal and official documents, especially related to motion of no confidence and such other strategies. CBOs could help them in these regards as well.

As regards providing social security to the dalit community, there are clauses in the Constitution of India, and various other Acts. There is a necessity to make the dalit community aware of them. More important is instilling a sense of confidence among them and assuring them of their consistent support. Similarly, awareness regarding various laws and legal provisions for legal security to dalits political role is equally crucial. Besides these capacity-building measures, the CBOs can also extend legal counselling to the leaders. Hence, as felt by the respondents, presence of the NGOs/CBOs is an important supporting factor.

Hindering Factors for Dalits in Leadership Role

As against these supporting factors, there are various deterring factors faced by dalit in leadership roles. The factors are overwhelming and, as the findings point to, are perceived as the real threats to them. Some of these are internal or psychological factors, but many among them are external factors, which deserve attention in order to have a full view of the ineffective and inefficient role of the dalits while participating in the PRIs.

Gender issues – Being a dalit woman is itself an inhibiting factor

The analysis reveals that caste continues to be a primary locus, along with gender of the felt oppression of the dalit women. The definition of the centrality of the caste compounded by intensities of the class oppression comes from the direct lived experiences of the debilitating social, economic and political conditions of masses of the poor dalit women. The educated middle class women experience casteism in modern relations in the economic, social and political domains. The culture of caste still affects the public domain, including the progressive arena of social movements. Class, caste and gender constitute every sphere of social relations. dalit women relate to the totality of conditions and to the centrality of the caste-class issues to their lives.

In context of the dalit women in the PRIs, an understanding of the prospects, constraints and the support structures of the women as they grapple to fit into the political roles would involve examining issues that this group is faced with on a day-to-day basis. Enabling factors are those that do not cause any impediments to the functioning of the marginalised in the new roles as political leaders. These factors would enhance efficiency and effectiveness. Against this, inhibiting factors are seen largely in the context of the socio-cultural environment and structure of the PRIs itself.

Hindering Factors for Dalits in Leadership Role

- Dalit identity and caste barriers: 65%
- Prejudiced mindset of the non-dalits and non-acceptance of dalits: 15%
- Being a woman, particularly a dalit woman, is itself an inhibiting factor: 40%
- Weaker financial base: 85%
- Illiteracy: 95%
- Lack of awareness about their rights as dalits: 25%
- Lack of confidence (submissiveness): 55%
- Lack of knowledge of the Panchayat Act and related rules, regulations, rights and duties, and other processes related to Panchayati Raj: 75%
- Motion of No Confidence: 45%
- Verbal and sometimes physical violence against elected dalit representatives: 10%
- Proxy representation and decision-making of elected women representatives by their spouses/male family members: 15%
- dalits represented by the upper caste representatives in decision-making: 35%
- Dependency of dalits on non-dalits for their livelihood: 45%
- Lack of no support for majority of leaders at the village level from the political parties: 55%
- Non-cooperative government machinery against dalits: 65%
- Gram Sevaks misguide in panchayat activities: 45%

The factors behind an alarmingly high proportion of the powerless women in the PRI are both intrinsic and extrinsic. The opportunity created by policy makers to bring about gender equity in governance is yet to be translated into reality. The socio-political dynamics at the villages are hampering this transition. Meanwhile, the incidents of harassment have been reported from different quarters.

Reasons for not attending various meetings by Elected Dalit Women Representatives

- Household chores and other such compulsions, do not find time: 24%
- Men of the house do not like it: 55%
- Do not get the information regarding the meetings: 55%
- Meeting timings are not proper and conducive: 10%
- Do not understand anything, hence do not attend: 45%

Spread of malicious rumours is a major impediment once the dalit women come to the position of power. These rumours question the individuals' character, honour and integrity. Till today, the women have been seen as the upholders of the family virtues and traditional values. The greatest fear that women have is that their character should not be associated with issues that might cause their family to lose face.

Proxy representation for women is another area of concern. If one were to acknowledge the fact that women would trust their husbands in all matters, what ends up happening is that this assistance does not come without the strings attached. Men see this opportunity to influence both their wives and community. For a woman the fight to retain the autonomy becomes fraught with risks and in a majority of cases she sacrifices her position for the sake of harmony at home.

Lack of knowledge of the Panchayat Act and related rules, regulations, rights and duties, and other processes related to Panchayati Raj

It is expected that the dalits and women who are entering the domain of the public life, majority for the first time, would not be as well versed as their *savarna* counterparts, who have mastered the skills of interpretations of rules and also internalised the rules and regulations required to run the PRIs. However, lack of knowledge about rules and regulations is the commonest of the impediments allegedly forwarded by the other elected representatives. There are several causes behind this unawareness. Illiteracy, coupled with inhibitions and lack of exposure of the dalit leaders, further makes the argument of the non-dalit representatives.

Atrocities (verbal and physical manifestations) against elected Dalit representatives

Over and above, the violence embedded inherently in the system of untouchability, the infliction of organised and systematic violence on its victims seems to occur in direct proportion to the intensity of challenges to its religious ritual basis. At the most basic level, atrocities signify violent outcomes of situations of social tensions and conflicts between the strong and the weak. The actual incidences of atrocities have been difficult to establish. It has numerous forms: physical assault, disfigurement, beating and lynching to death, rape, human sacrifice, social boycott, nude parades, destruction of property and crops, poisoning of wells, verbal abuses, etc.

Non-cooperative government machinery against dalits and the role of the Gram Sevaks

As regards the government machinery and its cooperation with the dalit leadership, many of them have been found only to pay lip service to the cause of upliftment of dalits. The nexus between the non-dalit upa-sarpanch and the village level officials, especially the Gram Sevaks (Village Secretaries), has proved to be counter-productive for the dalit leadership. The Gram Sevak is considered to be an important link between the villages and the Block Offices or other offices, especially with regard to the information and implementation of the various developmental schemes for the villages. However, it has been seen in most of the cases that the alleged nexus does not allow the sarpanch, especially a woman sarpanch, and inhibits their functional capabilities in more than one ways.

Motion of No Confidence

The traditional rural leadership has been disappointed with the reservation policy, and having tried and failed different strategy to keep the above-referred coteries of newly emerging rural leadership under their predominance, motion of no confidence has come as an overpowering stratagem in their hands.[28] In the context of the 73rd Amendment Act, this stratagem has allowed two distinct trends in the grassroots politics. On the one hand, there has been a rise in the political consciousness cutting across the caste-class strata. This increasing political consciousness has paradoxically disturbed the cohesiveness of the caste-based communities. The caste leaders or the representatives to the various panchayat bodies now can no more presume the support of their 'own' people in the events such as that of motion of no confidence because of the ensured reservation to their caste in the Gram Panchayat, thus indulging in the power dynamics vis-à-vis another representative from the same caste.

Hence, the stratagem of motion of no confidence is being adopted by the upper caste not only to destabilise and discourage the participation of the marginalised caste in local self-governance, but it has also come as a convenient weapon in disturbing the viscidity of the various caste groups. The second trend is thwarting of the opportunities for the dalit, especially women, representatives to come up as leaders through participation in the Gram Panchayats. Because of the excessive use of the motion of no confidence, there are no support structures created or allowed to be created, in absence of which the emerging leadership faces challenges and also feels de-motivated in the process of governance.

Nonetheless, even in the face of such a scenario of despondency and disheartenment, the presence of 20 million women and more than 60 million of the dalits in the process of governance and democratic functioning of the Indian State at the local level provides the ray of hope. The provision of motion of no confidence is a principal exigency of any democracy to function properly, but to render shield to the welling up woman and dalit leadership in the rural politics from the menacing effects of motion of no confidence is as well consequential. This shield is also significant because the lopsided rural developmental scenario must change, which is presently the situation in face of such counter factors. This can only be accorded with proper training in the art of administration, polity, and finances, as they are to be equipped to shoulder responsibilities.[29] As the recommendation of the study suggests, some measures for changes in the functioning of the officials concerned with the Gram Panchayats too are required, but what could be of far-reaching consequences is the political education and training of the members of the Gram Sabha in a sustained and focussed manner.

Against this scenario, it is natural to explore the alternatives to the situation.

The Way Ahead

Politics is the study of the exercise of power. Political participation should, therefore, mean participation in the exercise of power, the power to effectively influence decision-making processes and policies, to reverse existing situations wherever they are disadvantageous and to bring necessary social change. Political participation, therefore, is much more than physical or quantitative participation in formal institutions and processes, though this is necessary both for itself as well as for influencing decision-making processes. However, one observes that there is still a great hiatus between the constitutional guarantees, the quantitative participation and qualitative representation of the women and those belonging to the verging segment of the society such as Scheduled Castes (SCs), Scheduled Tribes (STs) and Other Backward Communities (OBCs), and who have hitherto been on the fringes of the political participation.

The questions, sought to address in this context, are whether the quantitative participation of women and dalits has led to qualitative enhancement of their lives, whether this participation has re-negotiated the gender and caste relations and increased awareness among them, and issues such as power dynamics and political manoeuvring before, after and during the motion of no confidence, the various actors and factors associated with the process of adopting the motion, and the buckler to be provided to the newly emerging leadership against various political strategies. Besides, the issue is to provide a set of strategies for these prime stakeholders in the rural politics, so that the presently reinforced hierarchies of power can be redefined.

One of the basic questions in the analysis of the problem of power sharing by weaker sections through the Panchayati Raj by way of reservation has been the perception of the villagers themselves. Such an issue needs to be debated from empirical point of view as it alone can be a pointer to the power-sharing scenario and direction in which the PRIs are moving in the aftermath of the Constitutional Amendment. Some argue that except in case of caste, other variables like sex, age and education are of lesser significance in forming opinion about reservation and thereby one could hypothesise that economic, political and caste considerations in varying degrees may have impact in forming opinion about reservation but this would require an in-depth study by re-defining reservation as a means of brining about uplift of poverty structure of masses. It has been concluded that the upper castes and classes find reservation as a challenge to their power, which they were enjoying for a long time.[30]

Further, the present development paradigm of activating the civil society organisations (CSOs) and empowering the local panchayats largely lacks concern and sensitivity to deal with the problems of the dalits. As has been argued, in the present context, most of the dalits have come to believe that the state should work in the interest of the rural poor. The situation demands urgent steps to check the deficiencies in the present strategies of rural development to make them sensitive to deal with the dalit issues.

Participation of the people in developmental activities of late has been realised to be ultimate path of development. Consequently, both the state machinery and the NGOs are striving towards this end. NGOs functioning in the rural areas are concentrating on making the popular participation work. This can be seen in the form of training of the elected panchayat representatives, forming community structures and *Mahila Mandals,* forming of SHGs, applying PRA techniques, etc.

The success of popular participation involves structural problems, as has been discussed so far. Caste stratification is the given social situation. This stratification has left the dalit not only economically backward but also socially vulnerable. This social milieu acts as an obstacle in ensuring participation of dalits in the developmental activities. Participation for dalits at present, means following the upper castes blindly, without questioning them.

The rural development plans/strategies so far have led to vertical mobility in the society and increase in social inequality. Keeping in mind the rise in rural poverty and the need to keep the fiscal deficits under control, the rural development plans should try to focus on the development of the dalits. Efforts have to be made to understand and incorporate the problems and sufferings of dalits while framing rural development strategies. To make popular participation and decentralisation work for dalits they will have to be empowered enough economically and educationally so that they can think and act for themselves. It is in this context the roles and responsibilities of the NGOs/CBOs become very critical.

As regards the present role played by the NGOs/CBOs in empowering dalit community, there are different perceptions. Some look at their role as big brotherly, patronising on the one hand, and guiding on the other. Many others see it as getting the wider community accept the role of dalits in all social, economic and cultural activities and encourage dalits for good work. The NGOs are helping the dalit community resolve their own issues and implement developmental schemes. But, the most important role has been capacity building and enhancing leadership qualities and spread literacy/education (formal/political) among dalits, especially on PRI subjects. NGOs are also believed to be bridge the gap between dalit community and government officials and thus accessing relevant information to the dalit community. Some NGOs have been engaged in advocacy for policy changes for the grassroots development.

The respondents have expressed varied contributions from NGOs/CBOs in empowering dalit communities. They are expected to provide training inputs and other capacity building measures. Some of the respondents feel that NGOs should provide action oriented active support for the preservation of the dalits' rights. As regards the contributions of NGOs/CBOs in facilitating dalits' political role, it is important that the specific political needs of the dalit community are identified, training module prepared and imparted to the dalits. Spread of political literacy, imparting skills to dalits to understand legal documents and analyse various government documents and awareness and capacity building of potential dalit leaders are some other possible intervention areas for the NGOs and CBOs. As has been stated earlier, the dalits are further stratified in various endogamous sub-castes, the external factors try to exploit the situation. Hence, what is important are the awareness campaigns during elections and forging political unity among dalits so that they remain united before, during and after the elections to avoid division among them and cannot be exploited.

To help dalits fight the atrocities NGOs/CBOs could contribute by providing social security to dalit community or canvassing 1985 Atrocities Act, and make dalits aware about it. Positive reconstruction of social history of dalits is far more important a task. Providing legal security is another important intervention for the civil society. This can be done through networking among various stakeholders and advocacy, and providing liaison linkages to dalits. Providing legal guidance and counselling on legal issues while dealing with the government officials is an important activity for the civil society. In short, what is significant in the given context is how to make the environment conducive for the dalit in the leadership role in panchayats, so as to have the qualitative representation of these hitherto marginalised sections of the society in the decision. making process. Quantitative aspects have long been met with.

PRIs and the Civil Society

Though PRIs have provided adequate space for the marginalised sections of the society through reservation, yet some barriers remain – principal among these being low levels of literacy, domination by village elite, lack of awareness, corruption and prevalence of patriarchal values. Compounding this is the lack of, or unavailability of adequate information, on PRIs. This has the effect of diluting the positive dimensions of the Constitutional Amendment.[31]

The inefficiency and the unresponsiveness of the state have led to a crisis of the state institutions. The failure of government agencies to protect the interests of the underprivileged groups has created a situation in which the disillusionment of marginalised groups and their consequent alienation from the process of governance has become conspicuous. It is in this context that civil society space becomes the arena for voluntary groups to raise their voices. Hence, the growing non-accountability of the state to citizens became the driving force of civil society.[32]

In the context of the PRIs acquiring a constitutional status, with time, these local bodies began to be treated as the third tier of implementation of development policies and programmes designed by higher tiers of government. This negates the essence of local bodies as institutions of local self-governance. Needless to state the lacking information flow, funds, lack of linkages between the three tiers and transparency in functioning, and coupled by bureaucratic procedures and non-accountability of line department officials. This reflects the inefficiency and unresponsiveness of the institution to the interest of the people. Hence, the civil society initiatives are concerned with the gap between what is constitutionally provided, and its frequent violations, appropriation of developmental benefits by the dominant groups, and the non-delivery of basic services.

Panchayats and civil society

The rural decentralised governments in the form of Panchayats which were revived in the late fifties on the recommendations of the Balwantrai Mehta Committee prepared the ground for participation of people and their organisations in the developmental processes. The series of rural developmental initiatives from sixties, especially with the adoption of the target group approach emphasising the targeting growth to weaker sections and backward sub-regions, gave primacy to decentralised planning. The latter emphasised participation of people, their organisations and NGOs in the planning and implementation processes, which in turn provided some space to civil society.[33] In its newly acquired posture, it is to play the role not only of assisting the panchayats by giving to them technical inputs on the basis of their own analysis of the prevailing socio-economic situation, but also to motivate people to participate in the development process including monitoring of, and taking up development projects for, the benefit of the weaker sections and backward sub-regions. In other words, the civil society is expected to play the role of capacity building among panchayat functionaries.[34] Increasing participation, especially of women and marginalised sections of the community, is another arena that civil society has influenced, and implemented programmes. Identifying local needs, prioritising the same and implementing programmes have been possible when capacity-building interventions have been made in collaboration with local civil society organisations.

Civil society intervention has enabled local bodies to engage in participatory bottom-up micro-planning processes to determine priorities and design programmes that address locally appropriate needs of different segments of society. This capacity-building intervention also enables greater engagement of different sections of the community/society in the planning process, thereby enhancing ownership of plans and programmes implemented by local bodies.[35] Promotion of citizen participation also requires sustaining authentic and timely information. Several interventions demonstrate the role of civil society in assuring timely information for informed and legitimised decision-making by local bodies.

Another important area of contribution by civil society organisations in effective functioning of the PRIs has been the capacity building of newly elected leadership, especially in the case of women, dalits, tribals and other weaker sections of the society. Building their confidence, providing timely information, enhancing their skills and creating opportunity for continuous learning for them, are some of the contributions that civil society organisations have made and will make in the future.[36]

Ongoing support is provided by civil society organisations to other voluntary organisations and community-based organisations interested in strengthening PRIs. Continuous support is also given to the Gram Sabha in rural areas to make it an effective, articulate and vibrant assembly. Internal divisions based on caste, gender, education, political affiliation and religious persuasion have created impediments in local governance. Unless these differences can be overcome through sustained action by civil society organisations, Gram Sabhas are unable to play an effective role in promotion of local self-governance.

By Way of Conclusion

In the final analysis, it is clear that the Ambedkarite agenda of caste mobilisation for emancipation has been hopelessly overtaken by caste politics of power consolidation, and the terms and conditions under which the current mobilisation of marginal communities is occurring, is likely to be more harmful than beneficial to their larger interest.[37] Politics has enlarged ethno-politicised identity, but it stands internally fissured and fragmented by the sharp political antagonisms between the major caste groups, sharp socio-economic differentiation within each of the scheduled castes, gender contradictions and the intense competitions that have surfaced.

This macro picture of Maharashtra politics, though has bearing on the micro situation, presents the challenging circumstances, but certainly not gloomy. It is evident that effective or ineffective women and dalit leadership is not the result of any one factor, but a combination of factors cutting across socio-economic conditions, culture, gender, caste and class. Hence, with all the constraints and hindrances, building of competencies and capacities through the process of political education for both women and men is seen as a must for democratic deepening, development of critical consciousness, and the recovery and development of people's knowledge. With this model, it is not only a recognition of the importance of political learning in the process of social change, but also affirmation that such learning begins with the reflection by the people upon their own experiences. Participatory training, awareness programme related to panchayats, distribution of simplified information are some of the strategies adopted by both governmental agencies and non-governmental organisations.

As regards the key question with which this paper has been initiated, i.e., whether affirmative action or reservation has helped dalits cross caste barriers, the analysis has revealed that reservation policy based on caste and caste-based social order has provided avenues of social and economic mobility through educational and occupational opportunities to the lower underprivileged castes. As regards reservation in the institutions of local self-governance, there is no or cannot be a direct or apparent opposition to the provision. There could be latent ideas against reservation for dalits, as this would help them climb the social ladder through political steps, however, these perceptions have largely remained unexpressed and latent. Whenever it has been expressed, it has taken many forms. On the face of it, reservation for the marginalised and underprivileged has been a more or less accepted fact.

One may conclude that the positive discrimination has provided an opportunity to the lower sections of the society to achieve those qualities and attributes on which the modern industrial society lays premium.[38] It requires a two-pronged strategy to bring out the lower castes out of their ascriptive syndrome. On the one hand, not making provisions for social justice but education of these groups through reservation, fee concessions, stipends, fellowships, etc. will help in self-emancipation and empowerment, despite poverty and adversity. However, this is one aspect of the desired social development.

On the other hand, if this process of social development needs to be long sustainable, then, the short route through the identity politics is certainly not the answer. It provides only the limited explanation and settlement. The long-term impact cannot be achieved until the access to natural resources, particularly the land resources are redistributed among the dalits and a class-based analysis is sought as a framework to understand the problem and answers are addressed and provided to in the same framework. Only these two strategies will enable the socially and economically peripheral section of the society to organise and fight their discrimination and subjugation and have a meaningful participation the governance process at the rural level.

Appendix
An Overview of the Findings[39]

A. Respondents' Profile

- *Major sub-castes among SCs taken up for Study*: Mahar, Matang, and Chambhar.
- *Total number of respondents*: 174
  - (68 women/76 men)
  - (129 SC/45 non-SC)
  - (53 SC/15 non-SC women and 16 SC/30 non-SC men)
- *Age profile of the respondents*:
  - < 30 years 43
  - 31 - 40 years 77
  - 41 - 50 years 46
  - > 50 years 8
- *Marital status of the respondents*:
  - Married: 170
  - Unmarried/Other: 4
- *Educational profile of the respondents*:
  - Illiterate 82
  - Primary and less 30
  - Up to X 36
  - Up to XII 9
  - Graduates 9
  - Post-Graduates 6
  - Professionals (Doctors) 2
- *Profession/Occupation of the Respondents*
  - Agriculture 91
  - Agricultural labourer 35
  - Service 33
  - Business 6
  - Agriculture/Business 2
  - Any other (Professionals etc.) 7

- *Average annual income of the respondents:*
    - Rs. 10000 and less 104
    - Rs. 10001 - Rs. 20000 33
    - Rs. 20001 - Rs. 60000 30
    - Rs. 60001 and more 10
- *First timers among dalit leaders* – 78 per cent; old or second timers – 22 per cent.
- *Various capacity building trainings received by the elected representatives*:
    - *Yes* dalits: 25 %
Non-dalits: 75 %
    - *No* dalits: 75 %
Non -dalits: 25 %

B. Has Reservation Helped Dalits Cross Caste Barriers?

- *Positive implications of the* dalits *in the panchayat process*: Yes: 56%, No: 44%
- *Necessary conditions for effective functioning of dalits in the leadership role:*
    - Knowledge of rules and Regulations of the panchayats: 85%
    - Knowledge of administration: 75%
    - Administrative support: 55%
    - Political knowledge and support from leaders: 60%
- *Any background in the political process of the self or the family and political affiliations* (asked only to the elected representatives):
    - Yes: 45%, No: 55%
    - Congress (I): 45%, NCP: 40%, BJP: 5%, Shiv Sena: 5%, RPI: 5%
- *Kind of support received by those affiliated* (asked only to the elected representatives):
    - Financial: 28%
    - Declared candidate of the party: 25%
    - Campaign: 32%
    - No support: 10%

- Any other: 5%
- *Dependency of the* dalits *for their livelihood on the non*-dalits:
  - Among dalit respondents: Yes: 75%, No: 25%
  - Among non-dalit respondents: Yes: 45%, No: 55%
- *Is dalit community further stratified from within on sub-caste, political, economic basis*:
  - Among dalit respondents: Yes: 45%, No: 55%
  - Among non-dalit respondents: Yes: 85%, No: 15%
- *Does this division affect their leadership role*:
  - Among dalit respondents: Yes: 25%, No: 75%
  - Among non-dalit respondents: Yes: 65%, No: 35%
- *How are the relationships of the dalit sarpanch with other members– both dalits and non-dalits, elected and Gram Sabha:*
  - Very Good: 5%
  - Good: 55%
  - OK: 20%
  - Not satisfactory: 20%
- *How are the relationships of the non-dalit sarpanch with other members – both dalits and non-dalits, elected and Gram Sabha:*
  - Very Good: 25%
  - Good: 45%
  - OK: 25%
  - Not satisfactory: 5%
- *Support required by the* dalits *in PRIs*:
  - Cooperation from the leaders at the higher tiers: 15%
  - Spread of education: 95%
  - Capacity building: 90%
  - Resolve issues related to economic difficulties: 55%
  - Support of family and larger community, not necessarily his own community: 70%
  - Support from his own community: 55%
  - Honorarium: 45%

- *Suggestions for strengthening the role of dalits in PRI*:
    - Sensitisation and awareness on the necessity of the dalits' leadership role in the community at large: 30%
    - Spread of education – both formal and political for the dalits: 80%
    - Political organisations for forging unity among the dalits: 25%
    - Measures for poverty eradication, especially among dalits for self-sustenance and self-dependence: 85%
    - Easy access to various developmental schemes and programmes to dalit leadership: 60%
    - Association of sarpanchas: 10%
    - Capacity building: 75%
    - Specific training needs for the dalits to be recognised and modules be created with a proper follow-up schedule: 15%
- How does organisation building help dalit leadership:
    - Build pressure groups of dalits: 50%
    - Forge unity among dalits: 65%
    - Solving problems of dalits: 45%
    - General good of the dalit community: 75%
    - Equitable and speedy justice: 30%

C. What needs to be done?

- *The present role played by the NGOs/CBOs in empowering dalit community*:
    - Big brotherly and patronising on the one hand and guiding on the other: 25%
    - Getting the wider community accept the role of dalits in all social, economic, and cultural activities: 40%
    - Encourage dalits for good work: 20%
    - Helping the dalit community resolve their own issues: 30%
    - Helping the dalit community implement developmental schemes: 40%
    - Extending financial assistance to initiate income generation activities, but without creating dependency among them: 10%
    - Capacity building and enhancing leadership qualities: 65%

    - Spread literacy/education (formal/political) among dalits: 35%
    - Bridge the gap between dalit community and government officials and thus accessing relevant information to the dalit community: 20%
    - Empowering dalits to tackle and address unjust situations: 10%
    - Advocacy for policy changes for the grassroots development: 10%
    - General awareness of dalit community: 55%
    - Capacity building of the dalit elected representatives especially on PRI subject: 75%
- *Contributions expected from NGOs/CBOs in empowering dalit community (except training inputs):*
    - Set up a help line desk at the taluka/district level to provide all sorts of assistance to the dalits: 10%
    - Conduct studies on dalit community, implement recommendations for them, and also influence policies: 5%
    - To reinforce dalit's cause, advocacy, lobbying and networking on the issues: 20%
    - Initiate activities for income generation tapping locally available resources for sustainability, and if needed, provide financial assistance towards the purpose: 45%
    - To have an overall development community, help them plan in a sustainable way, prioritising economic issues: 30%
    - Identification of potential future leaders from dalit community, which should start from the schools itself: 25%
    - Action oriented active support for the preservation of the dalits' rights: 30%
    - Informing dalit community regarding developmental schemes and help them implement it: 55%
    - Spread literacy/education to the dalits: 75%
    - Moral support to the dalit community in their activities: 65%
- *Contributions of NGOs/CBOs in facilitating dalit's political role:*
    - Having identified specific political needs of the dalit community, prepare training module and impart it to the dalits: 35%

  - Spread of political literacy: 45%
  - Imparting skills to dalits to understand legal documents and analyse various government documents: 55%
  - Advocacy for policy changes at the higher level: 10%
  - Launching campaigns for dalits political rights to have impact at the micro level: 25%
  - Awareness campaigns during elections: 65%
  - Awareness and capacity building of potential dalit leaders: 75%
  - Forge political unity among dalits so that remain united before, during and after the elections: 65%
- *Contributions of NGOs/CBOs in providing social security to dalit community*:
  - Canvass 1985 Atrocities Act, and aware dalits about it: 60%
  - Positive reconstruction of social history of dalits: 10%
  - Awareness of dalit community on the provisions of social security for dalits in the Constitution: 40%
  - Forge political and social unity among dalits: 60%
  - Assuring dalit community of the support of the NGOs/CBOs: 55%
  - Social security among dalits through spread of education: 75%
  - Social security through resolving issues related to economic insecurities: 25%
  - No role at the policy level but can influence policy by advocacy and lobbying: 10%
- *Contributions of NGOs/CBOs in providing legal security to dalit's political role*:
  - Through networking among various stake-holder and advocacy: 30%
  - Awareness on different laws: 70%
  - Providing liaison linkages to dalits: 10%
  - Providing legal guidance on legal issues while dealing with the government officials: 75%
  - Providing legal counselling: 55%
  - Action support: 40%

Notes

1. Homan, G.C., 1961, *Social Behaviour: Its Elementary Forms*, New York, Harcourt, p. 23.
2. Gill, Manmohan S., 2002, "Reservation-An Affirmative Action of Social Justice", *Social Change*, vol. 32, nos. 1-2, March- June, p.27.
3. Gill, *ibid.*, p. 28.
4. Sheth, D.C., 1987, "Reservation Policy Revisited", *Economic and Political Weekly*, vol. XV, no. 14, p. 1312.
5. Pawar, I.D., 1990, "Reservation and its Justification", *Kranti Jyoti*, p. 23.
6. Thorat, Sukhadeo, 1998, "New Economic Policy and its Impact on Employment and Poverty of the Scheduled Castes: Some Observations", *Ambedkar Journal of Development and Justice*, vol. 6, p. 34.
7. Krishna, Harsh, 2002 "Untouchability and Atrocities", in Shah, Ghanshyam (ed.), *Dalits and the State*, New Delhi, Concept Publishing Company, p. 275.
8. Census of India, special table on SCs and STs, 2001.
9. Census Report (1981), *Census of India*, Maharashtra, Series 12, Part IX (ii), Special Tables.
10. Lele, Jayant, 1990, "Political Mobilisation in Maharashtra" in Frankel, Francine and M. S. A. Rao (eds.), *Dominance and State Power in Modern India*, vol. 2, Delhi, Oxford University Press, p. 117.
11. Desarda, H.M., 1994, "Maharashtra's Economy: Myth and Reality", *Economic and Political Weekly*, vol. XXIX, no. 26, June 25, pp. 1565-68.
12. Palshikar, Suhas, 1994, "Politics in Maharashtra: Arrival of 'Bahujan' Idiom", *Indian Journal of Political Science*, vol. LV, no. 3, p. 39.
13. Velaskar, Padma, 2000, "The Politics of Untouchability and Social Change: A Study of the Scheduled Castes of Maharashtra", *Journal of Indian School of Political Economy*, vol. 12, nos. 3&4, July-December, pp. 473-99.
14. Dev, Mahendra S., 1995, "Alleviating Poverty: Maharashtra Employment Guarantee Schemes", *Economic and Political Weekly*, vol. XXX, no. 41-42, October 14-21, pp. 2663-76.
15. Omvedt, Gail, 1994, *Dalits and Democratic Revolution: Dr. Ambedkar and the Dalit Movement in Colonial India*, New Delhi: Sage Publication, p. 27.
16. Omvedt, Gail, 2002, "*Ambedkar and After: The Dalit Movement in India*", in Shah, Ghanshyam (ed.), *Social Movements and the State*, New Delhi, Sage Publications, p. 297.

17. Abraham, A., 1978, "A Report from Marathwada", *Economic and Political Weekly*, vol. XIII, no. 36, September, pp. 1536-40; also, Guru, Gopal, 1991, "Dalit Killings in Marathwada", *Economic and Political* Weekly, vol. XXVI, no. 51, December 21, pp. 2926-30.
18. Velaskar, 2000, *op. cit.*
19. Velaskar, Padma, 1998 (b), "Caste-Patriarchy and the Dalit Women's Subordination: Towards a Theoretical Framework", Sugava (Dr. Ambedkar Special Issue), pp. 54-67.
20. Narayana, R., 1978, "Social Background of Scheduled Caste Lok Sabha Members, 1936-71", *Economic and Political Weekly*, vol. XII, no. 37, 16 December, pp. 875-78.
21. Sisikar, V. M., 1995, *Politics of Modern Maharashtra*, Bombay, Orient Longman, p. 46.
22. Velaskar, 2000, *op. cit.*
23. Gokhale, Jayashree, 1993, *From Concessions to Confrontations: The Politics of an Indian Untouchable Community*, Bombay, Popular Prakashan, pp. 25-31.
24. Palshikar, Suhas, 1994, "Politics in Maharashtra: Arrival of 'Bahujan' Idiom", *Indian Journal of Political Science,* vol. LV, no. 3, pp. 37-45.
25. Nigam, Aditya, 2002, "In Search of Bourgeoisie: Dalit Politics Enters a New Phase", *Economic and Political Weekly*, vol. XXXVII, no.13, March 30, p. 1193.
26. Vora, Rajendra and Suhas Palshikar, 1996, *Maharashtratil Sattanantar* (Marathi), Mumbai, Granthali, pp. 98-99.
27. Rai, Manoj, Malini Nambiar et al., (eds.), 2001, *The State of Panchayats: A Participatory Perspective*, New Delhi, PRIA, p. 109.
28. Kumar, Santosh, 2001, Motion of No Confidence against Sarpanchs in Tuljapur Taluka: A Study Report, (Mimeograph), Tuljapur, Rural Campus – TISS.
29. Ibid.
30. Ibid.
31. Kripa, A. P. and Ganesh Prasad, 2000, "The Message of Panchayati Raj", *Frontline*, April 28, cited in *ibid.*, p. 233.
32. Tandon, Rajesh and Ranjita Mohanty, 2000, "Civil Society and Governance Research Studies in India: Preliminary Findings", draft of the paper, cited in *ibid.*, p. 234.
33. Aziz, Abdul, 2002, "Democratic Decentralisation and Civil Society", *Social Change*, vol.32, no.1-2, March-June, pp.135-46.
34. Ibid.

35. Tandon, Rajesh, 2000, "Partnership with Civil Society, Local Governance and Sustainable Economic Development". Paper presented at Commonwealth Local Governance Conference, September 12-14, cited in Rai, *op. cit.*
36. Velaskar, *op. cit.*
37. Zelliot, Eleanor, 2001, *From Untouchable to Dalit: Essays on Ambedkar Movement*, New Delhi, Manohar, pp. 48-49.
38. Gill, *op. cit.*
39. For a detailed information on these findings, please see, Kumar Santosh, 2003, *"Dalit Leadership in Panchayats: A Situational Analysis of Maharashtra"*, A Study Report, Tata Institute of Social Sciences, Rural Campus, Tuljapur, Study Conducted for PRIA, New Delhi.

12

New Panchayat Raj System in India as an Agency of "Bottom-up Approach" to Rural Development

A Review

Kunj Bihari Nayak

The passage of the 73rd Constitutional Amendment in 1992 was a turning point in the history of rural development in India. In fact, it has evolved as a watershed in the history of decentralised governance, planning and development of rural society in the country. It paved the way for a fundamental change in the way the public goods and services are delivered in rural areas of India. Since then, more than a decade has been passed, crores of rupees have invested and plenty of experiments have been made, but basic contradictions, which were haunting the rural self-governing institutions of India in the past, have continued to prevail. The success and failure of the system in the country varies from region to region and from state to state depending on the nature of their political economy, social structure and cultural diversity. An attempt has been made in this paper to critically view the system of Panchayat Raj in India – its evolution, transformations, contradictions, scope and limitations for sustainable rural development – on the basis of reviewing mainly secondary literature.

Origin and Growth of Panchayat Raj System in India

Since ancient times, a number of systems of community-based management of local affairs had been evolved in India. These institutions, in most of the country, were known as 'panchayats' which literally means a council of five persons. Their functions mainly focussed on local governance akin to what was developed in other countries during their agrarian phases like the Russian 'Mir', the German 'Mark' and the medieval 'Manor' of England. In most parts of India, however, the panchayat system was based on the traditional caste system, social status and family-kinship relations. The concept of 'local self-government' was first introduced in the urban areas and later in rural areas during the British rule in India, particularly in the later half of the 19th century. The colonial rulers constituted municipal corporations around the trading centres as early as in 1687 (Madras). In 1870, Lord Mayo got a resolution passed by his council for decentralisation of powers in order to bring about administrative efficiency. After a decade, during Lord Ripon's Viceroyship in 1882, the British government passed a resolution for providing local board with elected leaders (Mathew, 2003:155).

The apologists of the colonial rule in India generally aver that whatever might be the shortfalls of colonialism, the British government attempted to modernise various institutions of Indian society. Since then, it took more than one hundred year for the local self-government bodies to become a part and parcel of the Indian Constitution. These bodies are termed as 'panchayats'. Although the concept of 'self-governing system' and the welfare of villages were at the centre stage of the Indian Independence Movement, led by Mahatma Gandhi, but when the Constitution of Independent India was being drafted, they did not figure in its main body, except a reference in the Directive Principles of State Policy. But, the Directive Principles of State Policy are not justifiable. While Article 40 of the Indian Constitution says: "The State shall take steps to organise village panchayats and endow them with such power and authority as may be necessary to enable them to function as units of self-government." Even though no state government took Article 40 so seriously as expected. The Indian nation-state was functioning as a federation only at two levels – union and the states. The

Constitution, adopted by the Constituent Assembly on November 26, 1949, envisaged a strong Centre (Mathew, 2003: 155-62) and left the states at the periphery.

Even at the time of independence, the rulers of India and political leaders did not think it necessary to build up an alternative system of new institutions or to reform the existing ones for an independent local governance. Because, the most important goal for them was the task of nation-building and maintaining the unity and integrity of the country. This concern was so strong that the Indian Constitution retained a unitary bias and created a federal structure in which even the autonomy of the states was unreasonably curbed and the question of decentralisation of power at local level did not arise. Even, the pressure to retain the existing pre-independence system of district governance came from one of the main architects of our Constitution, Dr. B.R. Ambedkar, who argued against the empowerment of Village Panchayats on the ground of fear that the landed gentry of the upper castes would invariably dominate them and use them for perpetuating the exploitation of the lower castes people in particular and the poor in general (Bandyopadhyay et al., 2003: 3986).

The original Constitution of India had retained an entrenched administrative system at district and block levels. But, there was a strong pressure to retain the pre-independence, system in independent India. The system of local governance which was adopted, so much deep-rooted in the elitist understanding that the local self-government institutions became massively defunct in functioning and were accustomed to serve under the surveillance of local bureaucracy. In fact, the emergence of Panchayat Raj system in independent India could be seen from the point of view of development. The Government of India, after the transfer of power from the British in 1947, decided upon a path of major social and economic transformation in which the Union Government played a major role through a chain of hierarchical western bureaucracy.

Soon after independence, the Community Development Programme (CDP) emerged as the first gigantic project of rural development. It was launched on October 2, 1952. The First-Five Year Plan, through CDP, sought to initiate a process of transformation of social and economic life of the village India by increasing agricultural production, by promoting transport and communication facilities, and by providing adequate health and hygiene as well as educational services to the rural people. It was envisaged as a programme of aided self-help for individual and collective welfare of rural people. As an aided programme, the CDP provided for infrastructural facilities, technical help and material assistance to accelerate the development activities in the rural areas. In order to achieve the above-mentioned objectives, it heavily banked on extension service with block as its main unit of operation. Generally, a block consisted of 100 villages with an area of 150 to 200 square miles and a population of 60 to 70 thousands. But, in actual definition, it varied from region to region depending on the nature of communities concentrated or spread in an area.

The Second Five-Year Plan, however, simply extended the CDP with a view to cover every village in India. Towards the end of 1950s, it was observed that the programme was dominated by the official bureaucracy which, in reality, had complete control over its planning, decision-making and implementation. Soon after, it was discovered that its performance left much to be desired. While diagnosing the failure of CDP, the Balwantrai Mehta Committee attributed it to lack of people's participation in planning, decision-making and implementation of the programme. Thus, the Committee recommended that there should be decentralisation of planning and administration for the effective implementation of the programme. Accordingly, the CDP was put under the control of Panchayat Raj system as a formal organisation comprising the elected representatives of the people as well as an agency of democratic decentralisation for socio-economic development of rural people.

The Panchayat Raj system in independent India emerged as a system of local self-government. It stands for mainly decentralisation of power and administrative authority in the country. As a system of democratic decentralisation, the it emerged towards the end of 1950s mainly due to failure of CDP to achieve its desired objectives. Corresponding to the objectives of CDP, the Panchayati Raj system was based on the following principles:

(i) There should be a three-tier structure of local self-governing bodies from village to district level, with an organic linkage from the lower to the higher ones.
(ii) There should be a genuine transfer of powers and responsibilities to these bodies.
(iii) Adequate financial resources are to be transferred to these bodies in order to enable them to discharge their responsibilities.
(iv) All rural development programmes and welfare schemes at these levels should be channeled through these bodies.
(v) The system evolved should be such as to facilitate further decentralisation of powers and responsibilities in future.

However, the development administration remained with Panchayat Raj for a short period only, as Panchayat Raj eventually became defunct in many parts of rural India. The point needs to be emphasised here is that the basic motive for the support given to the panchayats was to enlist in a very limited way people's participation in a programme conceived and directed by the central government. Thus, legitimising a central government-led development programme was the hidden agenda behind the move. It is also not a surprising fact that out of three tiers of Panchayat Raj system, the Balwantrai Mehta Committee (1957) made the intermediary tier, namely, the Panchayat Samiti or the Block Panchayat, as the most powerful unit, which systematically marginalised both the Gram Panchayat and the Zilla Parishad because the block was chosen as a new administrative unit to implement the CDP.

Though the block was converted into an operational unit of the rural local power structure, but the definition of 'local' was determined by a bureaucratic fiat and was not left even to the imagination of the community. Though Pandit Jawaharlal Nehru considered the three-tier system of Panchayat Raj as a form of governance by the local self-governing institutions, but it was administered and controlled by the bureaucracy. In the meanwhile, the image of Panchayat Raj got transformed from an agency of decentralised development to more of a political body defining the new power structure of rural India. There was no attempt to replace the bureaucratic administration to democratic governance at the bottom level. The forces in favour of centralisation of power were so strong that even little concessions given to the first generation of panchayats were not tolerated for long (Bandyopadhyay et al., 2003: 3987).

Though the system had existed formally in most of the major states of India since the early 1950s, but in most states it was not an effective body of governance until the early 1990s. Even elections for the panchayat bodies were not regularly held for years and the panchayats did not assume any active role in the process of rural development (Chattopadhyay and Duflo, 2004: 980).

The system collapsed in almost all the states, except Maharashtra and Gujarat, soon after Nehru's death in 1964. The next decade was ruled by Indira Gandhi. Her tenure faced many political and economic problems like wars, internal threats, terrorism, inflation, communal conflicts, instability of government and period of emergency etc. Then, there was a period when other political parties strived to gain mass support for forming a government alternative to the dominant Congress. They promised to pursue some populist ideas including decentralisation and extension of local democracy. Realising the fault, the central coalition government formed another committee of eminent persons headed by Ashok Mehta in order to examine exclusively the question of institutionalising panchayats. This Committee also re-emphasised on the decentralisation of power. Because, by the end of 1970s, the lack of progress (in terms of outcomes) in the social sector, in areas like health and education, began to be taken seriously. Thus, the Ashok Mehta Committee, appointed by the Janata government in 1977-78, spoke strongly of the need for locally elected governments. The Committee made a number of recommendations for revitalisation of PRIs which included: (i) assigning more powers to PRIs; (ii) making Zilla Parishad as primary unit in PR system; (iii) political parties taking part in panchayat elections; and (iv) imparting training to panchayat members. Later, the Santhanam Committee was appointed to study the problems of resources and finances of PRIs. It also recommended measures like: (i) Giving powers to panchayats to levy special taxes based on land revenue, house tax etc.; (ii) sanctioning of grants to panchayats by state governments; (iii) handing over sources of revenue to PRIs;

(iv) evolving mutual financial relations between different levels of PRIs; (v) augmenting financial resources through gifts and donations; and (vi) setting up Panchayat Raj Financial Corporations to provide loans and financial assistance to panchayats and help them in providing basic amenities to villages (Ahuja, 1999: 336-37).

But, the Janata government that set up this committee fell shortly after and these recommendations were ignored by the Congress government that followed (Vyasulu, 2004: 2379-80).

Except appointing a committee, however, the coalition government of different political parties led by Janata Party did precious little to achieve the goal of democratic decentralisation. Only three states, viz., West Bengal, Andhra Pradesh and Karnataka, seriously accepted the recommendations of the committee and established or empowered their PRIs. In West Bengal and Andhra Pradesh, where regional opposition parties emerged with populist ideas and charismatic leadership by challenging the Congress Party. Only in Karnataka, there was a genuine attempt to develop autonomous local governing institutions at village and district levels. However, the experiment faced problems later when the party, which launched this programme of decentralisation, was voted out of power (Bandyopadhyay et al., 2003: 3987).

In the 1970s and 1980s, a series of movements occurred in different parts of the country based on ethnic, religious or linguistic assertions of regional communities who had developed a feeling of alienation from the mainstream Indian society. There were also militant movements in the north-east region, Kashmir and Punjab, besides the Gorkhaland movement, Jharkhand movement and Uttaranchal movement. The government was in difficulty in maintaining the unity and integrity of the country. The democratic republic of India was under stress and instability. In the mid-1980s, the danger of government's policy for maintaining India's multicultural society became apparent. Thus, a need was seriously felt to share power with the grassroots local communities. In the mid-1980s, the Congress Party was out of power in many states, though it continued to be in the government at the Centre. The opposition parties in different states were mounting pressures for more administrative and fiscal powers for the states and they were not ready to accept the centre's decision, which caused sufficient irritation to the central government. The Prime Minister was in danger as many stalwarts were forcefully asserting their views on national issues of integration, stability and progress (Bandyopadhyay et al., 2003: 3988).

Under this situation, it was thought by the central leaders that if decentralisation of powers takes place at local power structure, the autonomous local self-government institutions would create similar problems for the ruling opposition parties of the states, as these bodies would claim devolution of powers and resources from the states.

The idea to initiate a basic change in the administrative system at the district level and below – from a non-representative, autocratic and bureaucratic administration to a representative and responsive elected system of governance – was first mooted by former Prime Minister and the Congress Party President Rajiv Gandhi and it was placed before the conference of chief ministers by him for obtaining a consensus. The main reason behind this was his search for an efficient administrative delivery system. Initially, he had thought that if panchayats were used as supplementary to the existing administrative structure, the outreach of the government's development programmes could be enhanced and the leakage or misuse of huge resources for rural development could be curbed. Later, when he toured the entire country, and directly met the local leaders and interacted with the district collectors or magistrates in several regional seminars, then, he realised that there is a need of a systematic transformation of district administration from bureaucratic administration to democratic governance at the district level and below. Being a greenhorn in the political arena, Rajiv Gandhi could take an independent view and stridently advocated for strengthening local democracy (Bandyopadhyay et al., 2003: 3987). Even then, there were a number of causal factors, which led to the failure of PRIs in bringing about development in the country.

There were some crucial problems in the functioning of the Panchayat Raj system until early 1990s, which could be underlined as follows: (i) functions and powers given to panchayats were limited; (ii) panchayats were ill-equipped in terms of manpower in order to undertake planning; (iii) panchayats had no power to generate their own resources through taxation, etc.; and (iv) elections were not held on a regular basis. Therefore, the high expectations with regard to the panchayats were unfulfilled. The main reasons for the failure of the PRIs could be outlined as: (i) non-legalistic status of PRIs, (ii) irregular elections, (iii) frequent suppressions and suspensions, (iv) inadequate representation of the weaker sections, (v) insufficient powers given to panchayats, (vi) lack of financial resources, (vii) indifference and non-cooperation of the bureaucracy, (viii) lack of people's participation, and (ix) lack of genuine political will (Ahuja, 1999: 338). Barnabas (1998) has also identified five major causes for the failure of Panchayat Raj system before 73rd amendment. These are: (i) confusion about functions of PRIs; (ii) absence of autonomy; (iii) confusion in administrative arrangement; (iv) absence of coordination; and (v) fragmented and overlapping structure.

In 1984, the Prime Minister wrote to chief ministers to hold overdue elections to PRIs as well as to revitalise their functionings. Subsequently, two more committees were appointed in 1985 (G.V.K. Rao Committee) and in 1986 (L.M. Singhvi Committee). The former recommended the following measures: (i) PRIs have to be activated and provided with all required support in order to become effective organisations; (ii) PRIs at district and block levels should be assigned with the works of planning, implementation and monitoring of rural development programmes; and (iii) Block Development Office should be the spinal chord of the rural development process. The observations of the Singhvi Committee were as follows: (i) the PRIs were not functioning properly due to lack of political will; (ii) lack of evaluation and feedback; (iii) indifference to corrective measures; and (iv) reluctance of PRIs to raise revenue resources through exercising their taxing powers. Thus, the Singhvi Committee gave some suggestions: (i) locating proper means to ensure availability of adequate financial resources to PRIs; and (ii) making provisions for compulsory and optional levies (Ahuja, 1999:337).

In the early 1990s, while taking into consideration the views, recommendations and suggestions of these committees, the central government, led by BJP coalition, decided to amend the

Constitution, which was made by the Lok Sabha in December 1992, and by the Rajya Sabha in December 1993 and then after being ratified by 17 State Assemblies, it finally came to be known as the 73rd Constitutional Amendment Act, 1993. Practically, it came into force in 1994.

In this way, the Panchayat Raj system in India could be seen as evolved through six phases: (i) pre-formative phase, before independence; (ii) formative phase, between 1950-1960; (iii) readjustment phase between 1961-1964; (iv) critical phase between 1965-1985; (v) reformative phase between 1986-1993; and (vi) progressive phase, 1994 onwards.

Nature of Panchayat Raj System after 73rd Constitutional Amendment

The Parliament of India, on December 22-23, 1992, passed two Constitutional Amendments (73rd and 74th) and on April 24, 1993 they were incorporated as Part IX for the rural panchayats and Part IX-A for the urban municipalities. The salient features of the 73rd Constitutional Amendment are as follows: (i) formation of Gram Sabha at the village level; (ii) uniform three-tier system at village, block and district levels with exemption for intermediate level in states with a population of less than two million; (iii) direct election to all seats for all members at all levels; (iv) indirect elections for chairpersons at intermediate and apex levels (however, mode of election for the lowest level is left to the state; (v) reservation, on rotation basis, for the SCs and STs in proportion to their population both for membership as well as chairmanship of panchayats at all levels; (vi) reservation of not less than one-third of the seats and offices for women; (vii) tenure of each body at all levels as fixed for five-year term; (viii) fresh elections within six months in case of suppressions or dissolution of panchayat bodies; (ix) devolution of powers and responsibilities by the state in preparation and implementation of plans for economic development and social justice including implementation of schemes related to the subjects listed in the Eleventh Schedule of the Constitution; (x) setting up State Finance Commission, after every five years, in order to review the financial position of these institutions and to make suitable recommendations to the state on the distribution of funds among panchayats; (xi) setting up State Election Commission for holding panchayat elections under its superintendence, direction and control; (xii) while under the 74th Constitutional Amendment, a provision was made for constitution of District Planning Committee to prepare a Draft Plan of the whole district comprising panchayats as well as municipalities. Although this provision is a part of the 74th Amendment Act, all the states have been agreed to extend it to the 73rd Amendment Act (Pal, 2004:137).

The 73rd Constitutional Amendment Act (hereafter, also Central Act of 1992) was, in fact, a watershed in the history of decentralised governance, planning and development in India. As a land mark achievement, it has made the panchayats as the third tier of government with providing reasonable substance and content of powers and authority as well as creating adequate space for the empowerment of women and marginalised groups or communities in the Indian federal system. Following this episode, another Act was passed by the parliament under the name of Extension to the Scheduled Areas Act of 1996 (henceforth, also Extension Act of 1996) by which the decentralised democracy was extended to the Fifth Schedule areas of the states through the provisions of the panchayats. In December 1996, the parliament extended the 73rd amendment to the Schedule Fifth areas where tribal populations predominate (Pal, 2004:137). While the Extension Act of 1996 is an important step for enabling state legislatures to make laws for the well-being of the tribals that ensure their control and rights over natural resources as well as for conserving and preserving their identity and culture in a participatory manner through the institution of the Gram Sabha (Pal, 2004:138). The salient features of the Extension Act of 1996 could be identified as follows:

(i) Every village shall have a Gram Sabha consisting of persons whose names are included in the electoral rolls of the panchayats at the village level.

(ii) Reservation for the STs shall not be less than half of the total number of seats at all tiers of the panchayats. Reservation of the tribal communities shall be on the basis of proportion to their population. The chairmanship shall be reserved for the STs at all levels of panchayats. In case, some of the ST communities have no representation at intermediate (block or taluka) or district level panchayats, the state government shall nominate such underrepresented STs. But, such nomination should not exceed one-tenth of total number of elected members of the panchayats.

(iii) Every legislation on the panchayats in Fifth Schedule area shall be in conformity with the customary law, social and religious practices and traditional management practice of the community resources.

(iv) The Gram Sabha shall be competent enough to safeguard and preserve the traditions and customs of the people, their cultural identity, community resources and customary mode of dispute resolution.

(v) The Gram Sabha is empowered to approve plans, programmes and projects for social and economic development, to identify beneficiaries under the poverty alleviation and other programmes, and also to give certificate of utilisation of development funds for various plans and programmes.

(vi) The Gram Sabha or the Gram Panchayat at the appropriate level would be consulted before making the acquisition of land for development projects and before resettling or rehabilitating people affected by such development projects. However, actual planning and implementation of the projects shall be coordinated at the state level.

(vii) Recommendation of the Gram Sabha or the Gram Panchayat at the appropriate level is mandatory for the grant of prospecting licence or mining lease for minor minerals, and grant for the exploitation of minor minerals by auction.

(viii) The Gram Sabha and Gram Panchayats are endowed with powers to enforce prohibition or to regulate or to restrict the sale or consumption of any intoxicant, ownership of minor forest produce, to prevent alienation of land, to manage village markets, to exercise control over money lending, to exercise control over institutions and functionaries in all social sectors, to exercise control over local plans and resources for such plans including the Tribal Sub-Plans.

(ix) Planning and management of minor water bodies shall be entrusted to the panchayats at the appropriate level.

(x) The state legislatures may endow the panchayats with such powers and authorities, as that may be necessary to enable them to function as institutions of self-government. The statutes shall contain safeguards to ensure that the panchayats at the higher level do not assume the powers and authority of any panchayat at the lower level or of the Gram Sabha. So, the cardinal principle of allocation of functions has been provided to a greater extent in the Act itself.

(xi) The state legislatures shall endeavour to follow the pattern of the Sixth Schedule of the Constitution while designating administrative arrangements in the panchayats at the district level.

By introducing 73rd amendment to the Constitution, however, the Government of India has once again tried to revive and strengthen the Panchayat Raj system. Today, these democratic institutions have gained new contents. The Gram Panchayats, which constitute the lowest tier at the village level in the three-tier local government system, covers about 2,000-5,000 population in north India and about 10,000- 15,000 in south India. The next tier called as 'Panchayat Samiti' works at the intermediate level (at block\tehsil\mandal\sub-district level) and constitutes of about 40-45 panchayats on an average. The highest body of the Panchayat Raj system is known as 'Zilla Parishad' or 'Zilla Panchayat' is at the district level. At present, India has 594 districts (Mathew, 2003: 155-62).

The membership of these bodies, however, varies from region to region and state to state depending on the nature of constitution of population belonging to different communities and social categories of the society. In general, the Gram Panchayat consists of the elected representatives including those belonging to the SCs, STs, and women categories under reservation policy. Today, the PRIs are functioning in 22 out of 25 states and in six out of seven union territories of India, In 15 states, it is a three-tier system, in four states it is two-tier system and in three states it is one-tier system.

The functions assigned to panchayats may be classified as (i) obligatory, (ii) discretionary, and (iii) transferred functions. These include: providing civic amenities, infrastructural facilities and developmental activities. Broadly, these functions may be described as health and sanitation (control of epidemics, construction and maintenance of lavatories, maintenance of burial grounds, cleaning of roads, tanks, ponds and drains), public works (construction and maintenance of roads, drinking water pumps, wells and streetlights), agriculture and animal husbandry (distribution of improved seeds, and pesticides, planning for increasing agricultural production, arranging cattle fairs, improving cattle breeding, development of poultry and fishing), uplifting the weaker sections (arranging for their education, cultural activities and residential houses), and some miscellaneous works (meeting calamities, encouraging and strengthening cottage industries, strengthening co-operative societies, development of forests, welfare of women and children and adult education programmes). However, since their inception, the roles of panchayats have been gradually changed and the scope of their functioning has been enlarged (Ahuja, 1999: 337-38).

It is yet to be observed that to what extent, the 73rd amendment has been successful in achieving its fundamental objectives? Whether all the federal states in India have actually devolved powers and various functions to local self-governing institutions or not? Whether the reservation of seats for the STs, SCs, and other weaker sections including women, has practically helped them to improve their socio-economic and political status in rural India or not? Are there still forces continuing to inhibit in the genuine functioning of the PRIs in rural society? What is the current status of Panchayat Raj system in India? Possible answers to these questions could be explored in the section that follows.

Critical Observations of Some Studies and Comments

In the Panchayat Raj system, the most significant institution for direct people's participation is Gram Sabha (or Palli Sabha in Orissa, or Ward Sabha in Kerala or Gram Sansad in West Bengal) where the entire electorate actively participates in the debate, discussion and decision-making regarding development of village as a whole. In fact, all over India, the attendance of the people in these meetings has been unsatisfactory except that in Kerala. According to latest government data, even in the politically conscious state of West Bengal, the average percentage of attendance in the Gram Sansad meetings in May 2002 varied between 18 per cent in Jalpaiguri district and the low of 6 per cent in Howrah district. The percentage of women leaders' attendance was dismal. According to *Panchayat Raj Samachar* (November 2002, Kolkata), it varied between the high of 3 percent in Darjeeling, Cooch Behar, east Medinapur and Burdwan and the low of 1 per cent in North and South Dinajpur, Maldah, Howrah, Bankura, Purulia and Birbhum (Bandyopadhyay, et al., 2003: 3990-91).

After 73rd amendment, the Eleventh Schedule of the Constitution lists 29 items or functions that state legislatures could devolve to the local governments. In reality, most of the states have made such devolution as for mere ostentation. Some states and union territories have not yet fully transferred their earlier functions to local self-governing bodies in most of the states (Vyasulu, 2004:2383). However, only Karnataka, Kerala, Rajasthan, Sikkim, Tamil Nadu, West Bengal and Daman and Diu have transferred all 29 subjects. While Arunachal Pradesh, Assam, Bihar, Jharkhand, Goa, Gujarat, Andaman and Nicobar Islands, Chandigarh and Pondicherry have not devolved any function. The remaining states and union territories have transferred only some functions ranging from three in Dadra and Nagar Haveli to 25 functions in Orissa. Although several states have given a number of responsibilities to the panchayats, but these have not been put into practice. This, in turn, has adversely affected the efficiency and effectiveness of the panchayats (Pal, 2004:139).

According to Fernandes (2003:2873-74), "agrandiser government, in most states, continues to hold on to most powers, even as they have been formally devolved to local government through conformity legislations". In fact, the conformity legislations of most states have not significantly transformed the functional domains of Gram Panchayats, across the country. The studies conducted in Andhra Pradesh, Gujarat, Kerala, Madhya Pradesh,

Maharashtra, Tamil Nadu, Orissa, Punjab, Haryana, Assam and Goa also discovered the fact that most of the states granted a plethora of functional responsibilities without executive follow up of granting adequate powers, staff and additional financial resources. Bureaucracies in most of the states were indisposed to have elected PRIs. Quite obviously, the main issue was not devolution of additional responsibilities but granting them necessary powers, staff and funds within the present dispensation itself. Thus, it is evident that there is lack of political and administrative will in several states to strengthen their PRIs.

Although all the states have passed their conformity legislations within the stipulated time, but it is disheartening to note that most of the states passed them only on the eve of the deadline without having serious debate on the subject in their respective assemblies. This shows a lack of seriousness on the part of the states in piloting their legislation in conformity with the spirit of the Constitution (Pal, 2004:138).

Elections have been held, reservations for women and the depressed castes have been implemented, and finance commissions have been set up in almost all the states. These are formal steps required under the law. The 73rd amendment left it to the state assemblies to decide upon the details and the subjects which could be transferred and how. It was meant to provide flexibility to the states which differed from each other in so many ways. If any change needed, then, it could be possible only through the state assemblies (Vyasulu, 2004).

According to the Central Act, elections to all tiers of the Panchayat Raj had to be completed within six months of its coming into force. Even Article 243(N) also allowed the panchayats to complete their full term, if they were constituted immediately before enforcement of the Central Act. However, all the states and union territories, covered under the Central Act, have constituted the panchayats except Arunachal Pradesh, Jharkhand and Pondicherry. But elections were not held in time in a number of states. In most of the cases, the delay in holding elections was due to court cases, natural calamities or law and order problems. The Working Group on Decentralised Planning and Panchayat Raj for the Tenth Plan observes that "in most of the court cases, i.e., grievances of aggrieved parties related to reservation of seats for the SCs/STs/OBCs/ women, delimitation of constituencies, percentage of reservation of chairpersons from lower tier to higher tier, etc., the state governments have not pursued these pending court cases vigorously. This reflects the apathy of the states in ensuring participation of women and marginalised communities in their local self-governing bodies (Pal, 2004:139).

In most of the states, mere compliance with the law does not mean that local governments have begun to function. The existing governmental system is so large that its different arms speak with different voices. For instance, the Planning Commission has been urging for greater devolution of powers, while the Ministry of Rural Development has been insisting on the continued operation of the DRDAs, which systematically bypass local governments (Vyasulu, 2004:2381).

The DRDA, which shared major part of rural development budget, was not within the panchayat set up, though now it has been brought under the purview of Zilla Parishad. Though the Zilla Pramukhas are to be chairmen of DRDAs, which run all poverty alleviation programmes, yet in practice, they will only preside over the meetings of the governing councils of the DRDAs. While the financial powers will rest with the collector who would continue as the chairman of the Executive Committee of the DRDAs. Thus, the relationship between panchayats and DRDAs needs to be clearly specified (Ahuja, 1999:339-341).

In fact, the Panchayati Raj system, in its new incarnation, is designed to engage more as an agency of local self-government than as an agency of decentralised development in rural India. But, practically, the mode of delivering various rural development programmes and services continues to be bureaucratic even today (Sharma, 1995:77). Speedy development in rural areas depends on the quality of panchayat leadership and their involvement in local activities. The quality of leadership rests on the perception of panchayat leaders about their local problems which depends on their level of education, training, occupational pattern, age and frequency of their meeting with the common people. Furthermore, their efficiency also depends on level of income, sex and political alliance (Ghosh and De, 2003:135-48).

In 1998, a pilot training project was carried out by the Institute of Social and Economic Change, Bangalore in a district of Karnataka. with the help of modules and video documentaries while using locally available resource persons. The training methodology, developed in the project, was found to be appropriate, participatory and less time-consuming. A post-training evaluation of the project reveals that the training programme significantly contributed not only towards enhancing the level of awareness and self-confidence of local panchayat leaders but also towards improving their performance with regard to the provision of basic health facilities (Sekhar, 2002:359-377).

Though most of the states realised the problem of operationalisation and creation of a new tier of governance with a new set of elected representatives who had little previous experience and knowledge of governance, but they responded by designating certain institutions such as the State Institutes of Rural Developments (SIRDs) to undertake centralised two or three days training sessions in a classroom setting for the elected representatives. In some states, even some civil society groups were invited to help in the development modules and system of training of trainers (ToTs). But, given the mammoth task and the large number of elected representatives involved, the primary task of capacity building remained with the state government. In some states, non-governmental organisations (NGOs) like PRIA, Search, Rajiv Gandhi Foundation, and the UNICEF also contributed to some exercises of capacity building. However, despite the huge amount of energies and resources spent or invested by the state governments and other organisations, the capacity building of the panchayats remained weak and ineffective (Behar and Aiyar, 2003: 4937).

One of the most significant features of the 73rd amendment was the reservation of one-third seats for women in the panchayat bodies that has brought as many as 8,00,000 women into the formal political process. Besides, other hindering factors for their failure to perform their mandated roles, most of these elected women representatives (henceforth EWRs) had low capacities. The task of evolving a suitable future strategy for enhancing the capability of the elected representatives through training needs to be taken seriously (Pal, 2003:507).

The task of capacity building of these EWRs, therefore, became a vital responsibility of the pro-panchayat civil society organisations. By and large, the movement for networks of EWRs has been promoted by and unfolded in an environment dominated by civil society actors whose central focus is on governance issues and little effort has been made to include or interact with feminist groups or groups working on women's issues. There are a few cases where individuals from the feminist movement have informally contributed to these networks. On the other side, there is a growing success of networks of EWRs, which amply demonstrates the relevance of micro initiatives in institutionalising the Panchayat Raj system. While several of these networks were initially set up in order to equip EWRs with necessary skills and capacities, some of them have ventured into the political sphere (Behar and Aiyar, 2003: 4936-40).

Some recent studies in a few states have also observed other problems and given some suggestions for improvement in the functioning of the PRIs in the whole country as follows:

(i) Since 1978, in West Bengal, panchayats have played a significant role in the implementation of various anti-poverty programmes, i.e., land reform, delivery of credit and farm inputs, generating employment, establishing local infrastructural development projects, providing agricultural minikits and fiscal grants etc. A study (Bardhan and Mookherjee, 2004: 965-74), taking a sample of 89 villages covering four successive panchayat institutions, argues that while average level of poverty alleviation efforts within villages improved when land was distributed more equally, the poor became more literate, there were fewer low caste families and local elections were more contested. Another study by Chattopadhyay and Duflo (2004: 979-86) in two districts of West Bengal and Rajasthan maintain that the reservation of seats in PRIs introduced as a tool to ensure adequate representation and also assist in adequate delivery of local public goods to the disadvantaged sections of rural society. They suggest that a necessary condition for the efficacy of reservation policy in PRIs is that elected representatives have independent power and autonomy over and above not only the direct control of the villagers, but also they enjoy control over the bureaucracy, political party hierarchies and the local elite. The West Bengal government has made special legislation for effective functioning of PRIs in the state. However, a critique Bandyopadhyay (2003: 4825) charges: "In West Bengal, the legislation is creating tier after tier of non-functional Panchayati Raj bodies without resources, functions and functionaries. The creation of Village Development Committees (VDCs) under the West Bengal Panchayat (Amendment) Act, 2003 passed in July is a case in point. It is a grand exercise in shadow boxing."

(ii) The state of Gujarat does have a long tradition of PRIs. It is one of the few states that accepted panchayats as the self-governing institutions since pre-independence period. The PRIs in this state continued to function even when other states chose not to follow the Directive Principles of State Policy mentioned in the Constitution. This state made periodic reviews and changes in order to improve the Act, which regulated the functioning of panchayats. During last three decades, the Panchayat Raj system has brought about a certain degree of social transformation in Gujarat. Traditional leaders have got a setback. The women and Dalit leaders have gained self-confidence in the art of democratic parliamentary politics and have started to assert their rights, though in a small way. Young people have got some opportunities for participating in public affairs. New programmes have been initiated by local people in many villages. But, there is limited resources at the local level. The village communities do not enjoy control over public land, water and forest. The political power in planning is still largely concentrated in the union and state governments. The dominance of the upper castes has been challenged by the leaders of middle castes and OBCs. Though the small and marginal farmers, including the Dalits, have become members of panchayats, they have not been able to use their positions to improve their socio-economic status. Despite various measures, atrocities against the Dalits continue. Having only political positions in the panchayats do not necessarily empower them. In order to survive, the poor of these categories still depend upon those who control resources, especially upon the upper and middle strata of rural society (Joshi, 2003).

(iii) In the state of Maharashtra, politics has shown considerable transformation since 1960s when the Panchayat Raj system was introduced. A recent study by Ajit Kumar (2004:228-33) in Nagpur district shows that in the early years, caste considerations strongly influenced most of the decisions of the village panchayats. But, by the 1990s, institutional politics had a broader base which included many caste categories or groups. The author maintains, it may be too early to conclude that the feudal ethos of power is indeed giving way to a more modern orientation. Some studies have noted that the PRIs have been successful in bringing about qualitative changes in rural Maharashtra in terms of stimulating popular participation and local leadership. After 73rd amendment, the participation of the SCs, STs, women and the other weaker sections in the decision-making process of local bodies has considerably increased (Mohanty, 2003). A study by Patil (2003) in Kolhapur district reveals that though the women leaders in Maharashtra have been empowered but with some limitations in their role and status. In general, there is a mixed picture of both success and failure. Another study in the Latur district of Maharashtra by Kamble (2001) shows that after the implementation of the policy of reservation of 33 per cent of seats by the Government of Maharashtra, women in rural areas in the state are coming up to occupy leadership positions in PRIs. However, the goal of political empowerment of women does not end up only with their induction into the power positions in PRIs. The policy of political empowerment of women should aim at eliciting their active participation in the decision-making process in these institutions. After being elected for positions in these institutions, their actual role begins. The achievement of the goals of rural development depends on the active participation of the members of PRIs in the meetings of these bodies. Attending the meetings in these bodies could be considered as a pre-condition to exercise influence on the process of decision-making. Regularity in attending the meetings could be considered as an indicator of their involvement in decision-making, while women leaders' participation in the discussions in PRI meetings could be treated as an index of their active participation in decision-making. The findings of her study, however, reveal that majority (53 out of 175 or 30.3%) of the respondents' regularity in attending the PRI meetings was 'poor' (0 to 25% attendance), followed by those reporting 'low' (up to 50%) attendance and 'moderate' (up to 75%) attendance regularity in the attendance of the meetings. A very few respondents (20 or 11.5%) belong to the category of having 'high' regularity in attending the meetings. The variables, such as 'young age' (21 to 35 years), 'nuclear family structure', 'high educational level', 'high income level', and 'active family political background' were found to be positively associated with the respondents' regularity in attending meetings. The least regularity in attending meetings was observed in case of respondents belonging to poorest income category and various tribal categories. It was also observed that majority (nearly 62%) of the respondents take active participation in discussions while attending these meetings. The variables such as 'old age', 'higher levels of education', 'higher levels of income', and 'active family political background' are positively associated with respondents' active participation in the discussions in PRI meetings.

(iv) A study in Bidar district of Karnataka observes that after the 73rd amendment, the backward caste people seem to be learning more to wield political power at the grassroots level and in near future, they will dominate in the PRIs. Even women leaders have taken active interests in the administrative affairs denouncing the popular perception that they are mere dummies for their male relatives. On the dark side of the picture, it is observed that less than half of the OBC members have experienced caste discrimination, non-cooperation of officials and domination of local elite at the Gram Panchayat level. According to the OBC leaders, the transfer of power to the Gram Sabha has been harmful to the interests of the OBCs because it is just like conferring something by one hand and taking away that by another hand. The Gram Sabha, which is empowered through 73rd amendment, is predominantly controlled by the local/traditional elite and those with money and muscle power. It has to meet at least twice a year. In fact, it has become a farce in observing only a formality by proxy participation. It indicates that the purpose to decentralise power and development administration for the welfare of the underprivileged sections is in under threat (Bhatt, 1994; Bajpai and Verma, 1995; Bandhii, 2004:73).

(v) In the state of Orissa, the Panchayat Raj system has brought some changes in the local level politics. For instance, the reservation of one-third of total seats for women in the local self-government system has some implications for the empowerment of women. A study revealed that in 1994-95 around 66 per cent of women elected members in the state were from upper castes like Karans (Kayasthas and Khandaits). It also revealed that the percentage of non-SCs was 57 per cent in the post of vice-sarpanch which is higher than that of the SCs (28.6%) and that of STs (14.3%). While the lower castes dominated at the ward membership level in which the percentage of STs constituted 45.9 per cent. And that of the SCs was 27.3 per cent. In contrast, women leaders from the general castes constituted 27 per cent in the local self-government of Orissa (Mohanty, 1995: 3348). There are several factors responsible for the low participation of women and Dalits in the political process of the Orissa state such as (i) criminalisation and factionalisation of politics; (ii) emergence of religious fundamentalism; (iii) backwardness and underdevelopment of marginalised communities illiteracy as well as lack of their awareness regarding legal and economic aspects of society; (iv) gender bias in a patriarchal society; (v)

Adivasi-Dalit conflict in the electoral process where political choices are shaped primarily by factors internal to the social structures of villages; (vi) domination of upper and middle castes and classes in the state's politics; and (vii) political–economy of regional disparities within the state. Another recent study by Mohanty (2003) reveals that the PRIs in Orissa have not been able to pose a serious threat to the upper caste/class and the gender dominance, they have only generated a kind of consciousness among the marginalised groups regarding local governance. However, their participation in the elections, attendance and discussions in meetings and expression of viewpoints at various levels indicate some signs of changes in their living style and living standard. Today, rural people have stakes in the constituency level politics as the rural areas have frequently been entangled with developmental and ethnicity politics at the regional and national levels.

(vi) In the state of Madhya Pradesh, even today, the caste system defines social and political identity of rural people. The oppressed categories are represented by small sections from each group which are more or less integrated into the existing political system. The Panchayat Raj system serves as one of the instruments of this integration by opening the doors of opportunity for that small section of rural elite who in turn mobilise votes for the major political parties in the state. Whether the Congress or any other political party wins the coming assembly elections or not, the use of political decentralisation for the ruling class has been proved in reality (Kela, 2003: 2814). After all, the leaders of political elite have to change their former party membership and join the ruling party just for their self-aggrandisement. Under this situation, the limited fiscal and political decentralisation has not been able to bring any fundamental change in rural areas. Even, the problems of land reform, education and primary health are untouched by the Panchayat Raj system. The powers granted to the panchayats are narrow in scope. In actual terms, they usually involve little more than powers to decide how to implement various welfare schemes, use employment funds and select beneficiaries. The control of panchayats over the state functionaries is largely illusory. Since the state controls the flow of funds to the panchayats and also planning and implementation of all major development projects, the scope for the panchayat's autonomy is limited (Kela, 2003: 2814-16). Although Madhya Pradesh was the first state to set up three-tier Panchayat Raj system, its functioning has been severely affected by financial constraints and inadequate mobilisation of resources. Taxes assigned to them are by and large not too productive of revenue. PRIs should be enabled to levy local taxes on their own and mechanisms should be set up to ensure periodic re-evaluation of taxable properties (Palharya, 2003: 1024-28). The introduction of Gram Swaraj system by the Government of Madhya Pradesh on 26 January 2001 was most welcomed. While evidence from the field suggests that the system has made a slow and cautious beginning, the strong political will that was instrumental in conceiving and framing the system has not sustained itself during its implementation phase. On the contrary, it has been weakened mainly due to resistance from bureaucracy, lack of capabilities at the Gram Sabha level and inability of the governance systems to adapt to radical restructuring of the governance. However, the opportunities with direct democracy are still alive. It is critical for the state to invest substantial energies in revitalising, in order to comprehensively complement its ongoing efforts for effective governance where "people are viewed as solutions and not as problems" (Behar, 2003: 1925-27).

(vii) In the state of Haryana, the caste system and patriarchy in rural areas still exercise a stronghold on PRIs. In fact, it is making a mockery of decentralised governance. The caste prejudices emerged as a major stumbling block on the way of the functioning of Dalit women representatives of panchayats. The women elected representatives need adequate support systems (financial and legal) as well as education to make them effective leaders (Pal, 2004: 3581-83). Recently (on July 30, 2003), a three-judge bench of the Supreme Court upheld a Haryana government law prohibiting a person from contesting or holding the post of sarpanch or panch, if he/she had more than two children. The bench observed that "disqualification on the right to contest an election for having more than two children does not contravene any fundamental right, nor does it cross the limits of reasonability. Rather, it is a disqualification conceptually devised in the national interest". In fact, the Haryana order, demographically unnecessary, is not only a serious misreading of the relationship between population and resources, but also an agregious assault on democratisation which is proceeding fitfully in our country. Indeed, it is a thoughtless folly that laws, meant for empowering the Dalits, Adivasis, OBCs and other sections of the poor including women through PRIs, are being circumvented by these imaginatively anti-democratic population policies (Rao, 2003: 3452).

Experiences over the last ten years, however, show that the implementation of the 73rd amendment has been plagued by many problems and shortcomings. Broadly speaking, there are three main concerns that have emerged from the field experiences of working panchayats: (i) the inadequate functions, functionaries and funds made available to panchayats due to bureaucratic resistance and lack of political will; (ii) the overt or covert capture of panchayat institutions by local elite; and (iii) the lack of capacities of elected representatives and panchayat institutions to perform their constitutionally mandated tasks or responsibilities (Behar and Aiyar, 2003: 4937).

The main deficiencies in facilitating the potential of Panchayat Raj persist at three levels, i.e., state, PRIs, and society. The government at the state level, with a patrimonial perception of self and aggrandiser instincts, has pushed the 'self-governance participatory model' of the panchayats to the periphery, both at the level of discourse and praxis. This, coupled with conceptual inadequacies, epistemic as well as operational constraints, poor finances, and political interference – all have posed a serious challenge to the realisation of potential role as envisaged in the 73rd amendment. If Panchayat Raj system has to fulfil its fundamental goals of empowering the community, there is a need to recognise the primacy of societal well-being over individual interests and political goals. The PRIs have to transform themselves into community institutions fulfilling a societal contract with an all-inclusive participatory planning and associationalism as essential methodologies (Fernandes, 2003: 2873).

The concept of planning for economic and social development in rural areas is at the core of panchayat activities and it should be well enunciated. A second important focus should be in the area of mobilising local resources (Pal, 2003: 507-10), As already stated, the Eleventh Schedule of the Constitution lists 29 items or functions that state legislatures could devolve to the local governments. In reality, most of the states have made such devolution as a mere announcement. The state must desist from simultaneously functioning in the same sphere. Parallel institutions must be shut down, parastatals wound up or put under the control of local government. In fact, no state has taken action in this regard (Vyasulu, 2004:2383).

According to Vaddiraju and Mehrotra (2004:4139), since the enactment of the 73rd amendment, we find three broad views on the democratic practice of PRIs in India: (a) all the state Acts have been 'paper laws' and their implementation is nil (Upadhyay, 2002); (b) there has been institutional change and the impact of amendments is, to some extent, positive but that there is still a long way to go (Rai et al., 2001); and (c) local self-government in general and Panchayat Raj in particular should be made accountable. On the basis of field experience in mobilising and studying Gram Sabhas in some selected locations of Andhra Pradesh, Vaddiraju and Mehrotra suggest that strengthening people's participation in the Gram Sabha is a critical prerequisite for making panchayats accountable to people.

In fact, many of the arguments made in favour of participation do not capture the reality of the dynamics of community participation, as they exclude the inherent hierarchies, power differentials and socio-economic disparities in local communities. Thus, mere privileging the local people in policy formulations without understanding this important characteristic of local communities in rural India could mean the sanctioning of differences of money and social power which in turn could mean the exclusion of those who do not have such power (Puri, 2004:2511-17).

According to Mathew (2003:155), the institutionalisation of Panchayat Raj system, since 1990s, which has added greater momentum to the decentralisation process, has also had deeper implications for the human rights situation in India. Even as the democratic process has been extended, changes in the traditional society have invited conflicts and violence. The rights of the excluded people, particularly marginalised communities, had been violated over the years due to lack of democratic system of good governance at the community level where they could participate effectively. The system of local self-government, as manifested in the PRIs after 73rd amendment, has taken a leap forward in guaranteeing a life of dignity and respect to the citizens at the village level. It is with the increasing democratisation and intervention of civil society institutions that concern for human rights will assume its rightful place along with a vibrant as well as dynamic democracy.

Concluding Remarks

The Panchayat Raj system in India has evolved through five phases. On the one side, the new system after 73rd amendment to Indian Constitution in 1992-93 has been glorified by some social scientists, administrators, local elite and the well-off sections of our country—as being successful in bringing about actual decentralisation of power and as an attempt to improve the living standards of women, the SCs, STs and other vulnerable sections in the countryside.

While, on the other side, there are critiques who charge that the system has generated and sustained a number of problems in the rural society. Firstly, many elected women leaders seem to be like puppets dancing at the tune of their dominant male masters. While the patriarchal caste system continues to exercise its hegemony and influence over women's role and status because of which the elected women leaders have not been fully free to exercise their duties in their PRIs.

Secondly, in many places, the elected ignorant Dalit and Adivasi leaders have either continued to be influenced by the dominant leaders of mainstream society or they have been threatened to withdraw from their positions.

Thirdly, the reservation of seats for women, Dalits and Adivasis has often generated discontent among upper caste/class sections who have systematically and strategically created a space for conflict and violence in the rural society. However, the struggles of Dalits, Adivasis, women and the poor in general will determine the future of subaltern politics in rural India.

Fourthly, due to lack of sufficient financial support system, often elected leaders of PRIs either become accustomed to make black money out of PRIs funds or they feel discouraged to spend money from their own pocket for carrying on their official activities.

Fifthly, due to lack of will of the states to devolve their powers and functions to the PRIs and also the non-cooperative nature of Indian bureaucracy, the movement of democratic decentralisation is moving towards nowhere. However, the elected leaders can be truly empowered to work effectively only when proper legal and administrative training, sufficient financial support and cooperation of the police, court and bureaucracy are ensured.

Finally, without structural transformation through institutional reforms as well as a check on the intervention of party politics and politicisation of communalism, the Panchayat Raj system will be just "a new avatar with old wine in a new bottle". Besides, given this scenario, modern forces of social change like radical land reforms, welfare schemes, genuine cooperation of civil society, active role of mass media and authentic local bureaucracy as well as industrialisation in rural areas with a human value may not lead towards sustainable development in the countryside.

References

Ahuja, Ram, 1999, *Society in India*, Jaipur and New Delhi: Rawat Publications, pp. 335-41.

Bajpai, Ashok and M.S. Verma, 1995, *Panchayat Raj In India: A New Thrust*, Delhi: Sahitya Prakashan.

Bandhii, Madhusudana, 2004, "73rd Constitutional Amendment and Emerging Leadership Among the Other Backward Classes in PRIs: The Case Study of Bidar District of Karnataka", *Social Action*, 54(1), January-March.

Bandyopadhyay, D., S.K Ghosh and Budhadeb Ghosh, 2003, "Dependency Versus Autonomy: Identity Crisis of India's Panchayats", *Economic and Political Weekly*, XXXVIII (38), September 20, pp. 3985-91.

Bandyopadhyay, D., 2003, "The Caucus and the Masses: West Bengal Panchayat (Amendment) Act 2003", *Economic and Political Weekly*, November 15, pp. 4825-27.

Bardhan, Pranab and Dilip Mookherjee, 2004, "Poverty Alleviation Efforts of Panchayats in West Bengal", *Economic and Political Weekly*, February 28, pp. 965-74.

Barnabas, A.P. 1998, "Good Governance at Local Level", *Indian Journal of Public Administration*, July-September.

Behar, Amitabh, 2003, "Madhya Pradesh: Experiment with Direct Democracy", *Economic and Political Weekly*, May 17, pp. 1925-27.

Behar, Amitabh and Yamini Aiyar, 2003, "Networks of Panchayat Women: Civil Society Space for Political Action", *Economic and Political Weekly*, XXXVIII(47), November 22, pp. 4936-40.

Bhatt, G.D., 1994, *Emerging Leadership Pattern in Rural India: An Empirical Study*, New Delhi: M.D. Publications.

Chattopadhyay, Raghabendra and Esther Duflo, 2004, "Impact of Reservation in Panchayati Raj: Evidence from a Nationwide Randomised Experiment", *Economic and Political Weekly*, XXXIX (9), February 28, pp. 979-986.

Fernades, Aureliano. 2003, "Aggrandiser Government and Local Government", *Economic and Political Weekly*, Vol. XXXVII, (27), pp. 2873-74.

Ghosh, B.N. and U.K. De, 2003, "Leadership and Performance of Panchayat in Rural Development: An Experience From Tripura", *Man & Development*, XXV(4).

Joshi, Satyakam, 2003, "Panchayat Raj Leadership in Gujarat", a Seminar Proceedings, April-28-29,2003, TISS: Mumbai.

Kamble, Archana (Jagatkar), 2001, Women's Leadership in Panchayat Raj System: A Sociological Study, unpublished Ph.D thesis submitted to Department of Sociology, Shivaji University, Kolhapur.

Kela, Shashank, 2003, "Madhya Pradesh: Towards Elections: Disaffection and Co-option", *Economic and Political Weekly*, July 5, pp. 2814-16.

Kumar, Ajit, 2004, "Politics in Three Villages: A Study Nagpur District", *Economic and Political Weekly*, January 17, pp. 228-33.

Mathew, George, 2003, "Panchayati Raj Institutions and Human Rights in India", *Economic and Political Weekly*, XXXVIII (2), January 11, pp. 155-56.

Mohanty, B.B., 2003, "Panchayat Raj in Maharashtra and Orissa: An Overview", a Seminar Proceedings, April-28-29, 2003, TISS: Mumbai (see also in IASSI, 2003).

Mohanty, Vidyut, 1995, "Panchayat Raj Elections in Orissa", *Economic and Political Weekly*.

Palharya, Shakun, 2003, "Madhya Pradesh: Decentralised Governance Hampered by Financial Constraint", *Economic and Political Weekly*, March 15, pp. 1024-28.

Pal, Mahi, 2003, "Haryana: Capacity Building of Panchayats: Tasks Ahead", *Economic and Political Weekly*, February 8, pp. 507-510.

– 2004, "Haryana: Caste and Patriarchy in Panchayats", *Economic and Political Weekly*, August 7, pp. 3581-83.

Patil, R.B., 2003, "Constitutional Amendment and Changing Panchayat Raj Institution: A Study of Empowerment of Women and the SCs in Kolhapur District", a Seminar Proceedings, April-28-29, 2003, TISS: Mumbai (see also in IASSI, 2003).

Puri, Elora, 2004, "Understanding Participation: Theoretical Foundations and Practical Implications", *Economic and Political Weekly*, June 12, PP.2511-17.

Rai, Manoj, et al., 2001, "Grama Sabha: The People's Council", State of Panchayats: A Participatory Perspective, *PRIA and Samskriti*, New Delhi, pp. 77-104.

Rao, Mohan, 2003, "Two-Child Norm and Panchayats", *Economic and Political Weekly*, XXXVIII(33), August 19.

Sekhar, T.V., 2002, "Empowerment of Grass-Root Leadership in Health and Population: A Training Experiment in Karnataka", *The Indian Journal of Social Work*, 63(3), April, pp. 359-77.

Sharma, S.L., "Rural Development: Need for Reorientation", in U.R. Nahar and Ambika Chandini (eds.), *Sociology of Rural Development*, Jaipur and Delhi: Rawat Publications.

Upadhyay, Videh, 2002, "Panchayats and Paper Laws: Simmering Discontent on 73rd Amendment", *Economic and Political Weekly*, July 20, pp. 2988-89.

Vaddiraju, A.K. and Shagun Mehrotra, 2004, "Making Panchayats Accountable", *Economic and Political Weekly*, XXXIX(37), September 11, pp. 4139-41.

Vyasulu, Vinod. 2004, "Transformation in Governance Since 1990s: Some Reflections", *Economic and Political Weekly*, XXXIX (23), June 5, pp. 2377-85.

13

Representing Village

State, Rural Development and the Villager

Manish Thakur

Introduction: State-Village Relationship in the Post-colonial Context

After independence, the Indian state consciously took itself the task of modernisation and development of the society. This was natural in the sense that independence was energised not only by visions of democracy but also by a desire to modernise and develop a society that for so long had been systematically impoverished under the colonial rule. Democracy and development were taken to be cardinal principles of the post-colonial enterprise of nation-building. It was earnestly believed that the state had to play a central role in the development of the society in general, and that of the village in particular. In fact, the policies of development and change embarked upon by the Indian state has/had tremendous impact on the conceptualisation of the village and villager in post-independence India. The state has come to be seen as a positive agency of welfare and social change. The state, through a plethora of welfare policies and developmental programmes, aims to change the social structure of the village in its entirety. The growing pre-eminence of rural development, however, also meant the increasing incorporation and subordination of the village to the state.

In the changed context, there was no longer any opposition between the state and the village. Rather, around the patriotic image of the 'village' community countless administrative utopias were woven. In the process, contents of the village changed drastically:

> The picture of the Indian village as an idyllic but static rural community has also given way to one of that same village as the very 'epitome' of the 'grinding' poverty and despair of the 'third world.' It is either ripe for 'community development' or a 'green revolution': or a hopeless victim of its own past and a relentless world system that has forever shattered its former self-sufficiency (Inden, 1990: 151-52).

On another plane, various social groups aspiring for mobility invoked the protection of the state and used their rights as citizens to overcome the disabilities which the rest of the village imposed upon them. As early as 1957, in his ethnographic study of a village named Bisipara in Orissa, Bailey (1957: 13) noticed that such social groups "are passing beyond the political frontier of the village and seeking to establish themselves as citizens of the state". Corroborating Bailey's observations, Srinivas (Foreword in Bailey, 1957: vii) wrote: "It seems as though they [such social groups] are being gradually ejected from the village community of Bisipara into the political society of India. This situation is a familiar one in modern rural India, and if it proceeds unchecked, it is likely to alter the nature of Indian village community". In Bailey's words (1957: 3), "Until recent times the state was not concerned with the social and political organisation of the rural communities, nor did it interfere with methods of exploiting the material world. The state was interested in revenue ... The function of the government were fiscal and pacificatory and seldom reforming".

Even otherwise, historically speaking, the state has been powerful in relation to the individual village. Traditionally, the central axis of this vertical articulation has been the relation to land, with the state shaping property rights and revenue demands with the objectives of resource extraction as well as political accommodation and containment. Often, the basic unit for this relationship was not village at all, but smaller estates within the village, or much larger units comprising several peasant settlements. In terms of local political and power structures as well, the village *per se* was not universally the key unit. Simultaneously, land reforms have in many states broken down the earlier units and vested rights in individual peasant households, with the village being the basic unit for economic administration (Breman et al., 1997: 5-6).

The New Development Script for the Village

Curiously enough, as rural developmental gained momentum, the representation of the village got firmly entrenched in the globally unfolding narratives of development. It was seen to be characterised by backwardness, superstition, reaction, orthodoxy and resistance to change. The dynamic interface between development processes and village life rather than altering the well-ingrained conceptualisations of the village added its own weight to the obtaining ones:

> The fundamental dichotomy, for example, is assumed to be between traditional, meaning 'stable', and modern, meaning 'dynamic' as in the discontinuity postulated by nineteenth century officials in India between subsistence or commercial agriculture or between country and town. How complete is the division between urban and rural when few economic or social activities are restricted to one area or the other, and when the same trading, credit and social or religious networks pervade both? (Robb, ed., 1983: 2-3).

Even as the village landscape came to be dotted with agencies of the state, the national project of rural development encouraged the formation of a unified, monolithic Indian village crying for policy inputs from the state. This village of rural development, while transcending the differences of language, region, caste and ethnicity, marked off a common terrain to be developed under the benign guidance of development functionaries. What characterises the village is the common condition of underdevelopment at which development interventions are aimed. This characterisation of a social territory in exclusive terms of underdevelopment has many outcomes though.

In popular common sense discourse, development becomes the idiom through which the relationship between the village and state is articulated. This leads to the incorporation of the village into the state and the associated conversion of villagers into citizens irrespective of the real outcome of the rural development programmes (see Weber, 1979; Ferguson, 1990).

Along with this a temporal hierarchisation of the village takes place. Since villages are underdeveloped, they remain in the past or, at best, an inadequate present, while other places (non-villages) have already become part of the future by virtue of their being developed. In this sense, the category of the *villager* functions in the same way as the category of *the native* in anthropology (cf. Fabian, 1983). By being placed backward in time, the village typifies a particular social form and the villagers stand for a particular set of beliefs and values. Place and person fuse in the delineation of the essence of the village, as the village is made to stand for a kind of deprived culture-territory in relation to development.

In other words, whereas rural development aims to make development an integral part of the village, it also creates a dichotomy between the village and development. Development is concentrated in other places, while villages are places of little or no development. In this perspective, the village emerges in counter-distinction to development even though it is the prime target of development. As a consequence, rural development, while intending to bring development to the village, conceptually segregates it as a social world distinct and distant from development. For the practitioners of rural development, development is the solution and village is the problem. Seen in these terms, while villages are the objects of development and the villagers its recipients, the villages are also obstacles to national development. This conceptual opposition of the village and development, upon which much of rural development programmes is based, thus, leads to a paradox: rural development locates village on the periphery of development, yet, its ostensible aim is to make villages developed (see Pigg, 1992).

Dialectics of State and Village

One should not assume that the village does not contest and redefine the state: "the state is not only present in the village but the village also penetrates into the state" (Breman, 1997: 59). The dynamics between the state and the village is in no way unidirectional. As recent scholarship on development (see Pigg, 1992; Woost, 1993; Tsing, 1999; Moore, 2000) has shown, it is not merely the supra-local sphere such as the state that acts on the village, but the village does appropriate the state in its own image. However abstract the social map of the village for rural development functionaries, villagers have their own ways of reworking and appropriating developmental inputs of the state. The latter is not the focus of our discussion here. Suffice it to say that development apparatus is as much a pervasive and effective generator of categories as it is a potent mechanism of classification and knowledge control.

Rural development programmes[1] are, as a rule, accompanied by a certain conceptualisation of the village. The state, while devising, promoting and administering programmes aimed at improving the conditions of life of the villagers, necessarily relies on a set of images of the village and the village life. Development policy makers discuss what villagers do, how they react to exogenous inputs, how they visualise their needs, and what they think of development, and so on. At times, they collect what they refer to as relevant socio-cultural data in relation to development programmes. Their data and discussion provide them with images of the village and its developmental needs. However, very often, these images of the village coalesce into a typical, generic village, turning all the villages into *the* village for the purpose of rural development.

Rural development practices necessitate and perpetuate a kind of ersatz socio-cultural knowledge. An abstract village, devoid and dissolved of all its diversities and particularities, turns out to be template of rural development. To the extent the village becomes knowable in the wake of its systematic reduction from the diverse into the generalisable, it also assumes a concrete reality for the purposes of rural development. This generic village, thus produced, provides a comfortable framework for rural development agencies within which programmes can be planned, launched and implemented. Seen thus, it will be interesting and instructive to ask:

When policy makers talk of the *village*, and do they mean the same thing as the inhabitants? How does the village come to occupy the periphery of development in relation to the national society and the world of development practitioners including trained sociologists and social anthropologists? Are not real villages translated into the language of generalities spoken in the world of rural development? Does not this translation of villages into the village entail a definite reification of the village? Does not this reification of the village as the locus of national underdevelopment lend itself to political uses and serve political interests? and Does not the very act of rural development constitute a new meaning of the village?

Viewed thus, the village is not merely an ontological category reflecting the morphology of a society where the vast majority of the people are villagers. Instead, rural development alters the meaning of the village in our social imagination. While talking of the village in the context of rural development, we no longer talk in terms of the actual villages where these programmes are going to be carried out or for which they are meant. Rather, an implicit opposition guides us: the village is something that is characterised by the absence of development while a developed place is a non-village. The village is also portrayed in this thinking as a backward place by virtue of its being at a remote distance from development. This is precisely why it qualifies to be the recipient of the rural development programmes. This means that the images of the village have changed over time, especially with the acceleration of rural development programmes. The semantic association of the village with development leads to a definite alteration in the earlier ways of conceptualising what a village is.[2] Village as a kind of place (underdeveloped/undeveloped) come to stand for a kind of people (backward).

Re-creating the Village

Arguably, the discourse on rural development constitutes a hegemonic version of the village. Also, the developmental focus on the village helps Indian state in getting a renewed legitimacy as a crucial modernising agency. Only by maintaining and sustaining a rural developmental discourse the Indian state can justify its popular sovereignty as a modernising tool amidst an underdeveloped society. As a consequence, this discourse also recreates the Indian village in a particular fashion by making it the principal site where tradition-modernity problematic unfolds itself.

Evidently, the village ceases to be a mere territorial and demographic entity. It transcends the social morphological dichotomy (of the country and the city variety) by getting enmeshed with the varying modes of its representation: the specific ways in which it is ideologically approached, theorised and written about. The act of representation itself becomes constitutive of what is represented. In this sense, village as a universe of shared meaning having its own holistic logic no longer remains an empirically given fact. Rather, the apparent boundedness and coherence of the village can be seen as something *made* rather than *found*. Nonetheless, these shifts in understanding are yet to reconfigure the general sociological orientation towards the village. Inden (1990: 152) brings out this point when he writes, "...it [the new corpus of village studies] does not mean that we have totally transformed the predominant episteme for viewing the village. The idea that there is a village community, transmuted into 'peasant society' still persists".

If we look at conceptual categories as not merely expressive of reality, but also constitutive of it, in methodological terms, then it becomes possible to visualise a theoretical possibility wherein the practices of rural development constitute an image of the *village*. Impliedly, it may be possible to argue that rural development discourse privileges one particular construction of the village while marginalising other possible constructions. This problematisation of the *village* of the rural development should help us make sense of the shifting constructions of the *village*. It is true that there are various ways of approaching the village, and, these approaches yield a multiplicity of representations. Very often, such representations come to be informed by larger representations of state and society. Rural development discourse may be viewed as one such dominant representation that has been constitutive of the representation of the village.

Thus, central to the ideas of the village are much disputed issues of representation. Somehow, much of the literature on rural development has not focused on this profound ideological shift in producing ways of looking at the village. Very often, the concern with the actual outcomes in terms of policy objectives and other empirical targets make the ideological effects of such programmes go unexamined and unrecognised. At any rate, the analysis of the dynamics of representation of the village itself is a worthy scholarly endeavour. In this spirit, it would be interesting to examine in general terms various representational strategies and how these strategies inflate or deflate the content of social categories on which they rely.

Village as a Governmentalised Locality

The projection of the village as a template for nation building and a laboratory of 'directed cultural change' (Dube, 1964) meant that those very virtues that had recommended the village to the nationalists now became the sure signs of its backwardness and stagnation. The supposedly unchanging stability of the village called for external impetus for change in the form of state-led rural development. The village had to be regulated now so as to be developed. A series of carefully designed programmes had to be put in place for this purpose. It had to be ensured that these carefully devised programmes did not run aground while encountering the "benighted traditionality of the village".

The village, as the site of state-sponsored development vision, now appeared as an identifiable object to development administrators and bureaucrats. In the process, it also became an inalienable part of the official ideas and categories. Whether villages are projected as homogenous or united communities or socially stratified ones, their representations have always been vulnerable to the official categories of knowledge.

More importantly, success or failure of a rural development programme is immaterial so far as it leads to certain transformation of the terms in which villages are talked about. That is to say, village becomes a marker of social difference in the overall context of development and modernisation. It is employed as a term of social classification with connotations of the degrees of development. The theories and practices of rural development have changed concepts of the village for the villagers as well, and not only for planners and policy makers. As the development vision of society spreads, more and more people lay claims to it. At times, the ideologies of development come handy while segregating village from the non-village. They also serve political interests. The ways of imagining social difference get associated with political uses of identity as underdeveloped or undeveloped.

The pre-eminence of the state has, however, resulted in the gradual loss of the defining characteristics of the village as a social universe. In an interesting study of a village in Tamil Nadu, Daniel (1984: 61-104) demonstrates how the statist definition of the village has marginalised the villager's notion of the village. Contrasting *Ur* and *Kiramam*, he shows how Tamil villagers conceptualise the former as distinct from the latter. A *Kiramam* refers to the revenue village, and thus, to a political unit created for the purpose of taxation and the organisation of local government. Administratively, it is under the jurisdiction of the taluk, which is governed by the district, then by the state, and ultimately by the national government. There is no ambiguity about its boundaries, as *Kiramam* refers to the bounded, standard, and universally accepted spatial unit. The government determines what a *Kiramam* is, and it is the same for everyone. There is no contextual variation in the use of the term *Kiramam* even though it is abstract and distant.

While *Kiramam* is a term whose meaning is really context free, universal, and fixed, *Ur* is a person-centric term that derives its meaning from the contextually shifting spatial orientation of the person. In the words of Daniel (ibid.: 104), "*Ur* is not so much a discreet entity with fixed co-ordinates as a fluid sign with fluid thresholds". *Ur* is always in relation to a given person or jati that is known to have established a special relationship of substantial compatibilities with that particular *Ur*. In the reckoning of the villagers, *Ur* is culturally more significant as soil substance of an *Ur* mixes with the bodily substance of the human inhabitants of that *Ur*. In essence, *Ur* is an indigenous concept of territory. Villagers invariably draw the boundaries of the *Ur* with reference to "ritually vulnerable spots, flow and transit of substance, shrines of the sentinel deities, the points at which roads or the village streams enter the village, the haunted tamarind tree at the edge". In fact, "the villager's concern is not only with what substances enter the *Ur* and affect its inhabitants but with the effect of these alien substances on the substance of the *Ur* itself" (ibid.: 79).

Despite the fact that *Ur* and *Kiramam* are neither semantically isomorphic nor mutually substitutable, villagers misleadingly represent *Ur* as *Kiramam* in their routine practices. Irrespective of whether this isomorphism between *Ur* and K*iramam* is apparent or real, it becomes evident that, in terms of scope and political significance, *Kiramam* has been overshadowing *Ur*. This reinforces our argument that, in our times, the state has also become dispenser of socio-political identities. This means that the process of labelling (be it of territorial units or social groups) by the state contains the potential of unleashing new solidarities that the labelling might it engender (see Wood, 1985). In this sense, to label a given human settlement as a village is rarely just a taxonomic or classificatory exercise. The village becomes much more than a semantic slot or a lexicographic gloss.

Stereotyping Village

Rural development remains a top-down project for expanding the scope of the state administration, notwithstanding the rhetoric of people's participation. It brings villages in line with the national standards. The stereotyping involved in rural development programmes transforms "people into objects – as recipients, applicants, claimants, clients, or even participants" (Wood, 1985: 13). The rhetoric of rural development, thus, has a peculiar effect of marking the village as backward and underdeveloped. More importantly, particular images of the village are produced as representations by the state's standards of representation. In these development-directed representations of the village it becomes difficult to discern whether villagers are enacting their native conceptualisation of the village or someone else's understanding of the village.

However, these seemingly apparent changes in the wake of statist labelling are pregnant with fundamental political consequences. Very often, the statist organisation of the village leads to the severing of contemporary and historical connections to a place. Pre-existing identities are rendered week and fragile, and at times, are broken to be re-established on the basis of people's relationship to an actual or potential state activity. The designation [of the village] thereby acquires a logic in which specified kinds of behaviour and interaction are demanded or expected. People cease to be what they were. Even when they remain the same people, they come to establish their identity in strikingly new ways. For example, during the United Front government at the centre (1989-1991), the then Deputy Prime Minister Devilal had announced some discounts at the government-run five star hotels in Delhi for people hailing from the villages. Nonetheless, the latter (beneficiaries of these discounts) had to convince the hotel manager that they really belonged to the village through 'appropriate' village ways and rustic behaviour, such as wearing a *dhoti*, or smoking a *hookah*, or walking inside the hotel with an *angochha*. Similarly, the participants and beneficiaries of the state-sponsored rural handicrafts exhibitions, rural *haats* and *bazaars*, and the village fairs like Surajkund, have to conform to the statist representation of the village. Thus, there are situations where people (even the real living villagers) have to be authenticated as 'villagers' according to someone else's (most importantly, the state's) understanding of the village.

There are innumerable cases where particular settlements have used all possible means to retain their labels of the village even when all the census-based indicators would qualify them to be designated as towns. Such cases are widely distributed across the country. For the state of Rajasthan, Atal (2003) notes this process as far back as the late 1960s. Very often, people manipulate their way through officialese and political establishment to technically remain as 'villagers' (than 'town-dwellers' or 'urbanites') so as to attract more development funds from the state, and partake of other gains such as income tax rebate, the highly subsided supply of public utilities, which are meant for them by virtue of their being villagers. Based on D.N. Dhanagare's personal communication, Pandey

(2003, fn. 8) underlines this process for the State of Maharashtra. Similarly, in the state of Goa, the locality of Taleigao, which was formerly part of the Panjim Municipal Corporation, has been re-designated as a Village Panchayat. In fact, the preliminary analysis of the 2001 census data reveals this widespread tendency (except in the State of Tamil Nadu) where former municipal towns have been officially re-christened as villages for the official purposes. Observers have described these tendencies as constituting a peculiar syndrome of 'turning urban, staying rural' (see Sivaramakrishnan, 2002). A village is so much its own and so much not its own.

Tsing (1999: 171) perceptively notes, "A village has to present itself as needy, that is, backward and primitive enough to require a special development attention. At the same time, it must present itself as open to change, such that development attention will not be lost on it". Even as the village longs for change it must know that no development programme would come to it if it were not backward. Backwardness is its basis for negotiation with the state in the context of rural development. In this sense, the village always remains a transitional community caught between tradition and modernity. It has to present itself as needing help, and also as ready to change. Even when it is entangled in primordial cultural values, it has to project itself as a village already on the move. In fact, the village becomes the locus of development innovations precisely because it is supposedly tied to a traditional culture that does not support innovative efforts.

State and the Essentialisation of Identity

As a matter of fact, administrative categories have implications for social identities. Villagers come to conceptualise their social-cultural boundaries in the wake of administrative categorisation. For example, the essentialisation of people's identity as the villagers has been articulated in various farmers' movements in the country. These movements have attempted to articulate their interests in terms of an opposition between the country and the city. Twisting the populist contention about the failure of development to reach the poor, they would highlight the failure of development to reach the village (countryside). They would posit a sharp and irrevocable divide between the country and the city – the rural *Bharat* and the urban *India*, which in turn, is built on a critique of the strategy and implementation of development (see Gupta, 1999: 74-101). For our purposes, the political-ideological construction of a unitary rural *Bharat* emanates from a certain essentialisation of the identity of the village in the context of post-independent development. Furthermore, this essentialisation of the village gets ideologically charged where "one pole [the village/*Bharat*] is authentic, good, moral, just, true, responsible, the other [the town/India] is inauthentic, foreign, evil, unjust, immoral, false and irresponsible" (ibid.: 66). Thus, we see how the village forms part of a certain Manichean discourse, and facilitates the representation of farmers as a unitary category irrespective of social divisions and hierarchy characterising the latter.

Similarly, in the state of Karnataka, one's identity as a villager, was, till recently (when the Supreme Court struck it down), a basis of positive discrimination in the state government jobs (Rural Weightage Scheme). Leaving aside the legal-constitutional validity of the 'Rural Weightage Scheme', we can clearly see that the *raison d'etre* of the scheme is the facile equation between the village and the backwardness (or underdevelopment). It is to be noted that since the provision for quota is constitutionally meant only for the 'backward' (socially-educationally, classes-castes), the village automatically and effortlessly gets designated and identified as a backward place needing the benign favour from an external agency like the state. This corroborates our point that no development programme or external intervention (mostly state) would come to the village if it were not considered to be 'backward'. In fact, as said earlier, it is the essentialised backwardness of the village which invites and legitimates the state intervention in the context of rural development.

The statist vision of rural development requires the village to give up its sense of autonomy and community. It exhorts the village to ally its destiny to that of the nation-state. True, the village does not always conform to the wishes of the state. It has its own ways of bypassing, appropriating and transforming the development impulses emanating from the state. In many ways, it keeps alive the locally autonomous concerns. But then, the modernising zeal of the modern state is too strong to leave the village to its own devices. No wonder, the community represented by the village slips away in the developmental fantasies of the state and the village becomes the playground for the pompous ideologues of varying shades and colours.

Apparently, the village is an administrative unit that operates around a well demarcated given human settlement. Daniel (1985), we have seen how the meanings of the village keep fluctuating over, within, and around shifting clusters of human settlement. However, once the village becomes the diorama of national development, the villagers are persuaded, cajoled and coerced into becoming citizens of a modern state. The village also becomes the site for the manufacturing of disciplined citizens. No wonder, since independence the post-colonial Indian state has enormously multiplied its development efforts in the village. At times, rather than developing and disciplining the existing settlements, the state endeavours to create its own ideal villages, for example, the social justice villages in Tamil Nadu, or the Ambedkar villages in Uttar Pradesh.

Conclusion

Official-statist-administrative categories, once they gain currency, develop a dynamics of their own. They get essentialised in course of time and acquire the potential to undermine the pre-existing bases of people's identity. However, the undermining of people's earlier bases of identity does not necessarily lead to situations of conflict. In the particular context of the village, people have responded to the statist construction(s) in innovative ways to further their instrumental interests while continuing with their old ways of identification with the village in magico-religious and kinship terms. This collective splitting of the self in relation to the village is likely to be quite widespread. The phenomenon of 'turning urban, staying rural' could be seen as another such instance of the split collective self. Nonetheless, this need not be the norm. Ethnographers have also reported instances where the long-existing ritual universe of the village appropriates the statist construction of the same in strikingly new ways. For example, in Mel Ceval village of the Tirunelvelli district of Tamil Nadu, the president of the (village) panchayat offers the first goat (in the name of the village) to be sacrificed to the village goddess Muppidariyamman at her festival (Fuller, 2002: 171). Such situations might not be very uncommon in the country.

However, one should not be misled in believing that the ritual-social universe of the village has successfully weathered the statist interventions. On the contrary, there have been enough ruptures in that universe, and the grip of the village over its ritually low members has sufficiently loosened. More than ever, the social position of the low caste members is predicated less on their ritual integration in the cosmic universe of the village and more on the protection afforded to them by the state. Rather than negotiating their ambiguous ritual position within the village, they would prefer warming up to the promises of citizenship of a modern state. Processes like this would not have been set in motion had the state not intervened in the village. And, one of the most powerful interventions has definitely been the enterprise of rural development. In any case, the hegemonic influence of the statist construction of the village through the medium of rural development seems to have led to the loosening (and, may be, the possible disappearance) of the ritual-symbolic construction of the village.

Notes

1. By 'rural development programmes' we refer to interventions guided, or more usually, implemented by the state (or by aid agencies though routed through the state agencies). In the Indian context, such interventions generally include policies and attempts made for alleviating the socio-economic conditions of the poor in the villages or developing backward areas (see NIRD, 1999: 123).
2. There could be numerous ways of conceptualising the village apart from the census and other administrative definitions which privilege demographic, ecological and occupational factors. Studies of the ways in which socially mobile segments of the population relate to the villages they have already left, studies of the urban elite's images of the villages they have perhaps never seen, and the studies of the rural and pastoral

imagery in literature, film and other visual media have hardly been conducted in India. These studies would show other dimensions of the images of the village that are being discussed in this paper.

References

Atal, Yogesh, 2003. 'The Studies of the Village in India', in Yogesh Atal, *Indian Sociology from Where to Where: Footnotes to the History of the Discipline*. Jaipur: Rawat Publications, pp. 159-85.

Bailey, F. G., 1957. *Caste and the Economic Frontier*. Manchester: Manchester University Press.

Breman, Jan, 1997. 'The Village in Focus', in Jan Breman et al. (eds.), *The Village in Asia Revisited*. Delhi: Oxford University Press, pp. 15-75.

Daniel, Valentine E., 1984. *Fluid Signs: Being a Person the Tamil Way*. Berkeley: University of California Press.

Das, Raju, J., 2001. 'The Spatiality of Social Relations: An Indian Case Study', *Journal of Rural Studies*, 17 (4): 347-62.

Dube, S.C. 1964. 'The Community Development Programme in India', in Baidya Nath Varma (ed.), *Contemporary India*. Bombay : Asia Publishing House.

Fabian, Johannes, 1983. *Time and the Other: How Anthropology Makes Its Object*. New York: Columbia University Press.

Ferguson, James, 1990. *The Anti-Politics Machine: 'Development', Depoliticisation and Bureaucratic State Power in Lesotho*. Cambridge: Cambridge University Press.

Fuller, C. J., 2002. 'Rituals of the Village', in Vandana Madan (ed.), *The Village in India*. Delhi: Oxford University Press, pp. 271-97.

Gupta, Akhil, 1997. *Postcolonial Developments: Agriculture in the Making of Modern India*. Delhi: Oxford University Press.

Inden, Ronald, 1990. *Imagining India*. Oxford: Blackwell.

Moore, Donald S., 2000. 'The Crucible of Cultural Politics: Reworking 'Development' in Zimbabwe's Eastern Highlands', *American Ethnologist*, 26 (3): 654-89.

National Institute of Rural Development (NIRD), 1999. *India Rural Development Report 1999*. Hyderabad: NIRD.

Pandey, Vikash N., 2003. 'Re-presenting Rural: From Definition to Discourse', *Sociological Bulletin*, 52 (1): 32-52.

Pigg, Stacy Leigh, 1992, 'Inventing Social Categories Through Place: Social Representations and Development in Nepal', *Comparatives Studies in Society and History*, 34 (3): 491-513.

Robb, Reter (ed.), 1983. Introduction : 'Land and Society : The British Transformation in India', in Peter Robb (ed.), *Rural India : Land, Power and Society Under British Rule*, London and Dublin : Curzon Press, pp. 1-22.

Sivaramakrishnan, K. C., 2002. 'Turning Urban, Staying Rural', *The Hindu* (Chennai), 27 February.

Tsing, Anna L., 1999. 'Becoming a Tribal Elder, and other Green Development Fantasies', in Tania Murray Li (ed.) *Transforming the Indonesian Uplands: Marginality, Power and Production*. Amsterdam: Harwood Academic, pp.159-202.

Weber, Eugen, 1979. *Peasants into Frenchmen: The Modernisation of Rural France, 1870-1914*. London: Chatto and Windus.

Wood, Geof, 1985. 'The Politics of Development Policy Labelling', *Development and Change*, 16 (3): 347-73.

Woost, Michael, 1993. 'Nationalising the Local Past in Sri Lanka: Histories of Nation and Development in a Sinhalese Village', *American Ethnologist*, 20 (3): 502-21.

14

Inter-Associational Conflicts and Cooperation

Implications for Development: A Case Study of Two Villages in Karnataka

Ozmond Roshan D'Souza

The enormous changes that have occurred in the 20th century[1] in the field of politics both nationally and internationally have been of great importance to the academics. World polity witnessed several major events in the 20th century, viz., the two world wars, the Great Depression of the 1920s, the Cold War, disintegration of the USSR, rise of the United States as the unchallenged superpower, etc. But one of the major achievements of the century was that more nations than ever before have transformed themselves into democracies. More interestingly, in the last few decades, governments in many democratic states have shown tendencies towards gradually shedding their regulatory role and interventionist approach to a great extent. Governance is increasingly seen as a facilitation process and the state as a facilitator. Different economic and social forces within the state have become very active, engaging themselves in developmental activities. 'Market' and 'civil society' are now considered significant factors in the transformation process of the state. There is a clear shift in the development discourse in the 21st century. With the retreat of the interventionist and regulator state, development outcomes are seen as a result of partnership between the state and the civil society and great emphasis is laid on people's participation at lower levels.

Participatory development is seen as a major instrument of social, political and economic change in India. Participation takes place at different levels and in different forms. Panchayati Raj Institutions (PRIs), where participation of the people takes place at the grassroots level, were established in India to strengthen the grassroots and involve people in developmental activities. Though these institutions were not successful initially, they became stronger, with rising stakes – political, social and financial. Today, with these institutions attaining constitutional status, they are seen as government at the lowest levels. PRIs were in-charge of almost all developmental activities in their jurisdiction and they were unchallenged until recently in their role as development agencies. But, post-1990s with the emerging interest of the state and other international funding agencies, different associations have sprang up in the rural areas with a stake in development of rural areas. There are many associations like the Self Help Groups, Watershed Management Committees, Joint Forest Management Committees, Education Committees and others, to name a few. These associations in the villages are viewed as parallel bodies to PRIs and the direction of relationship between the PRIs and these joint participatory bodies or the community-based associations is a cause of concern.

Objectives of the Study

- To observe the pattern of participation in voluntary associations like the Village Forest Committees on the one hand and legally sanctioned institutions like the Gram Panchayat.
- To observe the socio-political dynamics operating in the relationship between (bridging social capital) and within (bonding social capital) the aforesaid associations.
- To observe the influence of external bodies on the functioning of the aforesaid associations and the role they play in the relationship between and within the aforesaid associations.

Study Area

The case study for the present paper was conducted in two villages (Hubbanahalli and Balekoppa) under Balekoppa Gram Panchayat of Shimoga district in Karnataka. The district is situated on the banks of the river Thunga, which originates from the Sahyadri ranges of the Western Ghats. The revenue district is spread over 10,553 sq. kms[2] and has a forest cover of over 4,97,239 hectares.[3] The population of the district is 16,39,595.[4] Both the villages come under the revenue jurisdiction of Shimoga taluk and district and is around 29 kilometres northwest of the district headquarters. The revenue administrative office of the village is in Kumsi, a Hobli on the National Highway approximately four kilometres from the both the villages and is called Nada Khacheri. An officer of the rank of deputy Tashildar heads it, with the support staff like the Revenue Inspector, who is called Rajasva Nirikshakaru and other Village Accountants.

Hubbanahalli is around 29 kilometres northwest of the district headquarters. Revenue jurisdiction of the village is confined to 711 acres and the rest is under the control of the Forest Department. According to official records the state forest in the village is spread over 285 acres. Hubbanahalli has no panchayat of its own and comes under Balekoppa Gram Panchayat, which is around seven kilometres from the village through *pucca* road and around two and a half kilometres through *kaccha* road. The village has a history of around one hundred and thirty one years going by the Nandi Kallu (a divine stone with the pictures of deities planted at one of the many entrances). People though trace the village history to many generations. Most of the villagers are settlers who came here for the purpose of agriculture from neighbouring villages.

Balekoppa is only six kilometres away from Hubbanahalli village through *pucca* road and around two and a half kilometres apart if one travels through the *kaccha* road or the village agricultural fields. A metre gauge railway track divides the two villages. The jurisdiction of the Revenue Department in the village is spread over 2,635 acres. According to official records, the state forest in the village is spread over 1,594 acres.

The surrounding forests of these villages are classified as the Sandal Reserve Forests. Though large chunks of forestland are now cultivated by the villagers known as Bageher Hukum, these do not find any mention in the official records either in Hubbanahalli or Balekoppa.

The caste composition is quite similar in both the neighbouring villages. There are people from different castes. In both the villages, the dominating Lingayats form the majority within whom are the Swamys or the Aiyahs, the priestly class and slightly higher than the Lingayats in the caste structure. Then come the Devangas, the traditional agriculturist class. There are some families of the craftsmen class from a caste called Vishwakarma. Then, there are Scheduled Castes (SCs) called Madigas or Adi Karnataka. A few families belong to the Talavar caste, which is the traditional informer class (Sarahakavaru) of any event in the village. There are also people belonging to the traditional hunter families and come under the category of the Scheduled Tribes (STs) and are called Beedaru (hunters). Another caste called the Bovis or Voddaru also reside in the villages who also come under the SC category, who are traditional stonecutters. Their presence in the villages is due to the availability of quarry or boulders in the vicinity. There is not a single house belonging to other religious communities like the Muslims and Christians.

Research Methodology

The present research work is an analytical and descriptive study based on both primary and secondary sources and data collection. The fieldwork was carried out in May and June 2004 in two neighbouring villages. The data was collected through observation method, formal interviews and informal discussions with individuals and various groups. The respondents included villagers – both men and women – from different age groups and castes. They were approached with both structured and unstructured questionnaires with both open-ended and close-ended questions. Interviews and discussions were also held with community leaders, local government officials associated with the villages. besides, a professional from a renowned NGO was also interviewed for the study.

Table 1
General Statistics of the Two Villages

	Head	*Statistics*	
		(2) *Hubbanahalli*	*(1)* *Balekoppa*
1.	Total Households	150 (including separated families)	290
2.	Population	903 (760 adults and 143 children)	1844 (excluding around 409 children)
3.	Men/Women	369/391	949/895
	SC:	160	399
3A.	Men/Women	74/86	211/188
4.	ST:	21	10
4A.	Men/Women	12/9	6/4
5.	Revenue Land	711.01 (in acres)	2635.38 (in acres)
6.	Forest Land	285.01 (in acres)	1594.20 (in acres)
7.	Schools	01 (Govt. Primary School)	01 (Govt. Primary School)
7A.	Anganwadis	01 (govt. pre-primary)	03 (govt. pre-primary)
8.	Irrigational Tanks	8	7
8A.	Major/Minor	2/6	4/3
9.	Total Agricultural Khatas	102	288
9A.	Large/Small-Scale Farmers	26/76	50/238
9B.	Agricultural Labourers (households)	60	93
10.	Wells: Open/Tube	4/6	5/6
11.	Temples	4	7
12.	Literacy Rate	69.88% (60.63% among women and) 79.13% among men)	67.68% (63.68% among women and 77.55% among men)

Source: Fieldwork Data.

Findings of the Study

It is a known fact that the establishment of Panchayati Raj in India in the late fifties (1959)[5] and its spread across India in the early sixties were a response to the failure of the Community Development Programmes of the Government of India started in the 1950s. It still remains a research puzzle for academics on how the government has fallen back on community-based associations, which were deemed unfit for many reasons few decades back. The data for the present paper is collected from two villages in Shimoga district of Karnataka. A comparison was made between these two villages.[6] The first village is Hubbanahalli, a small hamlet of approximately one hundred and fifty families and the second village is Balekoppa, has about three hundred families. Balekoppa is also the headquarters of the local Gram Panchayat. It is observed that the people of Hubbanahalli, who without a functional Gram Panchayat of their own managed to constitute a Village Forest Committee under the Joint Forest Planning and Management Programme of the Government of Karnataka in 1998-99 and as a result have contributed to many a developmental activity, the detail of which is given in this paper further. Whereas the other village, Balekoppa has not had any voluntary associations apart from the caste-based associations and the Village Education Committee and the Adult Education Committee, which was a result of the perusal of the cause by few enlightened individuals of the village. This apart, if one looks at some other development indicators like Anganwadis, agricultural holdings, water connections and electricity connections, Balekoppa ranks higher than Hubbanahalli.

In majority of the cases it is observed that there is tension between the PRIs and the other committees – be it Village Forest Committee, Watershed Management Committee, the Village Education Committee, etc. It is interesting to note that many other traditional committees in the villages have been living harmoniously with the PRIs for decades. These traditional committees or as it is called 'Samitis' in Karnataka are mainly based on the caste, trade or language factor. Conflicts between these traditional 'Samitis' and PRIs are negligible and normally in cases where PRI leadership was held by members of smaller communities, lower castes groups, etc.

But they never arose to the proportion that the state or the central governments had to intervene. The conflicts observed currently between local joint participatory bodies/community-based associations and PRIs has many contributing factors. The first and foremost is that the PRI leadership in villages see the voluntary associations and their leadership as a challenge to their own leadership. In many villages it is observed that since many. associations were formed and developmental activities were on a rise, people approach these leaders for the redressal of their grievances instead of PRI leadership, which they were used to doing before the establishment of these joint participatory bodies, as the local people feel that the PRI leadership is seen moving away from the masses. The villages[7] where there is a positive relationship between the PRI leadership and other associations have seen developmental activities taking place at a greater pace than the normal case is. The case of Hubbanahalli village is the best example, where the first leader of the local Village Forest Committee also happened to be a very prominent local traditional and political leader and was on Gram Panchayat Board and also served as its chairman for a couple of terms.

Another important factor that contributes either to conflict or cooperation is the agenda or the aim for which these associations have been established by the state. The overall agenda or the aim of these associations is the development of rural areas and development necessarily involves financial issues. Not that prior to the establishment of joint participatory bodies/community-based associations, all the development-related expenditures or rather finances went to the PRIs. But, the amount of funding that is pumped into the joint participatory bodies/community-based associations by the state and central governments on the recommendations of the funding agencies superseding the PRIs is enormous and certainly causes envy among the PRI leadership. Furthermore, these institutions also have a political and social stake. Leaders of PRIs in many villages do not stand the leadership of the community-based associations for these leaders have been able to gain more moral positioning in the village communities in a short time, which was never the same in the case PRI leadership.

One of the most important elements that separate the PRIs from joint participatory bodies/community-based institutions is the legal sanction behind the PRIs. With the 73rd amendment to the Indian Constitution and many rules and Acts passed and amendments made from time to time by different states, the PRIs have not only got a constitutional status as the third tier in the government mechanism, their powers and functions have also enormously increased. Out of the 29 subjects that have been transferred to the PRIs natural resources also form a list with water, forests, etc. But creating parallel associations to manage subjects that have already been entrusted to the jurisdiction of the PRIs creates suspicion in the local leadership. On the one hand, PRI leadership claims to have more power and social and political status based on the Constitutional status enjoyed by the bodies they represent, and on the other, there are these community-based associations whose leadership is purely voluntary. Although the by-laws of these associations (voluntary) provide for a democratic set-up within the committees, not many are ready to challenge each other for important posts with an intention that they exist to support the association and not compete for a post that brings them little supremacy. But, this element of legitimacy has had an adverse affect on PRIs.

The data collected during the field visit to these two villages and visits to the local Gram Panchayat and Taluka Panchayat offices suggest this. First and foremost, Gram Panchayat members see themselves as the legitimate leaders for the entire term, i.e., five years and that they cannot be removed or suspended from their office without serious criminal offences or accusations. This psychological trait makes them deal with the local populace as the most powerful and unquestionable leaders in the locality. They have little respect for the electorate after elections and not many of these leaders take the complaints or grievances from the people very seriously. Any advice or complaint or request that comes to them from the villagers is outrightly rejected and only some leaders in exceptional cases accept the people's requests, provided, either the leader is a very concerned individual or the matter involves some sort of finance or the other. Hence, the local people have little respect or trust in the PRI leadership. To a question on whether their Gram Sabha leaders would get their work done, a majority of the respondents felt that their work would be done only if they were very well connected to the Gram Sabha leader or if they could afford to pay the amount demanded by the leader.

Interaction with the Gram Panchayat members in Balekoppa was not very cordial. When the researcher told the members that their bargaining power for developmental activities would be higher with the establishment of voluntary associations like VFC, one of the members claimed that he had personally carried out more than half the developmental activities carried out in the neighbouring village (Hubbanahalli) with the help of VFC. He also claimed that he would carry out more developmental activities if he was provided financial assistance by the government as is provided to the MPs and MLAS under the Local Area Development Scheme. He felt that, when the Gram Panchayats were already satisfactorily working in the rural areas, this is purely wasting time and resources on voluntary associations. And, according to him, only thing that was needed by the PRIs in rural areas is regular sanction of finances by the state government. Another member questioned as to why leaders of the voluntary associations are provided with finances when there were already elected representatives available in rural areas. He felt that instead of creating parallel bodies, which contributed to conflict and confusion in the rural areas, the government should further strengthen the existing Gram Sabhas.

For a long time these people had no alternative but to pursue the matter with the PRI leadership. But, with the establishment of community-based associations, which are purely based on voluntarism, mutual trust and respect, people have started trusting these leaders and approaching them for all sorts of problems they face in the village ranging from drinking water problem to health, education and sanitation. This was witnessed by the researcher during the fieldwork. For a few days in the third week of May 2004, there was a severe water crisis in Hubbanahalli due to some technical problems. Though the water supply is the function of the Gram Panchayat, the people from a couple of localities in the village were seen grilling the VFC leaders for lack of water supply. Clarifying the fact that water supply was not under the ambit of VFC was not possible. In fact, the people were also abusing the VFC leadership for not being able to deliver basic necessities of the villagers. The leaders of voluntary associations, on their part, willingly offer their help and suggestions to the aggrieved villagers, the people find it easier to deal with them because there is an understanding that the leaders (of voluntary associations) are powerful but not unquestionable. The fieldwork also suggests that the villagers felt that they have the right to even scold and abuse the voluntary leaders, which is certainly not the same with PRI leadership. Informal discussions with the villagers revealed that they could abuse the leaders of VFC because they thought that the leaders were one among them and that they would not take the abuse very seriously and get the work done as opposed to the PRI leadership who were well connected and they feared that any abuse, which would be taken by them seriously would only prove to be detrimental.

Furthermore, these PRI leaders have a very common practice of interaction with the lower rung officials of the PRIs. There is an unholy nexus of these officials and local leaders due to the financial funding involved in the PRIs. The people also have realised this fact and so there is a fear among the villagers to meet the concerned officials for submission of their grievances. The officials of the PRIs on their part know very well that most of the PRI leaders will not return to their respective bodies in the coming elections due to their functioning and attitude and hence normally ignore the comments or directions of PRI leaders or at best take it lightly. Those villagers who have had interaction with both the PRI leaders and the lower rung officials of the department know very well that the request they will be making will fall on the deaf ears for reasons already discussed.

On the other hand, we have the joint participatory bodies/community-based associations and their leaders who have a very good rapport not only with the villagers but also with the officials of the concerned departments. Many conflicts arising between some erring villagers and officials of the forest or police departments have been solved successfully by the leaders of these associations because of the goodwill they enjoy with the officials of many government departments. The officials on their part are known for very good behaviour with the leadership of the joint participatory bodies/community-based associations knowing very well that these leaders enjoy a very good social position among the villagers. There have been cases in the surveyed villages, where police and forest officials have approached the leadership of the community-based associations to advice the villagers to keep away from illegal activities like gambling, illicit liquor trade, illegal tree felling and smuggling of valuable trees like rose wood, teak wood and sandalwood. There have been numerous cases of the aforesaid kind in both the villages in the past ten years. Police officials of the concerned station have stated off record that they have unsuccessfully tried to get the cooperation of PRI leadership in solving the problem in Balekoppa, but similar requests to the leadership of joint participatory bodies/community-based associations (Village Forest Committee in case of Hubbanahalli) in the other village have borne fruits and there is a vast decline in the cases involving Karnataka Police Act in Hubbanahalli. In many instances, the VFC leadership in Hubbanahalli has been successful in avoiding police officials from raiding their village in search of people accused of illegal activities.

The idea of consent (electoral politics) has also had a negative impact on the PRI leadership. PRI leadership is known to claim legitimacy in all the activities they do and hence in many cases state their inability outrightly in solving the problems of the villagers giving many irrational reasons. But, with the leadership of community-based associations such problems are not found. The consent given to the leadership of such associations is purely based on the trust and goodwill they enjoy in the village community. The leadership cannot give reasons for not doing their own work and that of their people, for there is an element of concern[8] involved, which is not there in the case of PRI leadership. Moreover, the relationship between the villagers and the PRI leadership is always formal[9] but the relationship between the leadership of the community-based associations is always informal and there is a sense of oneness between them.

On the question of relationship of PRIs and voluntary associations with other government bodies and other stakeholders within the village and outside, it is interesting to note that joint participatory bodies/community-based associations have been more successful and effective in dealing with other government bodies than the PRIs. It is evident from the field study that there is more trust in joint participatory bodies/community-based associations than PRIs as far as the government bodies are concerned. In the fiscal year 2004-2005 the Department of Education (Primary) sanctioned Rs. 35,000 for village schools in a phased manner under the *Akshara Dasoa* (mid-day meals) scheme for the construction of a fireproof kitchen. Initially, the government thought that the sanction is to be channelled through PRIs (as PRIs control educational institutions in rural areas come under their jurisdiction) and in fact those PRI leaders who could successfully bargain for the project got the finances sanctioned in the name of concerned Gram Panchayats. It was so in the case of Balekoppa, but the villagers in Hubbanahalli decided to get the money released in the account of the local School Education Committee. Once the money was sanctioned, the work on the construction of kitchens in both the villages began. It was observed that the construction of kitchen in Hubbanahalli was far better than that of Balekoppa. For this there is a major reason. The construction in Balekoppa School was done by private contractor and as usual a large chunk of the sanctioned amount went either to the contractor or to the PRI leadership who helped the contractor to win the bid. It is a custom[10] or convention, in case of PRIs, to invite tenders for any developmental activity, if the project money is routed through the PRI. It has almost become the practice that the bidder who quotes the highest commission or highest percentage in terms of sharing with the PRI leadership wins the bidding instead of the bidder who quotes the least amount. The reasons given for rejecting the contractor who quoted the least amount were mostly based on low quality work, low quality materials, etc. But, in Hubbanahalli, the villagers under the leadership of the VFC decided that the construction work will not be handed over to any private contractor, instead they would themselves supervise construction with locally available human resources like the carpenter, mason, helpers and so on. As a result, there was not only a good and strong RCC room that was constructed; in addition to it there was also a small stage, which the school could use for daily assembly and physical training (PT) classes. It was not so in the case of Balekoppa, one can clearly see the sub-standard construction near the village school.

Other stakeholders in the villages have also benefited from joint participatory bodies/community-based associations. PRIs have only been successful in providing part of funds that have been released to them by the state or the central governments. But community-based associations have successfully contributed to many developmental activities with the benevolent help from funding agencies. Among the community developmental activities carried by the VFC in Hubbanahalli include sealed or smokeless hearth (*Astra Vole* in Kannada) to each household in the village, construction of 55 permanent gobar gas plants with subsidies from the agriculture department and LPG connections to 31 households, who neither have smokeless hearth or permanent gobar gas plants. Initially, there was a hue and cry regarding the money people would have to spend at regular intervals on LPG connection, the VFC leadership stated that those households with LPG connections could work for a couple of days more every month on wage earning to contribute to refilled LPG cylinder an amount of man hours equal to what these households would spend in the forests to collect firewood. In addition, the VFC has contributed around Rs. 10,000 only to the school development fund and provided the school with ten cents of land adjacent to the school for a playground. The VFC has also contributed Rs. 5,000 to the village temple for developmental activities. None of these activities has taken place in the neighbouring village of Balekoppa though that heads the Gram Panchayat. On being asked, as to why the people in that village were never interested in the creation of a VFC as it could help many developmental activities, one of the Gram Panchayat member claimed that though they might not have done more than the neighbouring village, they had single-handedly done some developmental activities in the village with out the help of outside funding.

The members of the Gram Panchayat in Balekoppa do not want the VFC to be established in their village as they see an ego problem and challenge to their unquestionable authority in the form of parallel leadership of community-based associations and keep citing one reason or the other for not being interested in the formation of a VFC. They have even gone to the extent of accusing the government officials, especially the forest officials of corrupt practices. One of the members even claimed that the VFC is eyewash to gobble up the money coming in the name of foreign funding. On the other hand, the forest officials, have little respect for the Gram Panchayat members or the villagers in Balekoppa in general. They see them with utter contempt and even hesitate to enter the village without a valid reason, like the cases of tree felling or smuggling. In fact, many cases have been filed against the villagers in aforesaid cases. The officials also note that the villagers are very well known in the departmental hierarchy for their illegal activities in the forest. One infamous record of the village is that they fell forest trees, smuggle costly timber and sandalwood and create agricultural land in the forest, which is officially called *Bagerhukum* (meaning without permission in the colonial terms).

It is very important to note that in the last couple of years, government agencies at the state and central levels have superseded the PRIs in funding the rural development programmes and have successfully channelled the finances through community-based associations like the Joint Forest Management Committees and the Watershed Management Committees. In fact, even international funding agencies like the World Bank and IMF, in addition to unilateral agencies like the DFID and JBIC, have shown more interest in funding these community-based associations than the regular PRIs. In a recently held meeting between the World Bank officials and the Karnataka government, the World Bank made it clear to the state government officials that the funds (around Rs. 670 crores) sanctioned by it for the development of lakes and ponds under the *Sujala* (meaning pure water in Kannada) Scheme of watershed programme, should not be channelled through the PRIs, instead it should be entrusted to the Watershed Development Department, which is responsible for supervising the *Sujala* scheme in Karnataka.[11]

To get some clarifications regarding the World Bank approach in dealing with the PRIs and other joint participatory bodies/ community-based associations in relation to the funding of rural development activities, the researcher approached MYRADA, a Bangalore-based NGO working on rural development. MYRADA is also the nodal agency for the *Sujala* project in Karnataka. Discussion with the programme officer (Ms Yasmin Master) of MYRADA was very revealing and it provided an insight into the understanding of the working of associations involved in rural development. According to Ms Yasmin, neither the World Bank nor their own organisation, are per se against PRIs. Their argument is that the PRIs are not well trained to handle issues involving watershed management or other natural resources for the simple reason that they are more so there because of political reasons rather than social, where as community-based associations are well trained to handle these matters. All stakeholders, who are affected by a given project, should ideally be involved in the development process at all levels.[12] But, how much do PRIs involve grassroots people in various developmental activities? Moreover, most members of the PRIs are either members of political parties, or supported by mainstream political parties, in which case it becomes obligatory on their part to serve their political masters, and most members know very well that PRIs are only a stepping stone (or training grounds) for future political endeavours and hence their concentration is more on their personal political necessities rather than the social needs of their village. This notion of PRIs gives room to suspicion among funding agencies and agencies implementing the projects regarding the social concern or developmental interest on the part of PRI leadership in villages.

There is also a feeling within the NGOs sector that it is very difficult for them to hold PRI leadership accountable in case of any discrepancies arising in a development project.

In case the PRIs should be involved in developmental activities like the watershed management, they should be trained regarding the social accountability of the project, but here according to the project officer there is a problem. Because of the electoral politics involved in the PRIs, training members becomes redundant in case they are not returned to their respective bodies.[13] The issue becomes complex when the newly elected members are from rival groups. In case of community leaders, they can be retained in the process as members for as long as they like to serve on the committee or in the association.

The programme officer also feels that building trust in the PRIs, between its members and among the rural masses, is a very difficult task. Instead, what is suggested is that trust and awareness building should take place at the lower levels where there is no question of political or social status involved. These lower level groups are called affinity groups.[14] Through these groups a strong baseline needs to be built and train the leadership in a more systematic organisation, which is apolitical in nature. Stronger grassroots base and leadership gained through affinity groups help build trust and social accountability in the long run, which is presently lagging in the PRIs. This, in turn, can influences participation in the development process. Leadership training should be provided at the community level enabling them to represent their people on PRIs.

Another reason for official apathy with regard to the PRIs is in fact the idea of legitimacy based on consent or electoral politics. Firstly, anything that is connected with politics and elections in India are seen as a corrupt practice[15] and PRIs are not spared of this tag. The psychological notion behind such understanding is that the entry into politics (and PRIs being the stepping stone for bigger goals) is merely for making money and with the sort of connections politicians can have, it becomes very difficult to hold anybody in the PRIs responsible for any corrupt practice that is unearthed in the process of a developmental activity. Normally, there is a shifting of accountability and responsibility by the leadership in PRIs, and when nobody is ready to take the responsibility, not only is the existing project in jeopardy but it also creates suspicion for any future action with regard to developmental activities in the rural areas. But it is not the case with the joint participatory bodies/community-based associations. Leadership here is not very strong (politically). It is that much easier for officials to deal with them without the fear of any political activity being involved. Moreover, the moment officials find something going wrong, they may immediately withdraw from the agreement without any legal problems.

Conclusion

Conflict resolution mechanism within these community-based associations differ in many ways. Conflicts arising within the PRIs are normally resolved with the involvement of politicians at the higher levels or the government concerned. They bring in legal and hurdles in cases where the conflict is between members belonging to different or rival groups. Those conflicts which involve members from same groups create problems for the concerned political party or affiliate groups. And, many a time, political pressure is applied to resolve the existing feud. Thus, there is a scope for external parties to involve themselves in conflicts arising within the associations.

This is normally not the case with the joint participatory bodies. The conflicts arising within the association or the committee is solved within the group through mutual discussion, debate and based on the understanding that any conflict within the association can ruin the developmental process that has been smoothly taking place the village.

Conflict resolution mechanism between PRIs and joint participatory bodies/community-based associations is a very complex issue. Research in this area has been gaining pace in the last couple of years. Hence, it is very difficult to define the existing mechanism involved in conflict resolution. But one of the well-known facts that supports conflict resolution mechanism is that PRIs at least the village level should be based on traditional leadership rather than on electoral or consensual politics. It arises from the need to make the PRI leadership more accountable (both socially and politically). It is here that the concept of social capital needs to be addressed. There are three important variables that are involved in the understanding of social capital. They are participation, trust and developmental process.

In the course of the fieldwork, it was realised by the researcher that these three variables could not be located either as dependent or independent variables. The explanation on whether the developmental process depended on trust and participation by all stakeholders involved or vice-versa seems to be very complex. These three variables are interchangeable, depending on each other for successful outcomes and form a continuous circle, which is described in the form of following diagram:

Diagram 1 : Variables and their dependence on each other

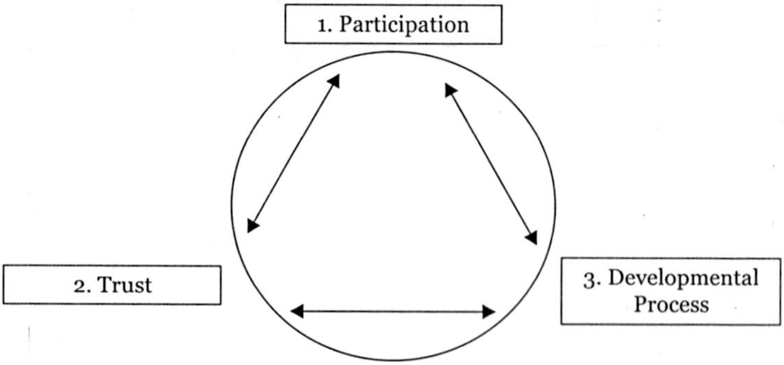

In the above diagram it can be observed that the process of development is directly dependent on the trust and participation of the people; similarly, the trust of the stakeholders is also directly dependent on the developmental process and the type and level of participation. And participation of the stakeholders in a given development process depends on the developmental process itself and the trust it can generate among the stakeholders on each other.

The complexity involved in the understanding these three variables is to some extent deciphered with the application of the theory of social capital, which has gained enormous popularity among the academicians and policy makers around the world in the last few years. This theory helps to explain, why and how developmental activities take place in some regions or among some communities and why it does not take place in other regions or among other communities.

The findings of the present study provide ample proofs as to why a certain community (Hubbanahalli) has been able to successfully utilise the social resources found within its community and why the second community (Balekoppa) has failed to convert its social resources into qualitative or quantitative development process.

The concept of social capital basically refers to features of social organisations, such as networks, norms and social trust, that facilitate, co-ordinate and cooperate for mutual benefit"[16] emerging from civic engagements or civic activities. As a result of which, there can be better schools, better management of resources, lower crime rate and faster economic development leading to an effective and efficient government.

The World Bank defined the term 'social capital' as "the institutions, relationships and norms that shape the quality and quantity of society's social interactions" (World Bank, 2000).[17] A definition that suits our present study is the one given by Sabel (1994)[18] who argues that "social capital builds up as a result of all actors committing themselves to ongoing negotiations based on shared understanding of a common goal".[19] Hans Blomkvist and Ashok Swain[20] (2001) define it "as a resource – a capital that consists of relations one has with other people".

John Harriss puts it in a nutshell as "resources that inhere in social relationships". They are resources otherwise labelled as 'trust' and 'reciprocity' that both underlie and derive from social network.[21]

But sustaining social capital in an association (bonding social capital) or among a group of associations (bridging social capital)[22] in the long run is more important and this is the function of participation. Accumulation of social capital in any association necessarily depends on how the process of participation takes place in it, who participates, why, at what level and how.

Acnowledgement

I owe special thanks to Prof. Arun Kumar Patnaik, Department of Political Science, University of Hyderabad, my research supervisor for his comments on the article, useful suggestions and constant encouragement. I also thank Dr. Uday Bhaskar Nidumolu, Hyderabad for his comments and suggestions.

Notes

1. The socio-economic and political phenomena of the 20th century A.D. is acknowledged by many authors. The present idea is basically adopted

from two works: (1) S.R. Sankaran (2002), 'Globalisation and Marginalised Sections', *Indian Journal of Human Rights*, Vol. 6, Nos. 1&2, January-December, p. 1.; and (2) Blomkvist, Hans and Ashok Swain (2001), 'Investigating Democracy and Social Capital in India', *Economic and Political Weekly*, Vol. 36, No. 8, p. 639.

2. — (2004), *Manorama Year Book*, Malaya Manorama, Kottayam.
3. — (2003), *Shimoga Vrutthada Varshika Varadhi 2003-04* (01-04-2003 rindha 31-12-2003 ravarage), Shimoga Aranya Vruttha, Karnataka Aranya Ilakhe.
4. — (2004), *Manorama Year Book*, Malaya Manorama, Kottayam. Original Source, 2001 Karnataka Census Report.
5. After the Community Development Project was inaugurated in 1952, it was realised that without an 'agency' at the village level which could represent the entire community, assume responsibility and provide the necessary leadership for implementing development programs, real progress in the area of rural development could not come about. In 1957, the Balwantrai Mehta Committee's report recommended the establishment of statutory elective local bodies. For information visit http://www.rlek.org/pragati/history.html
6. The details of these two villages are given under the sub-title Study Area and also Table 1.
7. For the present study it is Hubbanahalli.
8. The concern on the part of leaders of joint participatory bodies refers to the commitment towards social cause with which they have volunteered to serve as members of joint participatory bodies/community-based associations.
9. The term 'formal relationship' is used here to mean what a majority of the respondents in both the villages felt and how they related themselves to the leaders. A few respondents observed that many of their PRI leaders were not what they were before getting elected to the Gram Sabha. It is very difficult for an aggrieved villager to see the member of Gram Sabha, who in most cases asks the former to meet in the Gram Sabha office, especially if he/she is Adyaksha or Upadyaksha. Gram Sabha members, on their part feel that they have been elected to the office legally and hence, it is always advisable to keep formal relationship, which also is not envious for other villagers.
10. The process of tender was witnessed by the researcher during the field work. The Gram Sabha members claim that by inviting tender, they are displaying their honesty and are socially and politically accountable,

where as some villagers felt that the tender process was an eyewash, they felt that the contract was already pre-determined.

11. www.deccanherald.com/deccanherald/dec142004/s8.asp - 24k
12. Samuel Paul distinguishes between different levels of participation and categorises them into four, all of which may co-exist in a developmental project. The first two categories present ways to exercise influence and the other two categories present ways to exercise control. They are: (1) *Information Sharing*; (2) *Consultation;* (3) *Decision Making; and* (4) *Initiating Action.* As cited in Deepa Narayan (1995: pp.. 7-8). To refer to the original work see Paul, Samuel (1987), *Community Participation in Development Projects: The World Bank Experience*, World Bank Discussion Paper No. 6, Washington, D.C.
13. These bodies mean either Gram Panchayat, Taluk Panchayat or Zilla Panchayat, the ones, which the trained members represented in the immediate past elections.
14. For more details on the concept visit the web site of MYRADA-http://www.myrada.org/
15. Major works have been carried out on election related issues, by academicians, government agencies, independent bodies and the mass media organisations.
16. Putnam Robert D. et al (1993), *Making Democracy Work: Civic Traditions in Modern Italy*, Princeton University Press, Princeton, p. 167.
17. World Bank (2000), *What is Social Capital?*, it can be reached at www.worldbank.org/poverty/scapital/
18. Ibid. The original source is Sabel (1994), 'Learning by Monitoring: The Institutions of Economic Development' in Smelser and Swedverd, *Handbook of Economic Sociology*, Princeton University Press, Princeton.
19. Though there are many definitions and arguments regarding social capital only those related the present study are given in this section.
20. Blomkvist, Hans and Ashok Swain (2001), 'Investigating Democracy and Social Capital in India', *Economic and Political Weekly*, Vol. 36, No. 8, pp.. 639-43.
21. As cited in John Harriss (2001), *Depoliticizing Development: The World Bank and Social Capital*, Left Word Books, New Delhi, p. 29.
22. These terms are better explained in Putnam, Robert D. (2000), *Bowling Alone: The Collapse and Revival of American Community*, Simon and Schuster, New York.

References

Blomkvist, Hans and Ashok Swain (2001), 'Investigating Democracy and Social Capital in India', *Economic and Political Weekly*, Vol. 36, No. 8, pp. 639-643.

Coleman, James S. (1980), *Individual Interests and Collective Action: Selected Essays*, Cambridge University Press, Cambridge.

– (1988), 'Social Capital in the Creation of Human Capital', *American Journal of Sociology*, Vol. 94, pp. 95-120.

Dasgupta, Partha and Ismail Serageldin (1994), *Social Capital: A Multi-faceted Perspective*, World Bank, Washington, D.C.

Dreze, J. and Amartya Sen (2002), *India: Development and Participation*, Oxford University Press, New Delhi.

D'Silva, Emmanuel (2002), 'Participation and Empowerment through Community Institutions: Lessons from Adilabad District, Andhra Pradesh', *Journal of Rural Development*, Vol. 21, No. 3, pp. 369-94.

D'Silva, Emmanuel and Sudha Pai (2003), 'Social Capital and Collective Action: Development Outcomes in Forest Protection and Watershed Development', *Economic and Political Weekly*, Vol. 38, No. 14, pp. 1404-14.

Fine, Ben (2001), 'Social Capital and the Realm of Intellect', *Economic and Political Weekly*, Vol. 36, No. 8, pp. 741-45.

Fukuyama, Francis (2001), 'Social Capital, Civil Society and Development', *Third World Quarterly*, Vol. 22, No. 1, pp. 7-20.

Harriss, John (2001) *Depoliticising Development: The World Bank and Social Capital*, Left Word Books, New Delhi.

Jayal, Niraja Gopal (2001), 'Democracy and Social Capital in Central Himalaya', *Economic and Political Weekly*, Vol. 36, No. 08, pp. 655-64.

John, M.S. and Jos Chatukulam (2002), 'Building Social Capital Through State Initiative: Participatory Planning in Kerala', *Economic and Political Weekly*, Vol. 37, No. 20, pp. 1939-48.

Khatri, Rajkumar, (1998), 'People's Audit in Panchayati Raj', *Journal of Rural Development*, Vol. 17, No. 1, pp. 53-75.

Mayer, Peter (2001), 'Human Development and Civic Community in India: Making Democracy Perform', *Economic and Political Weekly*, Vol. 36, No. 8, pp. 684-92.

Milbrath, Lester W. (1965), *How and Why Do People Get Involved in Politics*, Rand MC Nally and Company, Chicago.

Mohapatra, Bishnu, N (2001), 'Social Connectedness and Fragility of Social Capital', *Economic and Political Weekly*, Vol. 36, No. 8, pp. 665-72.

Mukherjee, Neela (2002), 'Measuring Social Capital; Forest Protection Committees in West Bengal', *Economic and Political Weekly*, Vol. 37, No. 29, pp. 2994-97.

Nagel, Jack H. (1987), *Participation*, Prentice Hall Inc, New Jersey.

Nambiar, Malini (2001), 'The Civil Society and Panchayati Raj Institutions', *Journal of Rural Development*, Vol. 20, No. 4, pp. 615-34.

Narayan, Deepa (1995), *The Contribution of People's Participation Evidences from 121 Rural Water Supply Projects*, Environmentally Sustainable Development, Occasional Paper Series No.1, World Bank, Washington, D.C.

Pai, Sudha (2001), 'Social Capital, Panchayats and Grass Roots Democracy', *Economic and Political Weekly*, Vol. 36, No. 8, pp. 645-54.

Putnam, Robert D. et al (1993), *Making Democracy Work: Civic Traditions in Modern Italy,* Princeton University Press, Princeton.

Putnam, Robert D. (2000), *Bowling Alone, The Collapse and Revival of American Community*, Simon and Schuster, New York.

Rudolph, Susanne Hoeber (2000), 'Civil Society and the Realm of Freedom', *Economic and Political Weekly*, Vol. 35, No. 19, pp. 1762-69.

Sankaran, S.R. (2002), 'Globalisation and Marginalised Sections', *Indian Journal of Human Rights*, Vol. 6, Nos. 1&2, January-December, pp. 1-15.

Sen, Amartya (1999), *Development as Freedom,* Oxford University Press, New Delhi.

Serra Renata (2001), 'Social Capital, Meaningful and Measurable at the State Level?', *Economic and Political Weekly*, Vol. 36, No. 8, pp. 693-704.

Singh, S.P. (2002), 'Hierarchy of Developmental Functions of Gram Panchayats: An Assessment of Representatives' Response', *Journal of Rural Development*, Vol. 21, No. 3, pp. 317-49.

Stiglitz, Joseph E. (2001), *Wither Reform? Ten Years of Transition- Speech on Social and Organisational Capital,* Anthem Press, London.

Vyasulu, Vinod (2002), 'Development and Participation: What is Missing?', *Economic and Political Weekly*, Vol. 37, No. 37, pp. 2869-71.

Unpublished Papers

— (2002), 'Panchayati Raj and Natural Resources Management: How to Decentralize Management over Natural Resources? Karnataka: Situation Analysis and Literature Review'. This report is based on the ongoing study of Panchayati Raj and Natural Resources Management, jointly being carried out by Overseas Development Institute (London), Social and Economic Research Associates (London), TARU Leading Edge (New Delhi and Hyderabad), Centre for Budget and Policy Studies (Bangalore), Centre for World Solidarity (Hyderabad) and Sanket (Bhopal), and supported by Ford Foundation, New Delhi.

Kameshwari, V.L.V. (2001), 'Collective Management of Forest Resources in India, Lessons for Policy Formulation and Stakeholders Involvement'. Paper submitted to the 9th Biennial Conference of International Association for the Study of Common Property (IASCP), Victoria Falls, Zimbabwe.

Meenakshisundaram, S. S. (2001), 'Panchayati Raj Institutions in Natural Resource Management'. A Paper presented at the workshop, "Policy Frameworks to Enable Successful community-based Resource Management Initiatives," held at the East-West Center in Honolulu, Hawaii, between 5 February and 2 March 2001.

Ozmond Roshan D'Souza (2004), 'Social Capital and Joint Forest Management: A Case Study of a Village Forest Committee in Karnataka', M.Phil dissertation submitted to the University of Hyderabad.

Regina Birner and Heidi Wittmer (2001): 'Converting Social Capital into Political Capital- How do Local Communities gain Political Influence? A Theoretical Approach and Empirical Evidence from Thailand and Columbia'. Paper submitted to the 8th Biennial Conference of International Association for the Study of Common Property (IASCP), *Constituting the Commons: Crafting Sustainable Commons in the New Millennium.*

Subash Chandra Babu, P.V. (1998), 'Common Property Resource Management in Haryana State, India: Analysis of the Impact of Participation in the Management of Common Property Resources and the Relative Effectiveness of Common Property Regimes'. Paper submitted to the Biennial Conference of International Association for the Study of Common Property (IASCP), Vancouver, Canada.

Web Sites

http://www.caledonia.org

http://www.iifm.org

http://www.indiana.edu

http://www.relief.int

http://www.worldbank.org

www.deccanherald.com

Index